SON OF MINE

PETER PAPATHANASIOU was born in a small village in northern Greece. His writing has been published internationally by numerous outlets including *The New York Times*, *The Guardian*, *The Sydney Morning Herald*, *The Age*, *Good Weekend*, *ABC*, *SBS*, *The Pigeonhole*, *Caught by the River*, *Structo*, *3:AM Magazine*, *Elsewhere*, *Litro*, *Meanjin*, and *Overland*. He has been reviewed by *The Times Literary Supplement* in the UK and holds a Master of Arts in Creative Writing from the University of London.

SON OF MINE

PETER PAPATHANASIOU

CROMER

PUBLISHED BY SALT PUBLISHING 2019

2 4 6 8 10 9 7 5 3 1

First published in Great Britain in 2019 by
Salt Publishing Ltd
12 Norwich Road, Cromer, Norfolk NR27 0AX United Kingdom

www.saltpublishing.com

Salt Publishing Limited Reg. No. 5293401

A CIP catalogue record for this book is available from the British Library

ISBN 978 1 78463 168 0 (Paperback edition)
ISBN 978 1 78463 169 7 (Electronic edition)

Typeset in Neacademia by Salt Publishing

Printed and bound in Great Britain by Clays Ltd, Elcograf S.p.A

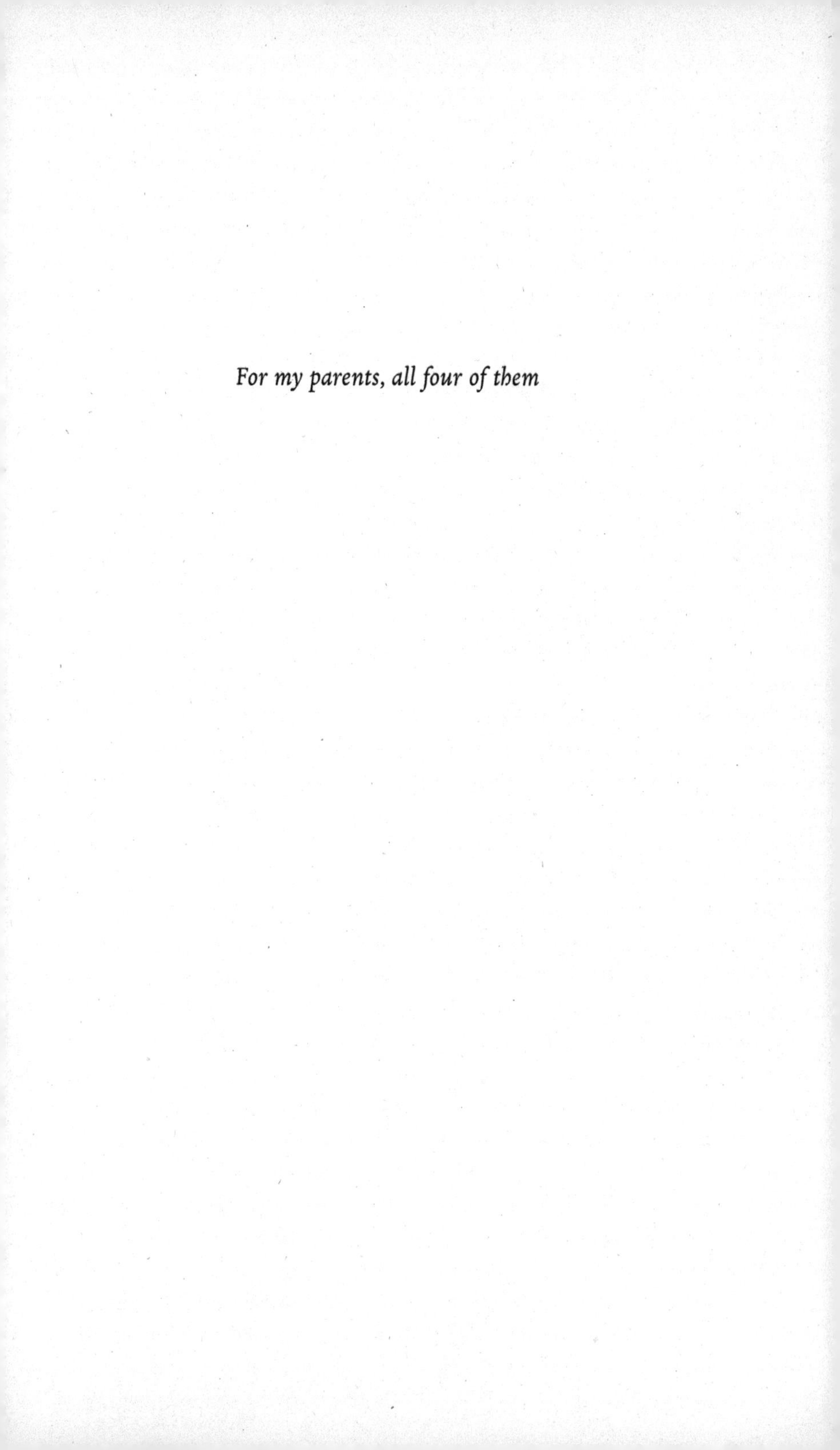

For my parents, all four of them

Prologue

YOU WERE ONCE a newborn. It's probably hard to imagine that now, sitting comfortably in your seat, wearing your clothes and reading this sentence. But there was a time when you were naked and new, bloody and blind, crying and cold. You were conscious in that moment, but will never remember it. You emerged from your mother's exhausted body in a moment. The cord was clamped and cut. The events that preceded it, and those that immediately followed, were beyond your control . . .

SON OF MINE

CHAPTER 1

1999

IT WAS THE hottest day of summer, a Saturday in January. I sat cross-legged in my study, surrounded by piles of undergraduate textbooks, flicking through them, leaving light fingerprints of sweat on the pages. Having studied science and law for six years at university, I was about to embark on a PhD in genetics, and so was packing my old textbooks away. Seeing myself on each meticulously highlighted page, I sighed lightly, remembering all the time I'd spent understanding, memorising, and ultimately regurgitating those passages in cold, cavernous exam halls. The focus was now going to be on experiments not exams, data not grades, discovery not curriculum. Occasionally I stopped to read an extract, which brought back even more memories of lectures, lecturers, tutorials and classmates. It was a job well done, graduation with honours, but all behind me now.

Mum looked into my room again. She had something on her mind. She hoped I wouldn't notice but it was impossible not to – she had poked her head in umpteen times that day. Having lived with my parents my whole life, I could tell when they were genuinely busy and when they were 'hovering'. The phrase 'helicopter parenting' could very well have been coined for them, and especially for Mum. I knew she loved me, but at times it was to the point of suffocating her only child.

'Mama,' I said, 'what's up?'

Mum stopped, leaned against the door frame. She didn't respond for some time. 'Eh,' she finally said, 'nothing.'

'You keep walking past my door. A dozen times now. It's not nothing.'

She rubbed her hands together pensively. Eventually, she asked: 'Are you busy?'

I returned to flicking pages. 'Matters of world importance,' I replied.

Mum was silent. Failing to sense my sarcasm, she continued to stare at me. After a few moments, I looked back up and met her gaze. It was as if she were assessing me, sizing me up for something. As she gazed longer and deeper into my eyes than I thought anyone ever could, I felt lightheaded. There were generations in that look. Mum's stature was small, and her hands tiny, with purple veins protruding, her fingers beginning to turn in with arthritis. But at that moment, she appeared like a giant.

Slowly, almost cautiously, I closed my book. 'Mama . . .' I said, '*ela*, what is it?'

Finally, she spoke: 'Can you come to my room? I've something to tell you.'

My stomach tightened.

As I followed Mum down the carpeted hall, a memory cut across my brain. The last time she had insisted we talk in her room was during my first year of university. My aunt in Greece had died suddenly.

Mum closed the door behind us. Her bedroom smelled of fresh linen. I didn't exactly know where Dad was – probably out the back in his shed or at the betting shop – but knew he wasn't in the house. The large, north-facing window amplified the hot summer sun like a magnifying glass.

'Please, Panagiotis, sit down.'

Mum always called me by my Greek name during moments of significance. It had been there in hospital during emergencies, in church during baptisms and funerals, and at home during lectures for teenage misbehaviour. I didn't mind it, but I knew what it meant. Someone had died, or was dying.

'I'll stand, Mum. Please, what is it?'

Mum took up position on the edge of the bed, her bare feet resting on a thick blue rug. Looking down at her hands, she began.

'When I was young, I tried many times to get pregnant. Although your dad and I succeeded three times, I miscarried each time. Three.' She held up three bony fingers. 'One, two, three babies I carried but never met. Even after all this time, those memories are with me, every day of every week.'

I listened, silently.

'Your *baba* and I wanted so much to have a family, we were losing our minds. Those weren't easy days. We'd been through a lot, coming all the way out to Australia after the war. In the end, the time came when we thought we had no other choice. We had to consider the option of taking someone else's child.'

Mum's eyes suddenly welled up and her face went red. She took a deep breath. Uncertain of what was to come, I did the same.

'Now there were places in Greece where you could adopt babies who weren't wanted. But you needed to meet certain standards, have money and status. And your dad and I didn't. So in the end, my brother Savvas and his wife Anna proposed to have a baby for us. They already had two sons who were almost teenagers, so their child-rearing days were well and truly behind them. But they were willing to help your *baba* and me. I felt terrible about my brother's wife having to carry and give birth to another baby for me, her non-blood relative. But our lives here were childless and, well, meaningless. In the end, an arrangement was made. Anna fell pregnant, and I flew to Greece.'

A tear rolled down Mum's left cheek. She pulled a folded tissue from her pocket and wiped her eyes. She fought hard to compose herself and not lose her place in the story.

'Your dad worked here while I was in Greece, and sent money when he could. During that time, I completed all the paperwork that was needed to bring you back to Australia. Six months later, we flew back. From that day, you haven't set foot in your country of birth, and the only contact with your birth mother was when she and I talked on the phone. To you, she was simply your aunt. And to her, too, this was the case. Even though she loved you dearly, it was for us to raise you in the way we chose. *You became our child.* She saw the benefits of life here, and it was why your dad and I came out in the first place. Your brothers, the two boys whom I've always said were your cousins, know everything you've been doing all these years.'

Brothers . . .

I put my fingertips to my temples, as if to steady myself, and let the new word nestle inside my brain. Brothers were such an unfamiliar concept. They had always been something the other kids in school had as I was growing up, in higher grades who protected them, or in lower grades whom they beat up.

'Your brothers were, I think, twelve and ten when you were born, so should now be thirty-seven and thirty-five. Both are unmarried. The eldest, Vasilios, was named after your grandfather but likes being called "Billy" to distinguish himself. He doesn't work and is somewhat handicapped, or "slow", as we like to say. The younger brother, Georgios, works for a power station. Unfortunately, Anna died six years ago. Your birth father, my brother Savvas, is old and weak and plagued by alcoholism. He blames it on having to look after Billy all these years.'

Mum wiped her face and eyes again, and took another deep breath.

'You're probably wondering why we took so long to tell you. I wanted to tell you long ago, and keeping this from you for twenty-five years has made me grey before my time. But your dad and I knew we couldn't tell you too young – you wouldn't have understood. And back then, I was still too ashamed that I hadn't had my own children. It seems so foolish now but it was cultural. The older you got and the further you went with your schooling, the harder it became to tell you. We didn't want to do anything to ruin all your hard work. I wanted to tell you before you started university six years ago but the timing wasn't right. The timing was never right. So we waited until you finished and were able to start work. But now, you're about to do *even more* study. Your dad wanted to wait longer, perhaps another year, but I imagined by then you'd be buried in something else. At least now, the news will have some time to sink in.'

She rubbed the soles of her feet back and forth on the rug. Her heels were dry and cracked from age and exposed footwear.

'You deserve to know this. Some parents don't tell their kids. They keep the secret forever. But I know that even if people don't see all that goes on, God does. There are no secrets from Him.'

Mum momentarily glimpsed skywards and crossed herself, before returning her eyes to me.

'So,' she said, 'that's it.'

While Mum spoke, I had leant against the wall, before slumping down, and finally ending up on the floor with legs bent. My skin rushed with heat. I frowned, looked away, stared out the window. I saw the empty street, the cloudless sky, and the tinderbox trees drooping in forty-degree heat. Not a single thing was moving; no birds, no branches. There wasn't even a hint of breeze to blow around the dry leaves on the lofty gums. It hadn't rained in months.

Mum wiped her now flushed face with another tissue. It was only then that I realised this may have been the hardest thing she'd ever done.

'Oh wait, there's one more thing . . .' Mum said.

I braced myself.

'I need to say sorry to you, *agape mou*,' she continued. 'I'm sorry for having deceived you your whole life by pretending my blood was yours. This is my confession. I hope you understand, I did none of this to hurt you. I love you. *We* love you – your *baba* and I. More than life. We're not bad people. We just wanted to be parents. It was our dream.'

There was a long moment of silence when no one said anything. Mum and I just sat listening to each other's breathing. And then, Mum uttered her final sentence.

'So,' she said, 'now that's it.'

Mum looked at me with the same honest brown eyes I had seen my whole life, and waited patiently for my reaction.

Georgios woke at eight. Despite the bright sunshine outside his window, the solid wooden shutters kept his room in complete darkness. The house was still. He rubbed his eyes, put on jeans and yesterday's shirt, and checked his brother's room. It was empty. He found his jacket and snow boots, crossed the laces, tied them tight. Opening the front door, he felt a blast of cold air, and closed it behind him with a gentle thud.

Georgios's breath appeared before him in slabs. He looked to the sky, then the ground below. There had been only a little fresh snow overnight. It would be at least a month before the accumulated falls could thaw. Icicles as long and as thick as baseball bats hung from the edge of the roof.

Descending the steps, Georgios sparked his first cigarette. He trudged across the lawn, feet sinking, heavy, the snow shin deep.

The roads had been sprayed with salt again and were dirty, grey slush, slippery, treacherous.

Making his way down the hill, Georgios approached the *fourno.* Two stray cats darted inside, then hurried out seconds later and dived into a nearby dumpster. The air was thick with the smell of fresh bread. Stavros offered Georgios a white loaf but hadn't seen Georgios's brother. Georgios thanked him and walked on.

He walked past the neoclassical houses near the Sakoulevas River, listening to the sounds of morning. He heard the gentle babble of pure mountain water over stones, the honks of grand white geese, and quacks from plump grey ducks. Love padlocks sat fastened to the many small footbridges that crossed the river. It was where couples kissed and took photos. The river was at its best after rain, flowing strong and full; the town's healthy pulse. At the height of summer, it shrank to a trickle, as lush green grasses sprouted and took the river's place beneath weeping willows. In the depths of winter, the storm water outfalls were snapshots, each a frozen waterfall in time.

Cars slowed down and let Georgios cross the next two roads. He thanked them with a polite wave. The *plateia* was in sight.

Long shadows stretched across the square in the new light. The village rarely came to life before noon, and then it was only with great reluctance. Across the road, Sofia was on the balcony beating her living room rug with a large paddle. Georgios waved. The winter was the worst for accumulating dirt inside. On the corner, Georgios saw a teenage boy with his arms wrapped tightly around a girl, as if hanging on for dear life. The girl had her hands in the back pockets of her jeans and was looking up at the big white cross on the top of the mountain.

Cutting across the square, Georgios heard raised voices coming from the corner *kafenion*. He knew he was close. The skin on his cheeks prickled with cold.

'*Etho eisai?*' Georgios called out.

'Yes, I am here, boss!'

Billy was propped up at the bar sipping a syrupy coffee. As he ended the life of one cigarette, he gave birth to another. In front of him, a toasted sandwich was getting cold.

'What are you doing here? Have you been out all night? Is he giving you trouble, Dimitrios?'

But everything was fine, as it usually was.

'Dimitrios made me a sandwich! And Yiannis was here earlier, I was telling him about when Papou won the lottery! You remember that?'

'Of course I do, of course. Come, we need to walk home. You need some sleep and I have to go to work today.'

'Yiannis said he would have some work for me too. I will be security!'

'Bravo! Wonderful news, Billy.'

'And when I have money, I will go and buy milk for the orphans.'

'That's very generous of you. But we better go now.'

'Good. Let's go.'

The two brothers walked unhurriedly, barely lifting their feet off the cracked and muddy pavement. They passed under the red illuminated sign at the pharmacy. It showed the temperature as minus eleven.

'So Billy, what were you doing last night?'

'Not much. Walking around. I got ink on my shirt.'

'That's okay. Where did you go?'

'I went to Costas's bar for a while. He gave me cigarettes.'

'Give me one, will you? I've run out.'

'Here.'

'*Efharisto.*'

'It's cold,' Billy said.

'Very cold,' Georgios replied. 'Your feet wet?'

'Yes. My toes hurt.'

'You need new shoes. Those ones aren't made for this weather.'

'I went to Takis's shop. Leonidas was there.'

'How is he?'

'Sick,' Billy said. 'His feet are still swollen. He can't sleep.'

'When did you last sleep?' Georgios asked. 'What time did you get up?'

'I can't remember.'

'Let's go home now. I'll make you something light to eat. You can sleep.'

'I got ink on my shirt . . .'

'That's fine, I'll wash it while you rest. It will be clean when you wake up.'

'Where is Baba?'

'Sleeping.'

'Where is Papou? You remember the lottery he won?'

'Of course I do, but that was a long time ago.'

'Where is Papou?'

'We'll go see him later, when I get back from work. We'll light the candle in the lamp and see everybody together. Papou, Yiayia, Mama. Sofia gave me some flowers yesterday. They're plastic, but they'll last outside.'

'And *o micros?*' Billy asked. 'When is Panagiotis coming?'

'Soon,' Georgios replied.

'When do we get to see Panagiotis?'

'Hopefully very soon.'

CHAPTER 2

1999

'HOW DO YOU feel?'

Mum's words barely registered. For a long time, I didn't say anything. I couldn't. I was in too much shock.

And yet, at the same time, it wasn't unexpected. When I was at school, I had always questioned why my parents were so much older than all the other parents. Other parents played sport with their kids at school barbeques, and every morning dropped off their kids at school on bikes, while mine saw specialists for osteoporosis. Once at parent-teacher night, my mum was mistaken for my grandmother. I had also questioned why I was the only kid at school without siblings. That was anathema during the 1970s and 1980s, and especially weird in large ethnic families. But I was everything to my parents and I looked enough like them to not question it.

My bottom lip quivered, uncertain of the new world in which I found myself. By contrast, Mum looked instantly younger.

Part of that came through realising she'd broken the news to me first.

'My biggest fear was if I died and never got to tell you,' Mum said. 'What you'd think of me the rest of your life.'

'Yep,' I finally said.

'I'm not young anymore.'

'You are, Mum.'

'Ha,' she smiled, 'I'm not, I'm sixty-eight, but that's okay. Is there anything else you'd like to know right now, any questions?'

'No. Not right now.'

Mum paused; I don't think she believed me. As it happened, I did have questions; dozens of them. But they were still ordering themselves in my mind.

In the end, Mum asked the most important thing that was on her mind: 'Are you angry with me?'

I took a moment to respond. 'No.'

'We're good? All okay?'

'Yes.'

'Oh wait . . .'

Mum left the room and returned moments later with a thick photo album. It was heavy and dusty and smelled of leather and must, its pages stuck together like fused vertebrae. She flipped through the pages until she finally settled on a few photos. Careful not to tear them, she extracted three photos, and handed me one.

'Here,' she said, 'your brothers. That's Vasilios on the left, Georgios on the right.'

Looking at the image, I saw my own features. I had Billy's eyes and ears and Georgios's mouth and chin. The resemblance made my head hurt. It was as if my own face had been pieced together. I touched it lightly, just to make sure it was real.

Mum then showed me a photo of my biological father, Savvas. I saw a thin, moustached man staring out at me from beneath a slouched cloth hat. His image made less of an impression; I was, after all, familiar with the notion of a father. Despite being limited with both his knowledge of the world and his emotions, Dad had been a good father and I loved him dearly. He always provided for the family and as a child spoilt me with presents, which suddenly made a little more sense. I was, after all, a gift for him.

Finally, Mum showed me a photo of my biological mother, Anna. With a thick mop of wavy brown and pearly grey hair as if she'd been caught in a snow flurry, she shared a significant likeness with the sister-in-law who had raised me. I was pleasantly and instantly comforted. Mum was one and the same.

'Wow,' I mumbled, more to myself than anyone else.

Mum smiled warmly. 'You can hang on to those,' she said. 'Maybe we can now finally put them in a frame all together.' The album spine cracked as she closed it.

The afternoon had clearly been painful for Mum. The moist lines down from her eyes made her cheeks resemble a river delta. How she must've worried all those years that someone else had told me the truth before she did. It probably played on her thoughts every day. But now, she was overcome with relief, which brought me joy.

'Who else knows?' I asked.

Mum scratched her chin. 'You mean, of our friends?'

'Yes.'

'Well, all our old family friends do. I know I'll always be grateful that none of them told you over so many years. I suspect they just forgot about it after a while. It was old news, and they knew I would one day tell you the truth.'

I felt a sudden urge to tell my friends the news of my brothers. And not just that: to call up my old school classmates, people I hadn't spoken with in years, whom I didn't even know the whereabouts of anymore.

The questions came at me. What were my brothers like? How did they feel all these years? What were their birthdays? What were their favourite foods, their favourite music? Did they dance? Sing? We probably didn't even speak the same first language; my Greek was conversational, and their English may have been non-existent. Still, I wanted to shout it out, to tell everyone I had siblings. To tell them – hey, I'm suddenly just like you.

'We'll talk more another time,' Mum said. 'This has no doubt been a lot to process. For now, I think you should sit back and let the news sink in.' She rose from the bed, extended her arms.

We hugged. Mum didn't want to let go, still sniffing and leaving a wet salt imprint on the front of my sweaty shirt. It was the same loving hug of the mother that I'd always known. Warm, reassuring, laced with the smell of fresh laundry.

'One more thing, Panagiotis,' Mum said. 'When you see your dad, give him a hug. He'll be waiting.'

'Sure,' I replied.

I walked back to my study and flopped onto the battered office chair, which rolled backwards to a natural stop. I considered going for a walk to clear my head, which felt like it had been turned inside out. I thought about walking up to the mountain at the top of our street. I often walked there in the evenings to watch the kangaroos emerge and see the sun set over the distant Brindabellas. There was a calm dam that was immensely therapeutic to sit beside. But my neck was tense, my shoulders heavy, and I felt a sudden exhaustion wash over me. I wasn't going anywhere. I sighed and stared blankly at the crooked piles of textbooks surrounding me, before closing my eyes. Left alone with my thoughts, my brain began to work, and the emotions started to flow.

In a flash, I made complete sense; a second later, no sense at all. I was no longer the person I thought I'd been my whole life.

But who was I now? Was I the product of some experiment? Whose life had I lived, who might I have been? And who might have been me?

I began to feel shock and confusion and anger – those who I thought were my parents were, in fact, my aunt and uncle. I felt deceived, and began to doubt. Was there anything else Mum was hiding from me? What else was untrue? They should've told me earlier, I thought. It would've been better to have grown up with this news, and always had it as part of my story. Then, I would never have had to endure this bloody agonising moment of truth.

Did my biological mother really give me up voluntarily? I found that hard to believe. What woman – what *mother* – could?

The next emotion to wash over me was sadness. It was at the realisation of having missed meeting my biological mother. I recalled a memory of a time she called our house and Mum asked me to come and speak with 'an aunty in Greece'. I had refused, claiming there was no point talking with another distant relative

I'd never actually meet; and if I did, I would probably never remember. That ridiculously immature attitude stabbed at me. I felt like a fool.

I snapped my eyes open and let them wander around the room, before settling on the wall above my desk. I saw a laminated photo of a football goalkeeper in mid-flight, an autographed band poster, a purple pennant from New York University, and an old exam timetable that I needed to tear down. Then my eyes drifted to a framed family photo taken when I was about seven. It was at a department store, in front of a fake blossom tree background. I was smiling innocently, joyously. So were my fake parents.

I thought about the mainstream view of family, of a heterosexual couple with biological offspring. Whether it was the inheritance of a business empire or corner store, blood relations were the basis of kinship and opportunity. Blood was where you came from and probably where you were going. And for ethnics like us, blood was everything. Family was everything.

But I had fallen through the cracks. I was adopted. I was *an adoptee*. Whose family did I actually belong to? I was neither here nor there, my blood was thin. 'Here' was nowhere I recognised anymore, and 'there' was an even stranger place I had never visited. I felt divided, my life torn in two: two families, but also two periods of time, the before and the after. The before became an illusion, a fallacy. While the after was a scary period of self-exploration in which I had already begun to question my identity.

Mum soon appeared in the backyard to tend her summer garden, which was bursting with plump tomatoes, crispy cucumbers, and jungles of basil and parsley. I watched her through the window move back and forth, more fluid than usual. Dad joined her not long after, picking ingredients for their evening salad. If they were talking about me, it didn't show.

I looked back to the family photo, and started to make sense of the new world.

'All the other kids were born here in Australia,' I would say after I got home from primary school. 'Mama, how come I was born in Greece?'

Mum would reply, 'Because I wanted you to be born in Florina, in the same village as your dad and me.'

'But you were here in Australia at the time, right?'

'I was. But I flew back to Greece and had you there, then returned to Australia.'

Mum lied. She never braved a day's worth of airline turbulence while pregnant as she claimed. Perhaps this was why Mum and her older sister, my aunt Soultana, occasionally slipped into speaking Turkish on the phone. They were talking about *this*.

I stared into the department store photo, into my father's bright smiling eyes. Dad's heart was warm, but always a degree colder than Mum's. My whole life, I attributed this to the palpable distance that men put between each other, even their own sons. Now, I realised there was more to it. I wasn't Dad's blood at all – I was Mum's.

Growing up, my identity had eluded me. Greek-Australian; what hyphenated beast was that? As a consequence, I had endured most of my adolescence trying to make sense of the world and how I fitted into it. At first, I had shunned my Greek heritage. Mum had forced me to speak Greek when I was younger, and sent me to Greek language classes and dancing lessons. I hated it all, and nearly died with embarrassment the day she made me wear a traditional *tsolia* costume with its kilt-like fustanella and pointed shoes. All I wanted to do was fit in with my Australian mates; to play cricket and footy and speak English. I found it hard to make friends. I often played games by myself, and also talked to myself, which made the other kids think I was weird. As the only brown-eyed, olive-skinned kid in my class, the only thing steeper than my learning curve was my accumulation of schoolyard bruises. My lack of siblings made me even more conspicuous. There was no bigger version of me to protect me. And if I ever fought back, reinforcements appeared quickly. At the end of the school day, Mum would laugh off my lamentations and say: 'One day, God will gift you brothers!'

It seemed like such a throwaway line at the time. Little did I realise. The language, the culture, the comments. Secretly, it was all preparation for the future.

A loud knock on my bedroom window broke my reverie.

It was Mum, smiling. Ostensibly, she was showing me the biggest garden tomato I had ever seen, the size of a volley ball.

But I could tell she was actually checking to see if I was okay.

CHAPTER 3

1999

BY THE TIME I caught up with Dad, he was out the back in his homemade shed. Dad worked his whole life as a professional handyman, albeit self-taught. It's what all Greek immigrant tradesmen were after the Second World War, there were no trade certificates then. Just an aptitude to work with your hands and a willingness to bend your back.

Dad's shed was his kingdom. Growing up, I'd always feared it. The shed was next to a play area in the backyard where I once kicked soccer balls and smashed cricket balls. Every time an errant ball flew into the darkness of the shed, I had needed to summon all my courage to enter. The shed was shadowy and smelly and home to poisonous spiders and slippery rats and greasy car parts. Balls disappeared into the shed, never to be seen again. For some time, Dad parked his fishing boat there; to this day, I could still picture a large outboard motor sticking out of the shed like an ugly protruding tooth. Over time, Dad had extended the shed further and further back, building new sections of wooden framing, adding sheets of aluminium as he found them, until he finally reached the perimeter fence and stopped. Then he enclosed the entire structure, stuck on some makeshift doors, and filled it with every single tool or piece of building yard scrap he'd ever found. Twenty years later, the shed had become more hazardous than ever.

Dodging cobwebs and dangling wires, I approached Dad, who was hunched over his workbench with cigarette in mouth. I placed my arm around his shoulder and gave him a quick squeeze. I didn't say anything. Dad looked up from the frayed electrical cord he was repairing with insulation tape and smiled. Mum briefly looked in through the doorway and I saw her smile, too.

Seeing Dad in his element suddenly made me realise why I'd never had an aptitude for manual labour. I suspect Dad would've loved to have passed on his labourer genes to his children. Instead, I turned out to be a myopic bookworm who didn't know one end of a hammer from its Phillips head. Although that didn't seem to matter to Dad who was always very proud of my academic achievements. And I respected his skills, too, whether they were carpentry or electricals or painting or car mechanics.

When I first wanted to buy a cricket bat, Dad said, 'No, I'll make you one', and promptly went to his shed. He returned several hours later with a flat piece of wood in the shape of a cricket bat, which proceeded to stab my palms with splinters and send shockwaves up my arms with every cover drive. But his intentions were good, which was what mattered. Over the years, Dad built a fence out of scrap metal, a pergola from irregular bits of wood, and used leftover bathroom tiles to finish our mismatched shower recess. We always took pride in his work and ingenuity, though his craftsmanship was limited, everything he did had an organic quality about it, and a junkyard finish. But it was still more than I could ever offer. Although my future lay in a different direction, I knew that lab experiments would still require some level of dexterity and physical prowess, whether it was to prepare a chemical solution or dissect a mouse. I hoped I could handle it.

I found out two days later when I arrived at the Australian National University's school of medical research. It was on the southern side of campus near an artificially constructed lake into which a murky creek slithered. Its stream was the cumulative refuse of half the city's population. The pathology department pumped its cadaverous waste into the stream. Dogs and rats drowned in its muddy grasp.

I arrived at nine sharp on a Monday morning. It was the time the professor had told me to come. But then his secretary informed me that he was in California all week; a minor detail he'd forgotten to mention.

'So what can I do this week?' I asked her.

She looked at me blankly. 'Not sure,' she replied. 'Can you read something?'

I ended up spending the whole day in a library study cubicle trying to make sense of two sheets of A4 paper. Onto them, the professor had scrawled symbols and text that mapped my upcoming four years of research. It had something to do with genes and mice and family trees and a lot of inbreeding. I wanted to bash my head against the cubicle's walls to make sense of the notes but found the student graffiti too interesting, distracting.

The professor probably wanted me to venture into the lab and get started on experiments, or at least learn a few techniques, but I was still too intimidated by the technicians and students and postdocs. They rushed across the white-tiled floor in their white coats and gowns, opening and closing white freezers, carrying small white boxes and white styrofoam coolers, working on white benches under white fluorescent lights. Magnetic stir bars rattled in beakers mixing solutions. Water baths bubbled. My nostrils flared at the smell of organic waste.

On the second day, I was reading the latest scientific journals, and focused on the articles about genomes and mapping DNA mutations. Most of them were from prestigious institutions in America: Harvard, Yale, Princeton, Columbia. The professor had only recently returned to Australia after many years as a successful immunologist at Stanford University. He had originally trained as a veterinarian but, like me, had been infected by the research bug and wanted to make great discoveries. His latest venture had been a large-scale mouse mutagenesis and gene mapping project. And I was his 'guinea pig', so to speak: the first student to take on a mouse mutant with an unknown gene at its core. I was both daunted and excited.

By the end of the week, I had secured a lab key and access card to the building from the security manager. My plan was simple. With the lab empty all weekend, I was going to stay until late and familiarise myself with my new surroundings. I opened drawers and freezer boxes and incubators, checking out the pipettes and monoclonal antibodies and bright red bottles of cell media. I couldn't start any actual experiments; the mice were in another building with security access I didn't yet have. Maybe I was hoping that if I sat in the lab long enough, the knowledge needed to cure the world of all disease would simply osmose into me.

When the professor returned the following week, we met to discuss my new mouse strain which harboured an unknown genetic mutation. The international rush to DNA sequence the genome of everything that moved, grew or was extinct was gathering steam, and I intended to stake a claim. The aim of my project was to analyse what was wrong with my mouse strain and map the mutant gene: the *genotype*. It was up to me to put meaning alongside the word in the genome dictionary that hundreds of supercomputers across the world were busily compiling. If it was something novel, my name would be forever etched within the dusty academic journals as the gene's discoverer. It was scientific immortality. Maybe I would name the gene after myself. Maybe not.

An animal wrangler working in the animal facility had first noticed the visual characteristics of the mutation: the *phenotype*. She saw a stout, tennis ball-like rodent puttering around in the cage that didn't look healthy. The animal's back was hunched over, as if it was walking on its toes. But what the wrangler first thought was obesity or possibly oedema turned out to be something far more sinister: cancer. An examination of the animal's siblings and offspring confirmed the same phenotype. The cancer was genetic. By examining the animal's tissues and organs, I discovered the cancer was a leukaemia: an abnormal growth of blood cells seen in half the offspring with one mutant chromosome inherited from an affected parent.

'A mouse with cancer often models the same disease in humans,' the professor told me.

I was excited. My mouse strain offered the chance to understand the onset and progression of the disease in a living organism. Anti-cancer drugs could then be designed to benefit patients with the same genetic mutation. This was done by targeting the signalling pathway in which the mutant gene was active. I wanted to be a drug designer, I wanted to help people. I knew that part of this came from having elderly parents and spending much of my adolescence beside them in emergency wards.

I took some time to overcome my squeamishness working with mice. I found them understandably cute, especially the tawny brown ones, but would never admit it for fear of looking unprofessional. I saw the other lab members working without emotion so followed suit. I had soon developed enough scar tissue on my fingers to render me impervious to any further bites. It was as if I had earned my lab stripes.

The lab phone rang each time another sick mouse was spotted. The furry black tennis ball was the scientific equivalent of a call to arms. I changed into my powder blue overalls with matching hairnet and booties to prevent contagion. The mice were cleaner than any human. Scientists traditionally used cervical dislocation to euthanise small animals. By applying pressure to the neck, the spinal cord could quickly be separated from the brain, which provided a fast and painless death. But the immense volume of mice that the lab used for experiments meant this was impractical. Instead, the mice were placed in a clear plastic bag which was filled with carbon dioxide gas. I always felt uncomfortable seeing the bag balloon with the air of death. Despite the university providing numerous courses into the ethical treatment of animals, their correct handling and husbandry and euthanasia, I still hated having to do this, and wished there was a better way. But I always reminded myself that this was research meant to save human lives.

Using syringe needles to crucify the subject to a polystyrene mat, I doused it with ethanol for necropsy. I scissored open the swollen abdomen and carefully dissected the organs. The odious smell emanating from the intestines required a surgical mask, while the sight before my eyes was both horrific and beautiful. Lymph nodes, normally the size of sesame seeds, bulged like marbles in the cancerous mice. The spleen wrapped around and strangled the abdomen like a red hangman's rope and the thymus filled the chest cavity, suffocating the pea-sized heart. The bone marrow, once a healthy crimson, was bleached a deathly white, smothered by leukaemic infiltrates. It was the dark power of Mother Nature through the modification of a single letter of DNA – a few atoms of carbon changed a C to a T or a G to an A. Given the complexity of the code for life, it was one in three billion possibilities. Incredible. Exquisite.

I carefully noted which number mouse was sick and where it sat within the large family tree that I was meticulously sketching. It was all about following the mutation, tracking its heritability. I was soon sticky-taping pieces of paper together as the pedigree grew in size with additional generations. Putting my notes to one side, I harvested the animal's enlarged organs, cutting them free of its body. I weighed them on ultrasensitive lab scales, and then gooshed them into a single cell suspension using a stainless steel strainer. The rest of the day was spent centrifuging the cells, washing them with saline, and attaching a series of light-sensitive markers to the cell surface through a series of incubations. The markers were recognised by the facility's cell analyser, a laser-propelled machine that distinguished cell types according to the fluorescence of the light-sensitive markers. What kind of leukaemia was it: B cell or T cell? Was it an early stage tumour or did it come from cells late in development? The panel of markers helped answer these questions. The cell analyser could run thousands of cells per second and count the number of cells in any tissue provided they were labelled correctly. It was painstaking work, though, which meant I wasn't able to analyse the cells until the evening. But then, a fireworks display of cellular colour materialised before my eyes with each sample, thousands of tiny dots exploding onto a blackened computer screen in a windowless room in the facility's basement.

It was only once an experiment was running smoothly that I could finally sit back and relax. The perishable nature of biological experiments permitted only certain stopping points; pull the pin early and the data was ruined, you may as well have not started at all. With the cells silently being analysed, I usually brought up a web browser and surfed the net. I often found myself entering the name of our family's village into a search engine. In Latin, Florina meant 'little flower'. Maps showed that it was closer to the Albanian capital Tirana than it was to Athens. Being so far north, Florina was perhaps the closest Greek township to the rest of Europe – thirty miles from Albania and just ten from the Former Yugoslav Republic of Macedonia. In some photos it was covered in snow, the rooftops and fir trees blanketed in white, the front of a Christmas card. It looked beautiful. I still couldn't quite believe that this was where I'd entered the world, and that this was where I might've grown up if things had been different.

I threw myself at my work, driven by the incredible prospect of discovering a new cancer gene. For weeks, I worked through the night, subsisting solely on a vending machine as my food supply. I then returned home just before dawn to sleep a few hours, before getting up and doing it all again. As the nights got colder, I often returned home to find my pyjamas wrapped in a hot water bottle and left on my bed. I was young, brimming with energy and ambition, and saw the world as full of promise. I felt indestructible and thought everyone else in my life was too. So it came as a shock when I returned home one night to see spinning red lights illuminating the driveway. Mum was lying on a collapsible gurney.

Dad was standing nearby in his flannelette pyjamas and robe, a worried look on his face. 'We've been trying to call you at work for an hour,' he said.

'An hour?' I said.

I had been down in the basement all evening, analysing my latest tumour samples. The phone in the lab would have rung out two floors above. At that hour, there was no one else there to pick it up and come find me.

'What the hell?' I continued. 'Did the ambulance take that long?'

'We only just called it, after we couldn't get hold of you,' Dad said. 'Mum's been having chest pains.'

CHAPTER 4

1999

I RUSHED TO Mum's side. She wiggled her fingers at me in greeting, unable to speak under her plastic oxygen mask. I laid my hand on her shoulder and stroked her thinning hair.

'You'll be okay,' I said. 'Yes?'

She nodded numbly.

The paramedics lifted and positioned the stretcher into the back of the ambulance. The familiar metal clank of the adjustable gurney filled me with an uneasy feeling of dread. I saw my breath. The night was cold.

'*Ela*,' Dad said, 'let me change and we can follow in the car.'

I reflected on the situation. It was usually Dad in the back of that ambulance with his unruly blood sugar and his nicotine addiction. Aside from the odd complaint, Mum was bulletproof.

I considered my experiments, my colony of mice, what they represented. The arrangement of their major internal organs was the same as any human, and they were 99 per cent genetically identical. But this specimen wasn't another data point. This was a human specimen, aged nearly seventy years. This was my mother.

Dad and I drove through the night to the hospital in silence. The air in the car was tense and not conducive to conversation. Hospitals are the bookends of life. Those big white buildings where most people enter the world and so many depart.

With such elderly parents, I had become aware of the notion of mortality earlier in life than most other primary-schoolers, and grew up much faster than I would otherwise have wanted. By the time I was in high school, the emergency room was my second home. The most senior paramedics knew me by name, as did all the nightshift nurses. Behind a thin paper emergency department curtain, I sat in a stiff plastic chair worrying about my school exams and distressed about my parents' health. It always seemed to be something different: a rapid heart rate, difficulty breathing, dizziness, numb body parts. And this was on top of accompanying my parents to a myriad of daytime medical appointments with doctors and specialists in order to translate for them. I approached it all with the same sense of duty as both an only child and a loyal son, but I knew these experiences had shaped my subconscious mind and eventual career choice.

Mum was taken straight in, hooked up, injected. I was soon sitting in the stiff plastic chair alongside her bed and together we waited for the doctors to complete their regime of tests: vitals, bloods, ECGs. Mum sat up in bed. Having been given several injections, she was now stable. She had removed her oxygen mask and changed into a hospital gown. On the floor beside her bed in a plastic supermarket bag were her slippers and clothes.

The late-night A&E freak show was in full swing. Angry men in open shirts and ripped jeans with bloody head wounds staggered past swearing at their police escorts. Comatose teenagers carried in for an urgent stomach pump were surrounded by a horde of delirious peers. Frantic mothers cradled young children, unsure of what they had swallowed when their backs were turned.

'That's the doctor there,' Mum whispered to me. 'See him? The man who walked past, the short one, he spoke with me earlier.'

'Mm hmm,' I murmured, overtired.

'And that fat nurse over there took my blood. See my arm?'

'Ooh yes. Bruised.'

'She couldn't find the vein.'

'No good.'

There was a long silence, punctuated by a regular electrical blipping.

'So, what else is new? How goes the work?' Mum asked.

'Good,' I exhaled.

'You haven't been home much.'

'Busy. There's all this new stuff I have to learn.'

'What are you doing?'

'Experiments.'

'Complicated?'

'Yes and no. It's messy. Stuff with mice.'

'And you'll be a doctor from this?' Mum asked.

'Yes and no,' I said. 'See all these doctors here? I'm trying to help them do their jobs, to understand what goes wrong in the body, and then design new drugs.'

'For?'

'At the moment, cancer.'

'*Poh poh!*'

'It's not that exciting.'

'But it is important. And plenty of money.'

'Ha. Not really. Only for the lucky few.'

'So long as you're happy.'

Mum told me her only experience with mice in a medical setting was something she called *pontikeleo,* which loosely translated as 'mouse oil'. In her village they would put baby mice in a small bottle of olive oil they later used to treat infections. The hairless mouse pups were naturally fortified with antibiotic agents on their hides. By placing them in oil, those substances were released, rendering the concoction as effective as an antibiotic. I was impressed. The village invention was ingenious.

'Are your experiments like that?' she asked.

'Sort of,' I replied. 'How are you feeling?'

'I'm fine now.'

'But before there was . . .?'

'Pain, heavy . . .' She pointed. 'Here, my chest.'

'Down your arms as well?'

'Not really, no. They gave me an injection in the ambulance. I've been fine since.'

'Probably stress.'

I tried to reassure Mum, although I imagined her life had significantly de-stressed since telling me the news of my adoption. It was as if a twenty-five-year weight had been lifted. Then again, people often got sick after stressful periods. I knew I often did when my exams were over. When the body's defences to ward off inflammation or infection during a period of stress phased out, a letdown reaction occurred. Stress hormones like cortisol and adrenaline were released, and illness followed.

'Your dad,' Mum said, 'he drives me crazy sometimes.'

'I know, I know. But let the doctors finish all their tests, see if it's anything.'

'*Endaxi*.'

There was another long silence. I tried to let out my tension with a long sigh. Mum chastised me.

'I told you before, don't do that,' she said. 'You're still too young to sigh like that.'

I shifted in my seat and looked away.

'So what are we waiting for now?' Mum asked.

'The second blood test,' I replied. 'They'll come take more blood, then take it away.'

'Ah.'

The midnight ward looked like a black and white cartoon, no soft contours or sense of optimism. With the footsteps of every approaching physician, I prepared for the worst. I imagined an advanced infection, a catastrophic rupture, an irreparable blockage, a malignant tumour.

Dad hadn't been able to sit still and left the emergency department before Mum had even settled in. He went outside to chain smoke and make small talk with the paramedics on break, trying to pump them for information. Dad hated doctors, specialists, surgeries, hospitals, in fact anything to do with the medical fraternity since he claimed they had misdiagnosed his diabetes for thirty years.

'It's easier for them to cover their tracks in here,' Dad had said about the hospital, eyes darting. 'It's all an inside job. And because one hand washes the other, they never get caught.'

Dad's medical conspiracy theories clicked into overdrive in hospitals, which only stressed Mum more. 'Let him go,' she'd said.

Mum was the polar opposite. She sat calmly, regularly asked where Dad was, reassured me that she was fine, and implored me to go home and get some sleep with each new yawn that I released.

Finally, the doctor appeared. He was smiling.

'Elizabeth?'

'Yes,' my mum said.

'Your tests are all clear,' he said. 'We'll do another set of bloods to confirm, but you should be able to go home in an hour or so.'

Mum sighed with relief. I squeezed her hand with glee. I couldn't wait to find Dad and tell him the good news.

'Leave him,' Mum said, 'at least, for a little while. This is my only chance to be the centre of his attention. Once he knows that I'm fine, he'll start pestering me, asking what's for dinner tomorrow.'

I smiled. This crafty old Greek lady knew exactly what she was doing. Not that that suddenly surprised me.

'So . . . how are you feeling since I told you the news, any questions?'

Mum's query seemed to come from nowhere, and yet was always lingering in the air.

'Umm . . . not really,' I replied. 'I've just been very busy at work.'

'Well that's understandable. But I have every hope that you'll meet your family soon.'

I was slightly suspicious. 'Do you have anything in mind?' I asked.

'It's completely up to you,' Mum said. 'You're old enough, and are clearly happy enough to travel long distances.'

She was referring to the previous summer, which I'd spent working in a lab in New York City. Before that, I'd only stacked supermarket shelves and delivered pizzas in suburbia. New York had been my first time out of home, and came after I had carpet-bombed hundreds of American academics looking for a short-term research opportunity before my PhD. In the end, I got one solitary acceptance, but one was all I needed. I ended up working for three months on DNA replication at New York University, eating a lot of salty bagels and oversized pizza slices, nearly getting mugged in Brooklyn, and even landing myself in hospital with a nasty virus.

'Your brothers want to meet you after all this time,' Mum added.

'Can't they come here?'

'Not really, no. Billy doesn't travel. I don't think he's even been to Thessaloniki or Athens.'

'So Georgios comes alone then.'

'That won't work either. Georgios won't leave Billy. Billy won't let him.'

'Not even for a holiday?'

'Unfortunately not . . . Billy's a good boy but my brother Savvas made some big mistakes along the way with him and how he was raised. The universe revolves around Billy now.'

I tried to picture what my mum was describing, but couldn't. The large nurse waddled past, her rosy face beaming a friendly smile.

'I'm less worried about your brothers because they're closer to your age,' Mum continued. 'It's more my brother Savvas, your *baba*, who weighs on my thoughts. How he's coping.'

I'd gotten used to hearing Mum call her brother my '*baba*'. Dad didn't seem to mind either. It wasn't news to him.

'Why, what have you heard?' I asked.

'Eh, reports here and there, mainly from my sister, Soultana. She's not married so she looks after three grown men now, her brother and two nephews. Billy's not quite independent and is still a handful. He's big like a bear, while his father and aunt are old, shrunken, like me. It's during times like these, when I'm in hospital, that I worry more. They're in a village high in the mountains, hours from the nearest city. They don't have doctors like we do, machines, blood tests, medicines. People are here today, gone tomorrow.'

I stared into space. I tried to relate to what Mum was saying. She was finally talking about the blood that flowed through my veins, but she may as well have been describing the blood of complete strangers.

I considered what she was proposing, but it was still too much. The timing was all wrong. I had worked hard to reach this point, and my immediate course of study had already been chartered. I couldn't even leave my experiments for a few hours, let alone a few weeks. What would the professor think of me if I suddenly asked to go on holidays so soon after starting such an important research project? It was as if all its success hinged on me as the test case.

But above all, I was intimidated, scared. I had never asked for any of this.

It was the idea of meeting my other father that made me the most apprehensive. Brothers were different; they were of my generation. Plus there were two of them to share the magnitude of the moment. But a father was singular, older, and ultimately more problematic because I already had one of those. Dad wasn't perfect, but what father was? He didn't have the qualifications for the job, but had all the experience.

'Sorry,' Mum said. Her light touch on my arm returned me to the room. 'I didn't mean to scare you. Don't worry about it. Concentrate on your work. I'm sure my worry for my brother is nothing. When the time is right. Until then, we'll organise a phone call with Greece. I've tried ringing a few times but they're never home, or they leave the phone off the hook.'

I exhaled, relieved. 'Okay,' I said.

The emergency ward went quiet. The nursing staff caught their collective breath before the next wave of late-night revellers hit. Mum closed her eyes and relaxed her neck. I stared at the blue paper curtain and started thinking.

'Well,' I finally said, 'I guess having brothers is the most intriguing thing. And how exactly was it that I ended up being "arranged" for you and Dad?'

Mum opened her eyes, sat up. 'Of course,' she said. 'I've wanted to tell you more about all those things but I've been waiting for you to come to me. I didn't want to overwhelm you.'

'My brother Billy, you said he's "slow". Was he born that way?'

Mum paused. 'I don't think so. It came later, from an illness or an accident. But I may be wrong. I wasn't there. That's just what I was told.'

I let out a light sigh. My fears that it was something genetic remained. I wanted an unequivocal answer. Instead, I was left to ponder my mutant mice and whether they could shed any light.

'I met your brothers twice over the years,' Mum continued, 'both times in the seventies when they were boys. The first was in 1973, a year before you were born. Your dad, my husband, had sent me to visit an orphanage in Thessaloniki. Needless to say, had I had any luck there, you wouldn't be sitting here today.'

I writhed in my stiff plastic chair. 'Gee, thanks,' I said.

'Sorry,' Mum smiled, 'blame your father.'

We laughed. I liked that we could finally joke at the situation. It brought us a little closer.

'Anyway, I guess the story started not long after your dad and I got married in Queanbeyan,' Mum said. 'Which itself was a process that began in our village many years before.'

CHAPTER 5

1930–1955

ELIZABETH'S PARENTS WERE Vasilios and Maria Paraskevaidis, Orthodox Christian refugees who fled to the Macedonian mountains of northern Greece from Turkish Anatolia during the 1923 population exchange. It was what those involved called 'the Disaster'. Maria had her first baby, Despina, when she was only thirteen. Over the next twenty years, five more children followed, with Elizabeth the last to arrive in 1930. Vasilios knew that Elizabeth was to be a girl when he tossed an orange seed into the fireplace and said her pregnant mother's name aloud. Elizabeth's seed didn't jump out of the fire. She was not a boy. Vasilios hung his head.

Elizabeth's eldest brother Savvas was a twin, but his doppelganger Prokopis died two days after birth. Soultana was her other sister and Vangelis her second brother.

'There's no part of our country over which more blood has been spilt than ours,' Vasilios often told his youngest, despite her meagre years. 'We're at the crossroads of three continents: where Greek meets Slav meets Turk meets Negro.'

Elizabeth was exactly the same age as the family home. Vasilios told her she represented 'the completion of the family' and was their beacon amid a wave of darkness and depression, when migration to America closed and their mountain village became a ghetto.

The family's whitewashed house was a sugar cube that sat on a small hill. Vasilios had dug its foundations with an old shovel. The blade brought up pieces of bone, white and smooth. Vasilios was told they were human remains, the bones of Jews. When the cornerstone was laid, Vasilios cut the throat of a cock and let the blood spill on all four corners of the house, starting with the eastern corner first. The small balcony had a panoramic view of the entire village of Florina below, all the way to the central square of Georgiou Modi *plateia* and the rolling Sakoulevas River. Three orange trees in the front garden were also as old as Elizabeth. Vasilios had planted them from seeds he found on the road to Florina using soil he'd carried in a bowl from Anatolia. At the base of the house, Maria had planted a creeping wisteria vine. In line with superstition, Maria claimed the plant's successful growth was due to having stolen the original cutting from a friend's garden. To Elizabeth, this seemed the wrong way round – surely it was better to ask for cuttings, not steal them. However, a star jasmine liana, similarly acquired, had also thrived, spreading across the lawn like a bridal train.

'And don't ever fall asleep under a fig tree,' Maria told her children. 'Christ was under a fig when he was taken.'

Being the eldest, Despina had selfishly inherited all the miserly scraps of beauty from each of her ancestors, pooled them together, and took people's breath away with her perfect porcelain face. She married in her twenties but had barely packed away her wedding dress when she fell ill and died before passing on her golden genes. Despite all her daughter's aesthetic blessings, Maria claimed it was a miracle Despina survived as long as she did, having emerged from such an underdeveloped body. Sitting in their cramped kitchen, Elizabeth wasn't sure what was going on and had asked to see her bedridden sister. As the youngest child, Elizabeth was never given any details, and her world was only ever painted with the broadest strokes. She didn't like it. To her family, a hapless blowfly bouncing off a window pane had more purpose in life than little Elizabeth.

Elizabeth was led to the bedroom by her mother. She stood beside the bed, staring at her sister, unsure of what to say. Elizabeth stepped from foot to foot until Despina took her uncertain hand.

'*Agape mou*, don't worry,' Despina whispered. 'It's fine.' She mouthed her baby sister a kiss like her own mother.

Despina's once dainty hands and feet were a vibrant red, her legs swollen with thick purple veins. The room smelled of new roses, a full vase Maria had picked that morning. Elizabeth's grandmother exhausted every incantation and herb she knew to rid Despina's flesh of the demon that had crawled into her chest and refused to leave. In the end, she slipped away without even a whisper.

'People die as they live,' Elizabeth's *yiayia* told her.

Her all-knowing *yiayia's* proclamation, sourced from a previous century, rattled around in Elizabeth's small head for years after. Every time she heard of the passing of someone in her village, Elizabeth tried to picture what their death was like according to how they lived.

The best man at Despina's wedding, Nikos, was a much younger boy from the village. Following Despina's death, Nikos had become involved with the rebel *andartes* fighting the Axis forces of the Second World War from the nearby mountain caves. Disgusted by the inactivity of the politicians during the Occupation, the youth demanded leaders who had no regard for pain or sacrifice. Nikos was one such individual, although it meant he ended up having a few altercations with the authorities, which soiled his official papers after the war. His imagination, however, was inspired. So it came as no surprise to Elizabeth's family when they learned that Nikos had decided to leave their village and take advantage of the new worlds opening up to migrants.

Through his connections, and an appropriate *fakelaki* or two, Vasilios helped Nikos's cause. So much of what happened in Greece took place because of connections and networks: jobs, contracts, goods, services. The word 'transparency' had yet to take root in the Greek lexicon, and probably never will. The other key component was the *fakelaki* envelope stuffed with money. During the war, the *fakelaki* was filled with food. It was what had kept Vasilios's family from starving through his job at the *foro*. Whoever came to Florina's square from the nearby farms to sell their produce – chickens, milk, vegetables – was required to pay for the opportunity to enter the town as a merchant. The *foro* was the small room on the outskirts of town where Vasilios collected the entry fees for the government, and for himself.

Vangelis had explained to Elizabeth when she was about ten that the *fakelaki* was the custom on which their country's economy was based.

'You want anything done in this country, you take a *fakelaki*,' Vangelis told his sister. 'You go see the doctor, you slip him a *fakelaki* under the table. The taxman or inspector comes to your shop, *fakelaki*. You open any business, build anything, go anywhere, you need the magic *fakelaki*. It's the way business works. Without it, nothing happens. It's an ancient and noble tradition. Like growing your best olives on land the taxman can't find.'

Vasilios had been reluctant to help Nikos because he knew of the young man's involvement with the rebel fighters. But he acquiesced, partly for the sake of Despina's memory, and partly to transplant the bad seed as far away from his family as possible.

Through nothing more than the stroke of a pen, Nikos ended up migrating to Australia. As Vasilios bade him farewell, Nikos pledged to make it up to him. Should any of his children ever want to follow him, Nikos would return the favour and take them under his wing in the new world.

The following night at dinner around the table's candlelight, Vasilios scoffed to his family as they slurped their onion broth.

'Can you believe that buffoon Nikos picked to go to Australia?'

Elizabeth swallowed a chunk of square bread. 'What's wrong with Australia, Baba?' she asked.

'Too far away, and too new,' Vasilios said. 'Did you know the British once sent their criminals there?'

But Australia was crying out for new migrants after the war in the Pacific. 'Populate or perish' was the rallying cry as the nation sought to boost its population in the interests of economic and military security. The doors were open, even amid global fears of Communism. Having also fought with the Allies during the war, Australia's bond with the Greeks had been forged.

Crammed in around their small table, Elizabeth's family listened to Vasilios's news with wonder, but it was Vangelis who listened most attentively. Having travelled to France and Belgium with the army, he sensed that this was his chance to escape the goldfish bowl that was his tiny village. Jobs were hard to come by in Greece, and the exodus of the nation's youth had already started. Crammed boatloads drained out from Piraeus harbour every day, as if some enormous plughole had been removed. The Greek Civil War of 1946–49 had torn the country apart and left it in even greater economic distress than during the Occupation. In the *kafenions* of Florina where the men gathered to drink and smoke and solve the world's problems, Australia's roads were said to be lined with shiny new pounds, not weak old drachmas.

Coming from a village in the Macedonian region of Greece, Vangelis's migration papers ended up being thrown in the same geographic pigeonhole as other Aegean Macedonians. Since the 1920s, they had settled in only a few dots on Australia's great map. One of them was a small town with a strange name: 'Queanbeyan'. On seeing the paperwork, Vasilios struggled to pronounce it. The first letter was throwing him. It was like nothing he'd seen before.

'And this is where Nikos is now living?' he asked his son.

'Yes,' Vangelis replied. 'In fact, Greek Macedonians first went there soon after the Disaster. They've been working as stone masons, construction workers and *efkaliptos* cutters.'

'What's *efkaliptos?*' Elizabeth asked, screwing up her own face at the new word.

'Trees,' Vangelis said. 'They call them *yoo-ka-lips*. There are farmers who use the leaves to make oil, dyes and honey. People pay big money.'

'And you will go all the way to Australia to make honey?' Vasilios laughed. 'You can do that here, my boy. Our bees are the best in all of Europe!'

'You're missing the point, Baba.'

'Am I? I don't think I am.'

'Do you want to know what I heard about Australia?' said a soft voice.

The family looked over to the stove in the corner of the room. It was rare Maria spoke while her husband was holding court. But she had sensed a change in the air, as if this was a pivotal moment in the family's history.

'I heard,' Maria said, stirring her saucepan, 'from Aspasia, you know, the lady who owns the fabric shop near the *plateia*. She told me about her cousin Froso who lives in Edessa whose son Petros had a friend Agamemnon who went to Australia three years ago. Agamemnon went to find work as an architect but was directed to a factory assembly line to sort screws. He's since come back and is now working in Thessaloniki, as an architect.'

'Madness,' Vasilios said, seizing on the opportunity, 'sheer madness. The country is backwards, it doesn't even recognise people with professional skills.'

Elizabeth swallowed her mouthful of rich rabbit stew. She wanted to believe that deep down, her father supported Vangelis's decision. Vasilios never shied away from his love-hate relationship with their basket case country from the day he'd arrived in Florina. Perhaps Vasilios even envied his son: younger, stronger, optimistic, and with an opportunity he never had, in a truly new country not plagued by war and corruption.

'My child,' Vasilios eyeballed his son, 'please listen to me. If you go, and our neighbour goes, and Antonis the tobacconist goes, and Nikos, and one day Savvas, and then probably your sisters too—'

Maria made a sharp noise as if in pain, dropping her wooden spoon into the saucepan. Her husband continued.

'If all that happens, how is this country ever supposed to get off its knees?'

At the same time as one family was questioning the new world around their kitchen table, a son from another was already standing on a bustling building site in the faraway Australian town of Canberra. His name was also Vasilios, but all the workmen called him the Anglicised 'Bill'.

Bill was an all-round maintenance man who fitted out newly constructed buildings with electricals, plumbing, painting and minor carpentry. Just across the border from Queanbeyan, the capital city of Canberra needed building, and Bill's joy came in seeing the tangible fruits of his labour rise from out of the earth. One nail at a time, he was bringing the untamed landscape to urban life. Bill saw his new city as an extension of his new self, and he was proud to be integral in the construction of both, building homes for young families and offices through which a fledgling government and country would function. Bill had never worked on a single new building in Greece; there, he simply applied band-aids to an ancient civilisation crumbling quicker than he could patch. Some Greek buildings were never completed, second storeys left intentionally unfinished to avoid paying tax. The chance to work with new tools, thick timber and fresh paint was enough to turn Bill's tired grimace into a gentle smile each night as he travelled home. The beer, when it finally reached his lips, was ambrosia.

After living in Canberra for a year, Bill moved to Queanbeyan and paid rent to his sister Melpomene and her husband for their spare bedroom. In turn, Melpomene was housekeeper for both her husband and brother. Melpomene's husband was a young man named Nikos – the same Nikos whom Vasilios had helped to leave the old country, and who met Melpomene not long after he arrived in the new. This was how Vangelis met Bill in 1955 soon after Vangelis set his Hellenic foot in the Antipodes.

Vangelis's farewell from Florina had been brief. It was what he wanted. Vasilios had long emphasised the need for a close-knit family, but Vangelis felt he was wearing a straitjacket.

Before Vangelis left for Australia, he had met a girl named Marika, two years his elder. Vasilios disapproved of Marika, which came after seeing her behaviour at a wedding party. She had been drinking and smoking and indulging in a large platter of food. But it all meant little to Vangelis who was in love and, free of his father's yoke, let his intentions be known. After emigrating from

Greece, he would set up things in Australia, before bringing across his future wife.

Over time, Elizabeth had come to be close friends with Marika. It happened secretively, as necessary in a small village patrolled by her father. Through exchanged letters with both his new fiancée and baby sister, Vangelis described a tall, handsome young man named Bill whom he had met in Queanbeyan. Even a country as sparsely populated as Australia threw up surprising coincidences: Bill was originally from Florina, born the same year as Elizabeth, but had moved to Thessaloniki as a teenager. He was now at a suitably eligible age. His chest was broad and his arms thick like lambs on spits.

'Vasilios, here, look at this photo,' Vangelis said. 'Isn't she beautiful?'

Bill took the image and saw a young woman with a fresh face and a dainty gap between her two front teeth. 'Like the Mona Lisa,' he said. 'Is she your wife?'

'No,' said Vangelis. 'That's my baby sister. She's still at home in the village. She's sweet and honest and easy to love. If you like, we can organise to bring her out here. And, if you like her even more, and my sister feels the same, then I'm sure we can work something out.'

CHAPTER 6

1956

THE ELDERS IN Elizabeth's village complained about the slow-moving wheels of Greek bureaucracy, and yet that was all their offspring aspired to. A dream job for life doing very little as an employee of the state, retirement in your early fifties, with a hefty pension till the day you died. All provided you knew the right people. If not, and you were a man, there was always the chance you could marry a woman with a dowry, which meant either a house or money. But if you were without connections, an inheritance, intelligence or a penis, there was little choice. You emigrated.

Soultana was stubborn. She stayed, determined to eke out an existence in the old country as a seamstress. Her little sister was not. The path of least resistance was to emigrate into the arms of a man at the other end of the line. The fact Elizabeth didn't want to and feared the unknown was irrelevant.

The paperwork was processed. Vangelis and Bill each sent

money as sponsors: Vangelis for Marika, his beloved, and Bill for Elizabeth, his stranger. There was an information night in the village where all the hopeful emigrants sat silently, not asking a single question of the migration officials in suits. Health checks and police clearances followed.

Birthplace? *In or near the town of Florina.*

Age? *Twenty-five and five-twelfths.*

Eye colour? *Chestnut.*

Height? *Five feet and four inches.*

Elizabeth and Marika were poked and prodded, made to feel more like horses. Eyes, ears, arms, hands, legs, feet, spine, head, teeth.

Elizabeth even made a special trip to Thessaloniki to meet Bill's mother, Artemis. She took a small box of candied almonds and a posy of pink flowers. Artemis slipped a silver ring on Elizabeth's finger with a diamond the size of a breadcrumb signifying that she was going to the new country as an engaged woman.

'There's a girl out there with a groove on her finger who fits this ring and this ring alone,' Artemis said. 'Maybe it's you. I hope it's you.'

Artemis reassured Elizabeth she could always return the ring if things did not work out. Elizabeth wanted to believe it would not come to that. She pictured herself married, with a new family, happy.

Elizabeth and Bill shared letters. Elizabeth sent a photograph of herself standing in a long black dress and black heels. Elizabeth and her sister chose the photo together. It was one of the few nice photos Elizabeth had, and one which she thought made the gap between her two front teeth appear small. Elizabeth didn't like to show her teeth in photos, but as Soultana had said: 'There's no point hiding this from him, *agape mou*.' The photo Bill sent showed a man in a grey suit, clean-shaven, with a square jaw, straight teeth and thick eyebrows, and with small curls perched carefully atop his brow.

'If this is Vasilios,' said Soultana, 'you're very lucky.'

On the sixteenth morning of July 1956, Marika and Elizabeth rose with the sparrows, preparing their belongings and clothes. They wore their newest and most modest summer dresses with crisp white gloves. Elizabeth descended the thirteen steps from the house, her fingers clasped firmly to the railings snaked by thin wisteria tendrils, and looked down to her parents below. Maria couldn't stop crying. Vasilios held her up, squeezed her shoulder tightly, whispered in her ear. No amount of dinner table discussion or imagining could ever have prepared Elizabeth for this moment. Seeing her mother so hysterical made her want to drop her bag and run into her arms and say she'd never leave. But Vasilios kept ushering her on with a sodden handkerchief, his moustache and nose dripping with sticky salt from under his cloth flat cap. Maria cracked open a pomegranate, spilling the cornucopia of crimson seeds as a sign of fertility, while the split fruit embodied her broken heart. When Maria gave Elizabeth her last glass of water, she couldn't bring herself to drink without her father tilting the glass.

The *parea* of family friends accompanied the two travellers to the train station. Elizabeth's friends carried her bags the whole way, as if she were a soldier going to war and they were carrying her weapons to conserve her energy. All of Elizabeth's worldly belongings fitted in two bags: a small suitcase for the trip, and a chest full of blankets, sheets, towels and clothes. All those items rested in the chest on top of her mother's blue rug from Anatolia, the one she'd woven in an underground workshop as a child. Maria had worked fourteen-hour days while the village men ploughed the fields without the aid of oxen or horses, before they all retired to sleep on a pounded earth floor. This was the extent of Elizabeth's dowry – a random collection of fabrics, along with stolen cuttings from grape vines and fig and olive trees that Maria insisted she take in case her baby daughter needed her own supply. Maria had told her daughters many times over the years: 'Don't ever sit on your dowry chest or you'll never become a wife.' Elizabeth never had.

One by one, the *parea* kissed the two girls farewell. Elizabeth's head swam as the train chugged slowly out of the station towards the Athenian port of Piraeus twelve hours away. She clung to Marika's arm. Without her there, telling Elizabeth 'all will go well', sharing her handkerchief and kissing her gently on the forehead, Elizabeth was convinced she would have stopped breathing and died.

'Don't cry,' Marika kept saying. 'Don't let them see you crying.'

Outside, Elizabeth looked terrified. Inside, she was screaming. She wore a false smile and had a hard knot in her chest. Her lungs felt like they were choked with wool.

'And don't worry you don't speak the language,' whispered Marika. 'When you're at home, it'll be the same as here. And there will be people in Australia who will love you just as much. You can't see it now but you must believe it.'

❧

The image portrayed to Elizabeth during the immigration information meeting was of a short journey, comfortable, exciting, a continuous dream floating past romantic scenery, docking at exotic ports, meeting interesting people from different countries. Instead, it was a full month aboard a leaky boat which left Elizabeth so sick she was barely vertical, hardly able to leave her bunk bed, let alone her room.

Her first evening aboard the *Neptunia* had been without incident. She had not been ill; she was simply weighed down with a heavy heart. Elizabeth spent most of it on the deck, admiring the indigo water and the novelty of the coastline rolling past, watching the shore lights of Greece until they became tiny specks.

It all changed the next morning. She couldn't eat, drink, sleep or stand. She sweated through her clothes and could not stop shivering. All her nostrils could smell was the noxious effluvium of fuel oil combining with rust and salt, a bitter tang suffocating the air. For a month, the only thing grumbling louder than the bowels of the *Neptunia* was Elizabeth's stomach. Marika, on the other hand, hadn't a care in the world. She partied every night like it was New Year's Eve.

Having traversed the Suez Canal, Red Sea and Indian Ocean, and following stopovers in Ceylon and Fremantle, the *Neptunia* finally docked in Melbourne on the holiest of name days

– Panagia's day, the Feast of the Assumption of Mary, fifteenth of August 1956. The bright, temperate Mediterranean summer had transformed into a grey Melbourne winter with rain of biblical proportions. Vangelis, Nikos and Bill had driven down from Queanbeyan in a Bedford truck that they planned to load up and drive back.

'Hello, baby sister!' Vangelis said when he saw Elizabeth. He embraced her mere shadow.

'*Geia sou*,' Elizabeth said. '*Pos eisai*, Vangelis?'

'Wonderful!'

Elizabeth had to admit that her brother looked fantastic. His skin was clear, eyes bright, grin wide. His spirit was renewed.

And then, Elizabeth and Bill saw each other. The first thing she noticed was his brown skin and eyes, as if shaded with the same crayon. Bill's photo had failed to do him justice: he was as tall as a sapling, rugged, and with a broad back. Next to Bill, Elizabeth thought her brother appeared like a little boy. Bill told her he understood how long and tiring the trip was. 'I made it myself last year,' he said. 'And I was once a fisherman, so even more used to the water.'

Elizabeth didn't say anything. She could only smile. She thought Bill's eyes hinted at a warm heart.

'Well?' Vangelis prodded Bill with a sharp elbow. 'How does she look?'

'Lovely,' was all Bill said.

That night, Elizabeth, Bill and Nikos attended a party given by a local Melburnian man named Pavlos, whose family had emigrated from Florina around the time Elizabeth was born. Surrounded by loud strangers and burdened with a lingering queasiness, Elizabeth ate nothing. She sat in a corner, as shy as a kitten, watching Bill, the boisterous lion and life of the party. All she could muster that evening was her same forced smile.

Vangelis and Marika didn't stay for the party, flying to Canberra that same afternoon. Pavlos leaned in to Elizabeth's ear to be heard over the blaring *bouzouki*.

'Your brother, eh?' he said. 'Off like a bride's nightie!'

'Sorry?' she bellowed back, pretending not to have heard him. But Elizabeth had heard. She just didn't understand.

Pavlos smiled. 'Never mind, my dear,' he said. 'It's just an expression. Not important.'

The next morning, Elizabeth was still dizzy, and her day was to only get worse. A twelve-hour, diesel-laden journey north to Queanbeyan lay ahead along roads with the consistency of a cheese grater. She barely had a chance to take in the enormity and sparseness of her new country as she drifted in and out of consciousness. In western Macedonia, even the tiniest scrap of land had been cultivated, divided up in inheritances, and had blood spilled over it. In southeastern Australia, the land was dry, endless, virgin bush. Skeletons of trees, fingers and arms outstretched, begging for rain. Everything appeared vivid, as if the entire world had been polished with a fine sheen of wax.

The hard knot was still in Elizabeth's chest.

CHAPTER 7

1956–1963

Elizabeth was still fixing her hair in the mirror when she heard the beep of Bill's motorbike on the road outside.

'A relic from my days in Europe,' he told her. 'I had one there, too, but better than this jalopy.'

With some convincing, she hopped on the back and they rode together around Queanbeyan on their first date. Never having known a man, Elizabeth was cautious. But Bill came with her family's blessing. He didn't speak much English, which only served to bring them closer. By their second date, they already looked to each other for support.

They were soon laying out traditional Greek picnics on the red Australian soil. Bread, Kalamata olives, big chunks of goat's feta, garden tomatoes and cold *keftethes* that Elizabeth had prepared the day before. They discussed the old country, the new country, the heat, the people, the heat, the old country. Gunshots rang out in the distance, which Bill explained as 'young boys hunting rabbits', something he was known to do from time to time.

Little by little, excursion by excursion, story by story, and after weeks clinging to Bill's torso as he sped his piercing motorbike through the bush, Elizabeth's shyness started to fade. Where Elizabeth was from, few knew what it meant to be with a man outside of marriage.

Things moved fast. They had to – Elizabeth couldn't stay long with Vangelis and Marika, who wanted to embark on their own independent lives free of paternal control. The same went for Bill with his sister and her husband. Bill proposed by burying Artemis's ring in the *taramasalata*, which Elizabeth scooped up with a chunk of bread. She feigned surprise, said yes, and they kissed. She rinsed the ring, slipped it on her finger, and they finished the roe dip.

The wedding was a month later. There was no plump-domed Orthodox church in which they could marry, nor was there a local Orthodox priest to conduct the service. The nearest solution was the monthly Orthodox service the priest from Sydney performed at the Anglican Church on Rutledge Street. For all the fabrics in her chest, Elizabeth's dowry did not include a wedding dress. Instead, she and Marika bought their own material and sewed two dresses: one for Elizabeth's wedding in October and one for Marika's in November. The dinner reception was out the back of a small café on Monaro Street. There was circle dancing and plate smashing until midnight, before everyone then helped clean up and stack chairs.

Elizabeth and Bill's first house was a rental – a small

demountable in the suburb of Narrabundah on the eastern outskirts of Canberra that exclusively housed the city's poorest workers. When they pulled up on a wintry Saturday afternoon, the underside of the car's chassis was so heavy that it scraped the road. Elizabeth took one look at her new house and thought, 'I want to go home.' It was painted jaundice yellow. The dream she once had of her husband carrying her across the threshold was replaced by a box of heavy copper saucepans.

The house was basic. It smelled like fresh cut timber and was one of many identical prefabricated houses the government had erected side-by-side. The street resembled a movie set. The plywood walls were as thin as cigarette paper and the raw wooden floorboards birthed splinters the size of souvlaki skewers. Elizabeth placed her mother's blue Anatolian rug next to their bed along with an icon brought from Greece to safeguard the house.

Within a few weeks, cracks opened in the floorboards. The pipes froze. There was a cast iron stove in the kitchen with baked-in food detritus and a fireplace in the living area which Bill fed sticks he'd foraged from the bush. The tin flue from the fireplace to the outside was not insulated in the roof.

'Well, our box of matchsticks is quite literally that,' said Bill. 'One spark and we'll burn to death.'

Elizabeth remembered Florina's underground air raid shelters, and the prospect of being roasted alive. Like a bunker, her house had only one external door.

'It's a hen house,' Bill said. 'It'd be safer to pitch a tent in the yard and build a bonfire.'

The only redeeming feature for Elizabeth was her independence. Her own kitchen. Her own laundry. A Hills Hoist rotary clothesline. These were all things that a modern woman had.

But the novelty didn't last long. Elizabeth fast became bored and lonely, isolated on the sprawling flats of suburbia. Throughout the day, her only companions were blowflies. She complained to Bill, who was working five and a half days a week, about how she would sit and listen to the kitchen clock tick. She had even noticed it was maddeningly out of sync with the bedroom alarm clock.

'Leave it with me,' Bill said. 'After a shower, I'll make it so they tick together.'

He refused to let her get a driver's licence. 'We only have one car,' Bill said. 'And I'm the man, so there's no point.' She tried to navigate the bus routes but the local roads were a jumbled snarl of streets and circuits, as if weaved by a caffeinated spider.

Spending all her time in her own company, Elizabeth grew to expect a lot from her husband in the evenings. She found herself losing patience and getting frustrated when she saw he was not listening or did not think along the same lines. Bill often went to bed early citing 'exhaustion'.

In the end, he bought her a radio. Elizabeth played it all day and all night. In the evening, the soft mandarin hue from the lighted station dial cast an intimate glow across the living room that often made her fall asleep on the sofa. The wireless alleviated Elizabeth's boredom but until she could learn more English, it remained white noise. Her Australian neighbour often said hello and tried to strike up a conversation, but neither could understand a word of what the other said. The neighbour once invited

Elizabeth for afternoon tea with two upright fingers: 'Come at two o'clock, alright? Yes?'

She served an enormous layered sponge cake and coffee that Elizabeth thought tasted more like strained mud. The two women then sat like cuckoos, listening to clock ticking. The invitation was not repeated. And when Elizabeth thought she saw a pair of binoculars watching her from across the street, Bill was forced to bring home a roll of brown paper from which Elizabeth constructed 'blinds'.

Elizabeth's father sent letters detailing the news of the village – births, deaths, marriages. Her isolation eased, and yet her home felt further away than ever. Elizabeth would shuffle the thin pages through her hands over and over in case she had missed some small piece of news. It didn't feel right. She was living her life vicariously.

Elizabeth went to Bill. 'I want to work,' she said.

'No need,' he replied. 'I make enough money, and I'm the man. The men work, the women stay home.'

With each negating comment from her husband, Elizabeth felt her airway narrow. She was suffocating. She had equated marriage with freedom, having grown up as the baby in a family where she was granted none by her father. In Bill, it was as if she had swapped one guardian for another.

It was only after Bill broke his arm at work that he finally let his wife follow an opportunity she'd heard about through the local church. It was waitress work at what they called the Lolly House, an annex to a workers' hostel where they served meals and drinks.

The Lolly House had linen tablecloths and napkins starched pristine white like Elizabeth's new apron and cap. All around her there was movement and gossip and life. The female guests fixed their hair, freshened their make-up, and made sure they looked good; the men the same. The dining room was the place to be seen, a stage where the latest outfits were paraded and new images created. Even with her limited English, Elizabeth recognised that social events were being organised, dates and parties and outings, the beginnings of new lives together. It was heaven.

And then, a letter from Greece arrived. It was again from her father, and dated six weeks earlier. Elizabeth opened it while leaning against the letterbox.

My darling daughter, I write with sad news. Mama died last month. The funeral was last week. She had her blood tested in Thessaloniki and stayed at the clinic for an operation. But problems followed and she never recovered. We're all deeply upset, this happened so unexpectedly. I am so sorry this is the only way to tell you the news. Tell Vangelis that –

Elizabeth stopped reading. She dropped the letter as if it were infected and started to shiver. She cried. A three-dimensional image of her mama standing at the bottom of the steps the day she left home materialised inside her head. She struggled to stay on her feet and called to Bill who had just returned from work. He bolted outside to see what was wrong before the neighbours got any ideas. He helped her inside and sat her on their olive green vinyl sofa. He held her close and finished reading the letter.

He ran her a bath and fried bacon and eggs for dinner, but Elizabeth wasn't hungry. Bill then sat quietly and listened to his wife's rants and regrets: about how she never should have left Florina, never should have left her mama, never should have left for bloody empty, barren Australia.

Vangelis and Marika visited that night. Elizabeth showed her brother the black page.

'Why is it they write you and not me?' Vangelis stammered, a salty drop of condensation forming on the tip of his red nose. He handed the letter to Marika who by now wore a ring on each finger.

'Because I actually write to Baba,' Elizabeth said. 'Do they even have your address?'

'When your mother dies, you become old,' Marika said curtly. 'You always save things to tell your mother. No one else's embrace ever feels as warm or as comforting.'

The letter had enclosed a final photograph of Maria, one that Elizabeth had never seen before. Her mother was standing on the balcony of their house by herself, looking down. The house looked the same as when Elizabeth had left it. Even though Maria's face wore no obvious expression, Elizabeth felt it reflected a heart full of sorrow and loss.

For weeks afterwards, Elizabeth barely ate. She was numb and couldn't stomach anything. Bill let her be. To think a single sheet of paper could shatter Elizabeth's everything, the pain like being beheaded with a plastic knife. That Maria would never lay her eyes on Bill or see herself in Elizabeth's unborn children. That Elizabeth would never again sit with her and sew and talk and cook and eat. It seemed so unfair, to have her taken away like that. She was only sixty-three.

During her quiet moments, Elizabeth pictured her family performing the ablutions on Maria's body, covering it in almond blossom. She wondered how many people from the village went to the funeral. Hopefully there would be a crowd. Elizabeth remembered that her *mama* always went out of her way to pay her respects to the departed. She sometimes travelled miles out of town on the back of a donkey to attend a memorial service, even when she wasn't feeling well. On Maria's return, Elizabeth would hear her outside in the yard, washing her face with cold water from a bucket before she could enter the house. The ritual washed away the spirits of death so they could not be dragged into the house.

For months thereafter, Maria came to her daughter in random, nonsensical dreams. Elizabeth would wake in a panic and turn to her left to make sure her mother's blue rug was still on the floor next to her bed. She wanted to return to Florina to visit but it was too expensive, even with their extra income from the Lolly House. Instead, she bombarded her father with letters, almost one per day, asking how they were and requesting more information about Mama. Vasilios replied when he could, but never as often as Elizabeth. Sometimes he just sent an envelope with no letter but stuffed full of old family photos from younger days when they were all together. Elizabeth wasn't sure whether he wanted her to have them or if he simply did not want them any longer.

In her grief, Elizabeth often wondered how she got herself into such a mess. Why go all that way to spend her life with a stubborn, controlling stranger? Why tear herself away from all she held dear to travel to an abyss at the bottom of the world once founded by felons? Her father had warned her.

To Elizabeth, life meant family. To be a woman was also to be a mother, and without a baby she knew she would always feel like a little girl. Her chipboard hovel wasn't the Parthenon, but both she and Bill had been raised in less.

Elizabeth lost her first pregnancy there, not long after she married. After a blood test, her doctor had told her she was pregnant, and she and Bill held their glasses high, thankful for the blessing. But ten weeks later, the baby was gone without Elizabeth even realising. In almost every conversation they had, she and Bill found themselves ending on the phrase: 'If only we had a child.'

'Little by little, our child will come,' was the inevitable response to each other.

But there was nothing. The doctors couldn't find anything wrong with either of them.

'*Skata!*' Bill would later wail at home. '*Gamo to kerato sou!*'

Elizabeth learned early that swearing was a way of life for her husband and that rarely a job was successfully completed without it, whether it was unblocking a drain or impregnating his wife.

Elizabeth lost a second pregnancy, and then a third, in similar circumstances. Not long after, she found a long rose growing up through the cracked floorboards in their spare bedroom. It was new life in the room that was meant for the baby. Surely, Elizabeth thought, surely it's a sign.

'It may well be,' Bill said, 'but let's leave it a while, put it out of our minds, and see what happens.'

But nothing did, and Bill was soon frustrated again. Elizabeth's job helped ease her feelings of worthlessness. And yet, her subconscious mind continued to tick over, sending maternal messages to her every pore. Elizabeth didn't think it was possible for anyone to long for anything more in this world than she did for a baby. But there he was, a hundred hulking kilos, in the same room as her each night, grumbling, finger to his temple, wanting exactly the same thing. The noise became deafening.

Elizabeth and Bill's outings, which once were fun, had started becoming onerous and frustrating. There was a mass of rosy babies and sticky toddlers at every gathering, as if the entire world was teasing them. Elizabeth and Bill stood out like two foxes in a chicken coop, both suddenly self-conscious, almost voyeuristic. They were the kindly couple no one pointed out was childless. Even Bill, the heart and soul of social occasions, showed signs of cracking. And in every round cherub face, Elizabeth saw her mother's distant smile.

One evening, as they sat in their own empty hen house, Bill clicked his fingers. An idea had arrived.

'We should take one.'

Elizabeth looked up from her sewing. 'Take one what?' she asked.

'A child,' Bill said. 'Eliso, don't you see. It's so simple. We should take someone else's child.'

CHAPTER 8

1964–1970

THE CHOOK PEN was Elizabeth and Bill's home until land opened up in new suburbs on the northern side of town. After the Depression and war, materials were finally available for the construction of domestic dwellings that were not 'cow sheds or ex-army barracks', as Bill called them. Elizabeth didn't want to move to another sterile location. She'd had enough of Australia's gaping spaces and crushing skies. She longed for the security of her metropolitan embrace, the marketplace, the square, the kafenion, the church. In her village, Elizabeth couldn't walk five minutes without seeing a familiar face. In Australia, she could walk five days.

'Now now,' Bill reassured her. 'You'll see. It won't be so bad.'

But the northern end of town was exactly what Elizabeth had expected, great tracts of nothingness, wide expanses of flat paddocks, the odd tree. Except, their new suburb of Hackett had one significant difference – the backdrop was a verdant mountain erupting with thousands of eucalypts. It transported Elizabeth back to her village and the mountain alongside, heavy with chestnut trees.

'Oh . . . my,' she said, her breath escaping.

'I told you,' Bill winked. 'And this time, our house will be brick, double brick. Solid, like all those nice privately built houses we always drive past. It'll be beautiful, you'll see.'

Elizabeth closed her eyes and imagined her suburban palace. Perhaps her luck was finally going to change. Perhaps her new house would tumble with new life.

'In time, the suburb will expand,' Bill said as they surveyed their new outlook. 'Even bigger houses will appear in the streets on the side of the mountain.'

'So long as the peak is still visible,' Elizabeth said, picturing the large white cross on top of the peak in Florina.

Elizabeth and Bill moved in during the pit of winter. Each day, Elizabeth watched the magpies carrying around twigs and spinifex grass in their beaks. The birds were preparing their nests high in the ivory gums that towered opposite their house. Come the thawing warmth of spring, the magpies would descend with their demanding offspring, squawking and cheeping and skipping as they followed their parent in pursuit of food. Bill's big heart liquefied at the sight of the birds drilling for worms in the dirt.

'They're so trusting and tame,' he said.

Elizabeth often found him throwing them small crumbled pieces of feta.

'Stop it!' she implored him. 'You're teaching them bad habits. And besides, that feta is expensive, and I need it for salad.'

By summer, ancient lizards with protruding blue tongues began warming themselves on the mint concrete slab. By contrast, the front lawn was brown and patchy and each morning littered with fresh kangaroo droppings.

Elizabeth's job at the Lolly House was a world away now, on the far side of town that suddenly had a lake in the middle after the Molonglo River was dammed. The commotion some mornings with everyone in a hurry to eat breakfast and start their working day was like bottles smashing inside Elizabeth's head. In and out of the revolving kitchen door, the Lolly House girls carried precarious pyramids of porcelain and reams of clattering plates. Salt and pepper shakers were refilled, ashtrays rinsed and tablecloths changed with military precision. Weeks became months, months blurred into years. Elizabeth was a hamster on a wheel, with a mountain of household chores awaiting her at home. Sleep was her only refuge, every night beside a man who snored a combination of stale tobacco and antiseptic mouthwash.

With so much to do, the inevitable happened. Elizabeth slipped on the floor at the Lolly House and fell hard. Lashings of food went flying. There was an almighty reverberation in her spine that shook her whole body like a walnut cracking.

An ambulance arrived and she was taken to hospital. X-rays revealed that Elizabeth was fortunate.

'It's just bad bruising,' the attending doctor said. 'But the spine can be like black magic. The simplest thing you can do is take six months off work and do very little at home. Lie flat on the floor when you can.'

With Elizabeth out of commission, Bill called in his mother

from Greece. There was no consultation. Artemis arrived with a single suitcase.

Elizabeth had not seen her mother-in-law since their only meeting in Thessaloniki a decade earlier when she gave Elizabeth her engagement ring. Artemis had aged terribly. She had shrunk, her hair was grey and thinning, and her face had shrivelled like a withered leaf. On seeing Artemis so frail and mortal, Elizabeth recalled her own mother. Overcome by distance and loss, Elizabeth rose from the blue living room rug to greet Artemis warmly, proud to show that her marriage to her son Vasilios was still going strong. To Elizabeth, Artemis smelled of aniseed. But to Artemis, Elizabeth stank of failure.

'Humph!' Artemis said, rolling her head from side to side. She eyeballed Elizabeth and said, under her breath: 'And just *where* are my grandchildren? Vasilios desperately wants to be a father. It's all I ever hear from him. And *you* can't give it to him.'

Elizabeth did not respond, and looked away.

'You're not much of a woman, are you?' she continued. 'I'd had six children by the time I was your age. *Six*.'

Elizabeth never told Bill what his mother said. But every day after that moment, the temperature dropped when Artemis and Elizabeth found themselves in the same room. Elizabeth's heart twinged, as if one of its valves had frozen over. Did Artemis not have any love left for her daughter-in-law? Did she not respect her in any way? Artemis had not emigrated, assimilated, learned another language, or ever done any paid work. But Elizabeth had. Perhaps Bill would never see her efforts either and always side with his mother, like so many dutiful Greek sons did. Elizabeth and

Bill were more equals than he would ever realise. Elizabeth knew she had the same back and arms and legs. She just happened to also be the one born with the incubator.

'Don't use so much olive oil . . . Your *spanakopita* is undercooked . . . Why are you adding walnuts? Add more sugar . . . I said more!'

Artemis's comments on Elizabeth's cooking tore at her soul. Because Elizabeth knew what she was really saying: 'Where is my grandchild?'

By now, many of Elizabeth and Bill's compatriots were starting to reap the rewards from sowing an early harvest in the new country. Those who had arrived well before them, during the 1920s and 1930s, had started businesses or purchased great tracts of land. They now arrived at the cinema or to weekend football matches in shiny new Mercedes and BMWs, before returning home to their big houses amid the leafy streetscapes of the established suburbs. Even Vangelis had bought a second house. Bill felt jealous; not because other people had more money or bigger houses. But rather, because of what reverberated off their walls – the laughter of the next generation. Money and children, security and heirs. Elizabeth mused at how it all came so readily to some people. Some of it as a result of smart decisions that were to be applauded, but most of it was due to factors beyond anyone's control.

Returning to work after nearly half a year, Elizabeth moved like a marionette and could no longer perform her duties at full pace. Thanking the Lolly House for the opportunity, she bade goodbye to the dear old ducks in white. Tears filled her eyes as they presented her with a large farewell card. The girls who did not know English simply wrote their names or something in their own language, and then added a long row of x's and o's. It was a dishonourable discharge; honourable would've been to have had children. Elizabeth returned home to again move unobtrusively in her husband's orbit. She was now a broken woman of forty years with a pipe cleaner for a spine, eyelids that scratched when she blinked, and a pleated neck like corrugated iron. She sighed as she stared at her white belly in the mirror, picturing a round, perfect baby bump. Instead, all she saw was flabby middle age.

Elizabeth's miscarriages dogged her into the new decade. Artemis looked straight through her most days, while Bill kept climbing the walls and complaining. Not satisfied with the small nation of syrupy children who followed them at every social gathering, Bill was unable to contain himself around strangers anymore, stopping at stores he went to with Elizabeth and gazing at the children absently, then talking to them. They would giggle and stare back, intrigued at the sudden attention from an unfamiliar source, while their mothers would endure Bill's advances with forced smiles, but eventually politely turn and walk away.

CHAPTER 9

2000–2001

FOR OVER A year, I must have dissected and analysed more tumours than a retired oncologist. But the results were clear: my mouse strain had a T cell leukaemia that had arrested during the early stages of maturation. It likely started in the thymus – the organ that produced the vast majority of T cells – before spreading to the peripheral lymphoid organs – the spleen and lymph nodes – via the bloodstream. The average age of leukaemia onset was four months. But not all carriers of the mutation developed leukaemia; only about two-thirds did. This was consistent with cancer as a disease that occurred after cells incurred multiple genetic alterations caused by either single point mutations in DNA or recombinations, amplifications or deletions of genes. In our case, the chemical mutagen that we'd used on the pedigree founder mice – ethylnitrosourea – caused DNA point mutations, so while the mice that inherited this mutation were predisposed to leukaemia, they still needed at least three more DNA insults before cancer developed.

And so, my project moved into its second phase: identifying the culprit gene by mapping. To do this, I used a panel of repetitive DNA markers called 'microsatellites'. These were short tracts of DNA which had certain motifs repeated, but which differed in length between mouse strains. By breeding our founder black mouse strain with the cancer mutation against a white strain, we produced grey offspring with mixed tracts of DNA: some from the black parent, some white. By using the microsatellite markers to identify the black segments, we could then narrow the interval in which the cancer gene resided. In short, this stage of my project involved observing which grey offspring mice developed leukaemia, generating a sample of DNA, and amplifying different sections of the genome represented by each microsatellite using the famous polymerase chain reaction, a discovery that won the 1993 Nobel Prize in Chemistry. It was an even more laborious process than labelling the tumour cells with fluorescent markers. It took nearly a year to breed the grey mapping mice, and then another six months to optimise the microsatellites because the vast majority of reactions didn't work. But then, nearly two years after I began my project, a common region was identified near the start of chromosome 11 that was inherited by all the grey mice that developed leukaemia. Because we knew these mice all had black regions of DNA in that region, and because all developed cancer, we could finally link the cancer gene to that chromosome 11.

The professor was overjoyed. My discovery meant he could adapt the microsatellite mapping panel to all the other mutant mouse strains he'd generated and share it with the other PhD students to map their DNA mutations in the strains they were studying. Two competing groups had only recently published the very first draft sequence of the entire human genome to much scientific fanfare and intense media attention. The timing was incredible, and I was grateful to have contributed to the lab's mutagenesis project in such a significant way.

Unfortunately, the initial excitement of locating my cancer gene on a chromosome faded when I realised there was already a known gene on the same chromosome associated with T cell leukaemia. Standing between the shelves in the dank medical library, my heart sank when I read the research paper. It was published in the prestigious journal *Cell* by a lab from Harvard University in 1995. There it was, in black and white and grey, as if they had cracked open my skull in the middle of the night and transcribed the contents of my brain. The same phenotype, the same gene. I was gutted; I had wanted to find a completely novel gene. But such was the sport of science: an endless international race to submit that groundbreaking research paper a day before anyone else. And if you weren't first in science, you were last. Even without the head start, there was no way I could compete with such a lab – better funded, better resourced, better networked, and with all the thunder. And to think they'd only beaten me by a handful of years. The best I could hope for now was some low-rung publication documenting my find for the sake of completeness. It would be a piss in the ocean, not a tidal wave. In perhaps the greatest of ironies, the researcher who discovered my candidate gene was Greek-American, and had even given it a Greek name: *Ikaros*.

It felt like a mortal blow. I had worked so hard, harder than any time in my life. The professor stopped me in the corridor as

I shambled back to the lab with a still-warm photocopy of the 1995 research paper. I handed him the article; he scanned it, and somehow remained upbeat.

'I know this gene,' he said. 'Don't worry about it. It may not be *Ikaros*. Let's try to narrow the chromosomal interval to an even smaller region, and you may find that you can rule it out.'

But I couldn't. I successfully narrowed the linkage region down in size, which cut the number of candidate genes in half. And again, another half. But no matter how I sliced it, *Ikaros* remained firmly within the interval.

'Go ahead and resequence it,' the professor said. 'Let's check first if there are any DNA mutations in it before we get carried away. We've already got the sequence, so we'll know if there's a mutation. We're looking for a mutation, remember. If there's no mutation in that gene, then the cancer must be caused by another gene.'

It was hopeful thinking, but it was still hope.

I presented my data at a small scientific conference in Mount Buffalo in the Australian Alps. I made a new friend from Melbourne, who appeared to be a kindred spirit: he was about the same age, did research on mice, worked all hours, and wanted to help people after a health scare in his family prompted him to do medical research. We decided to stay in touch and perhaps even work together on a project one day.

With all this going on, thoughts of my biological family slipped further into the background. That was until I returned home late one night, having once again been thwarted by the gods of molecular biology. The *Ikaros* gene wasn't resequencing from my leukaemic mice, and I couldn't get a decent read of DNA sequence from their cancerous tissues. Dog-tired, I drove home with the windows down and stereo blaring. The night was warm and conducive to falling asleep at the wheel.

Dad's blood sugar often dropped during the night so it wasn't a surprise to find him fixing a snack at some ungodly hour. But on this particular night, I returned to find all the house lights on and both my parents drinking black coffee.

Mum's eyes were bloodshot. She had been crying.

'Your father,' she said.

'What about him?' I said, looking over. 'He looks fine to me.'

'No, my brother,' she said. 'My sister Soultana called earlier. He died a few hours ago.'

Oh . . . no.

I sighed and walked over to hug Mum who rose from her chair as if to embrace me. She was clearly upset but was already a step ahead of her son, ready for the fact that I may be more upset.

I knew this day would come; today, tomorrow, next week. My family and friends had been fortunate to have escaped the touch of the Reaper's bony finger for a long time. But now, even though he had taken someone I'd never met, I knew I wouldn't have been standing there without him. And Mum had told me that the adoption proposition had always been *her brother's* idea.

I knew I should have felt sad. And I did. But it was a more automatic reaction, in response to hearing of the death of anyone, rather than a deeply personal one. How do you mourn someone you've never met? I was sad for Mum's loss and guilty for my own. Uncle Savvas wasn't just anyone. He was the architect of my creation, and also one of the engineers. Biologically, he *was* my father. The reality that I would never meet him bulldozed a pit into my stomach when I realised that I'd also let my mum down. She'd always held out hope that her son would one day meet his family. That I never met my biological mother was Mum's fault, but that I never met my father was mine. An opportunity had passed forever. And it was all because I was busy with my bloody research. Because I was ambitious. Because I was a coward. Because because because. Fear is frightening, but it's never as frightening as regret.

Mum sat back down. Her hopes were dashed, more so than mine. For despite all my remorse, both immediate and future, I would've been lying if I didn't acknowledge that part of me was also relieved.

Ever since I was told of my adoption, I had been trying to reassemble the mother of all existential jigsaws. The pieces never fitted or I was content to merely push them around the kitchen table. Or I procrastinated and got distracted by more immediate, less daunting problems. Now, the jigsaw would never be complete. In truth, I didn't want to get to know another set of parents.

Dad drained his cup and went to prepare another coffee in his copper *briki* pot. It was a slow, careful process he had mastered over the hot sands of the Mediterranean as a fisherman. I had never developed a taste for his sugary black sludge but Dad was so determined to cook it properly, he'd installed a fast gas burner in the kitchen to circumvent the slow electric stove.

We'd had a phone call with my biological family a few months earlier. The phone line to our village of Florina crackled like an open fire. My hand trembled as Mum passed me the receiver, my palm sweaty, my head throbbing. I expected to hear my own voice on the other end.

'*Ela*,' a voice said, '*ti kaneis*, how are you?'

It was my brother Georgios. He was a baritone, reflecting my own deep voice.

'*Ela!*' I said, a little too eagerly. '*Kala*, I'm good.'

'You know who I am, yes? Your *mama* explained it to you?'

'Oh yes.'

'I'm your brother, eh!'

'You are. Yes!'

'And Billy too, he's our older brother. He's sleeping now but you can speak with him next time.'

'Great!'

I heard my voice, speaking a faltering Greek and sounding overly enthusiastic.

'So,' Georgios cleared his throat, 'when are you visiting?'

I laughed nervously. The question came far too quickly in the conversation and had probably been brewing for decades.

'Ah, um . . .' I tripped over my words, stumbling to buy time. 'Soon.'

'When?'

'Ah . . . not sure yet. My job here is very busy.'

There was a long, thoughtful pause. '*Endaxi*,' Georgios said coolly. 'Soon then. We'll talk again. Now that you know, we'll talk more often.'

Ever since the call, I had wondered what my brother thought of me, of our short, awkward exchange. Surely that I could even communicate had left a good impression. Mum beamed as she took back the receiver to continue the dialogue at a million miles an hour. No wonder she had been so vehement insisting I learn Greek when I was little, even sending me to language classes run out of an old convent building built in 1886. Other hyphenated kids had been less pressured by their parents, but Mum knew this day would come. Georgios didn't mention our deceased mother and then-ailing father, still working as a fruiterer at age seventy-seven.

I sat next to Mum on the couch and took her hand. Her fingers relaxed in mine. A familiar hiss of gas was heard from the kitchen.

'What happened, Mama?' I asked. 'How did Dad . . . er, I mean your brother . . . how did he die?'

I had my geneticist cap on, in case it might be anything hereditary. I could no longer respond to doctors when asked if there was any medical condition which ran in our family. It made me feel surprisingly self-conscious and apologetic.

'I'm not exactly sure how Savvas died,' Mum replied. 'Soultana mentioned *gangraina*.'

'What's that?'

'Eh, you know.' She pointed to her slippers. 'His foot, all black.'

I thought a moment, trying to assemble the pieces.

'Oh, you mean *gangrene*. His blood probably got poisoned.'

Mum nodded solemnly. 'My sister mentioned an infection, a bad smell.'

I winced at the thought. Gangrene, in this day and age? The mere mention of the word evoked diseases I thought had been eradicated. It was like hearing someone died of smallpox or polio or croup. I wondered precisely how underdeveloped my family's village was and whether I would need a raft of vaccinations to visit.

'Gangrene,' I repeated. 'Really, people still die of gangrene?'

Mum wiped her eyes. 'I told you,' she said. 'The medicine and doctors they have in our village aren't like it is here. People still die of things like *gangraina*.'

'Georgios or Theia Soultana never told you any of this on the phone?' I asked.

'No,' Mum sighed. 'Not a word.'

I was suddenly annoyed, and a little angry. How could Mum's family justify not mentioning her brother was unwell, let alone at death's door?

'Probably didn't want to worry us,' she added. 'It was the same with your mother.'

'How so . . .?'

'She apparently had a lump in her breast, and didn't tell anyone in the family because she didn't want to worry them.'

I shook my head lightly, rubbed my eyes. It sounded so utterly tragic at a time when doctors continued to emphasise the importance of early detection. My biological mother had been only sixty-four.

'When's the funeral?' I asked.

'Later this week, I think Friday,' Mum replied.

'Are you going?'

'No. No time. Or money.'

'You sure? I can give you money. I've been saving my scholarship.'

'That's sweet, *agape mou*, but save your money. Soultana's

taking care of all the arrangements. I feel for her and also pray for her.'

I sensed Mum didn't want to go. After not seeing Greece for twenty-seven years, to return to something so traumatic could do a septuagenarian more harm than good. But not me. Now, I knew I had to go more than ever.

I squeezed Mum's hand. 'You'll be okay, Mama?'

She exhaled, eyed the heavens. 'Eh, I'll survive. I'm used to this kind of thing now, and it's only going to happen more.'

Three mornings later, as I prepared to go to the lab, I was surprised to see Mum's smile had unexpectedly returned.

'I got to say goodbye to Savvas,' she told me. 'When they took his body home before the funeral, Soultana phoned again. She put the telephone receiver on our brother's chest. I spoke direct to his heart. I said goodbye.'

CHAPTER 10

1973

ELIZABETH SAT ON the olive green sofa, her bare feet on her mother's blue rug, making anxious fists with her toes. Her hand trembled as she held Soultana's letter. Her other hand rubbed the gold cross hanging on a long chain around her neck. It was late afternoon, the house was quiet.

'Baba's unwell,' her sister had written. 'It was a harsh winter and he's an old man now.'

Elizabeth's heart stuttered at the prospect of never seeing her father again. A tear ran down her cheek at the thought of her mother.

It was an easy decision. She told Bill as soon as he got home from work.

Elizabeth purchased an airline ticket and two weeks later, boarded her very first airplane. Bill had no interest in returning to Greece. Not even to visit. He had worked so hard to break free of that busted country, why should he ever go back?

Up close, the Boeing appeared sleek and welcoming. Thin and pointed like a sharpened pencil, with sparkling contours and warm corporate colours. It reminded Elizabeth of the paper planes she and Soultana once folded and tossed off their balcony to their father's annoyance. Her sister's always soared further because she was older. Elizabeth found herself wondering how this metal bird could possibly be of the same species as the grey predators that had rained down so much death over her village three decades earlier.

After six thousand days in exile, Elizabeth knew her family was only a day away. Too excited to sit still in her cattle class seat, she wrung her handkerchief between two clammy palms. Meanwhile, her breast pocket was burning. In it, she carried a mission of vital importance.

'While you're in Greece, go to Thessaloniki, visit *Agios Stylianos*,' Bill had told her the night before she left. 'See if you can get a baby.'

This was an orphanage – the Municipal Home for Foundlings. Elizabeth thought there was something very nineteenth century and poetic about the notion of adopting and raising a waif. As the 747 jumbo rumbled along the tarmac, her head was giddy at the prospect of being a child's second chance. Sitting back, she looked out the porthole window, and watched the world fall away.

When the plane had reached cruising altitude, Elizabeth closed her eyes. She had something on her mind. Something big. Perhaps even bigger than adopting a baby.

Tired of being childless, frustrated with doctors and his wife,

Bill had told Elizabeth that he was reconsidering their marriage. In a word: divorce. Elizabeth's knees went weak when she first heard the word. She knew divorce existed but didn't know anyone who'd had one. Certainly no Greeks. Bill said that a divorce was possible on the grounds of 'wilful and persistent refusals to consummate the marriage'.

'But that's not true,' Elizabeth said.

'I know it's not,' Bill replied. 'But if we'd consummated our marriage, then where are our children? There's no proof.'

As sad as it was to realise it, Elizabeth knew that Bill was right. She resented feeling manipulated, but Bill was also all she had. She'd moved half a world away to make a family with him. His motivations to be in Australia were different – he went for opportunity.

In the end, she decided not to say anything to her family. But it meant her visit to *Agios Stylianos* was now doubly important. Her potential to be a mother and her status as a wife were both on the line.

Compared to Elizabeth's month-long nausea riding the undulating seas, flying across the globe was over in an instant. The final eight-hour bus journey to her village over rocky terrain was seen through only semiconscious eyes. The bus stopped with a squeaky jolt, propelling Elizabeth awake. And then, there they were, no longer a hazy image in her mind's eye. Elizabeth's sister, brother and father, all walking towards her with open arms. A tidal wave of familial love she craved more than oxygen.

'My child,' Vasilios cried. 'Elizabeth!'

The family collapsed into each other, a sobbing mess.

'Look at you, a woman now!' Vasilios said. 'You left here a scared little girl.'

'Oh, Baba,' Elizabeth said through flushed cheeks, 'I'm just older.'

Soultana was playing with Elizabeth's hair, which was much shorter than when she had left. She kept asking Elizabeth why she had cut it, asking her a dozen questions at once, and rubbing her hands all over Elizabeth's pink face. But if Elizabeth's sister was a warm cardigan rediscovered in a bottom drawer, then her brother was the stiff, ill-fitting shirt that she never wore. Savvas stood back, letting a hand-rolled cigarette slowly turn to ash between stained fingertips. He let his sister and father carry on with the bulk of the hysterics; he was above all that. The passing of time had plucked Savvas of his thick plumage and turned him bald. Elizabeth thought he looked more like their father than ever before. Standing together, the men had the appearance of a set of *komboloi* worry beads.

'Eh,' Savvas said as Elizabeth patted his shiny new head, 'grass doesn't grow on a busy street.'

The family walked back to the house slowly, their arms interlocked, moving as one. A few old friends recognised Elizabeth, stopped her on the street, kissed her; she promised to see them soon. The family home was just as she remembered it: the whitewashed stone, the three orange trees and tang of citrus in the front yard, and the balcony where she last saw her *mama*. But the neighbours were now unrecognisable. New multi-storey blocks of *polikatikeia* flats reached for the heavens like long fangs rudely squeezed out of the gums of the earth.

'*Poh poh!*' Elizabeth exclaimed, craning her neck. 'What happened here?'

'Greedy people,' Vasilios scoffed. 'People I thought were my friends, my *parea*, all sold their blocks, moved away, all in the pursuit of the drachma. But not us. Come, come inside and see.'

As Elizabeth climbed the front steps, she noticed the heavy drapes of her mother's purple wisteria vine were now overflowing and dripping down over the balcony railings. Its thick woody arms were like spaghetti twisted around a fork, strangling the balcony prongs into unnatural contortions. The creamy vanilla scent flooded the pleasure centre of Elizabeth's brain and transported her back two decades.

Even though the facade was the same, the interior of the house was different. It was quiet and felt empty. Maria's stolen wisteria was thriving but her absence, the loss of her warmth, the aroma of her cooking, was palpable. The little house once tumbled with youth, with life and laughter. Now the old kitchen smelled only of bitter coffee and tobacco and onions. It was more cramped than ever.

'*Agape mou*,' Vasilios said, taking his chair, 'you must be exhausted. I know I am. I didn't sleep a wink last night.'

Apart from a sharp cough and being perhaps a little underweight, Vasilios appeared healthy. Elizabeth didn't know what to make of her sister's letter, which had made their father sound like he was close to death.

'Tomorrow,' said Savvas, preparing coffee, 'we'll go visit Mama.' It was one of the few things he said all evening.

'Yes of course,' Elizabeth replied. She was relieved that someone had finally mentioned the unmentionable. 'And there's one other thing I need to do tomorrow. Can we go in the morning? My train leaves for Thessaloniki in the afternoon.'

'Train? Thessaloniki?' Soultana asked. 'But you only just arrived. What business have you there?'

❧

The next morning, Elizabeth walked with her brother and sister down to the plateia. They crossed the bridge, past a knot of swans floating gently in the river.

'Baba's not coming?' Elizabeth asked.

'Best not,' Soultana said. 'Let him rest. He can't go as often as Savvas and me.'

The old cemetery was not how Elizabeth remembered it. The brick walls surrounding the perimeter were overgrown with ropes of ivy. The grass was hip high. A row of white poplars against the back wall were being strangled by rampant creepers. A sour cherry tree heavy with rotten fruit and caterpillars wept a large sore of saffron sap. The whole place smelled of mildew and felt cold, as if seeking to repel all worldly visitors. Under a pine tree, a family of stray cats curled around each other on a cracked concrete bench, sleeping. As Elizabeth entered, the mother cat woke and hissed at her like a cobra.

Savvas and Soultana walked on ahead of Elizabeth. The white pebble path crunched with every step like a million insects dying.

'*Etho*,' said Savvas. 'Here.'

He pointed to a grave being suffocated by a lattice of long

octopus tentacle vines. A small candle was burning behind a glass door that contained an icon and a washed-out photo of Maria that Elizabeth barely recognised. The inscription was fading. Alongside Maria's grave was a vacant plot already reserved for Vasilios.

'*Theos mou*,' Elizabeth said, feeling her knees buckle.

Elizabeth knelt, doing her cross. Soultana crouched and put an arm around her little sister as she started to sob.

'It's okay, let it out,' Soultana whispered. 'She kept asking about you, you know. Almost every day, wondering how you were, what you were doing.'

Soultana's honesty made Elizabeth weep harder. Savvas turned away, cupping his hands to light a fresh cigarette. Weighed by his thoughts, he started on a slow lap, the crunch of gravel fading.

'Did I do the right thing, going away?' Elizabeth asked.

'Of course you did, *agape mou*. Don't ever doubt it for a moment. Mama just missed you more than she thought she would, more than we thought she would. You were her baby, always and ever.'

'I missed her too,' Elizabeth said between short gasps of air. 'She knew that, right? That I loved her?'

'Of course!'

'Ah.'

'Mama was incredibly sad with Vangelis leaving, and then you not long after. She ate less and took to bed earlier. Not a day went by when she didn't cry for you. Eventually it all became black for her, her melancholia, and she never recovered.'

Elizabeth frowned. 'Sorry?' she said. 'What do you mean?'

'She just lost the will . . .'

'I thought Baba wrote she died from complications after a test on her blood and operation at the—'

'Listen, Elizabeth,' Soultana's tone had changed, become firmer. 'We had to tell you *something*. You were so far away. And not that we can be absolutely sure either. But there was no clinic, no blood test, and no operation.'

Soultana's words struck Elizabeth like pellets of hail. Soultana took her younger sister's hand. Elizabeth felt its lack of warmth.

'And if anyone asks, I didn't tell you any of that,' Soultana added.

The sisters sat quietly, watching their flame flicker behind the glass, and listening to the hosts of sparrows flittering overhead. No wonder Soultana had been so nice since Elizabeth had arrived. She was building her up to tear her down.

Savvas appeared.

'*Ela*,' he said, '*pame*. We'll come again. I need to return anyway, to clean things up around here. But we better go now or you'll miss your train.'

CHAPTER 11

1973

ELIZABETH BOARDED THE train heading east to Thessaloniki. She napped sporadically. Maria's image had returned to her with a clarity not seen in a decade. Bill's face came to her, too, dark and shadowy. She was met on the platform by his cousin Lefteris, a tobacconist.

Artemis had disapproved of Elizabeth's visit to her home town. She'd heard the story behind Vangelis's family, and was outraged. It made her spit vitriol at her daughter-in-law through her gummed mouth with its single gold tooth.

Like Elizabeth and Bill, Vangelis and Marika's nest had remained empty. Although both couples could plainly see the other's deficiency, they failed to talk about it. It was a sign of the times. Infertility was not discussed in the open; such topics were taboo.

After seeing his family's attitude towards his wife and decision to emigrate, Vangelis's distrust of his family had never dissipated. He pictured his blood cells as weighed down with atomic-sized anchors. Had it been possible, he would have had a whole body transfusion.

But Vangelis was proactive. In the autumn of 1972, he added his name to the register at an Australian adoption agency. By the spring, he and Marika were offered a newborn baby girl. Vangelis named her Maria after his mother. Two years later, an adopted baby boy would complete their nuclear family.

'What do you think?' Elizabeth had asked Bill.

'Think? Of what?'

'Of what Vangelis and Marika did.'

'What about it?'

'Do you think we could also—'

'Hell no.' Bill's eyes were wide. 'At least, not from here, not some convict's child, a mixed mutt with a dozen different blood types.'

By contrast, adopting a child from the old country was a much more appealing proposition.

'We'll get a much better baby there,' Bill said, 'a pure one.'

But Bill also had something else in mind other than just breeding stock: the paper trail.

'If we adopt an Australian baby, the parents could always try to find us, and then them,' he told his wife. 'But if they're ten thousand miles away, in a country where official papers get lost like tourists, where nothing can be believed, it's much safer for us. Go to *Agios Stylianos*.'

Elizabeth and Lefteris walked slowly along the platform. 'What do you think our chances are at *Agios Stylianos?*' she asked.

Lefteris puffed on his pipe. 'Buh,' he said. 'How would I know?'

It was a quick but honest remark that drained Elizabeth of all confidence.

'It's not like I've ever had any reason to go there myself,' he added. 'But you're here now, and I know how much it means to my cousin.'

Positioned between Dikasterion Square and the polytechnic school, *Agios Stylianos* was on 28th October Street, at the end near the port. Lefteris and Elizabeth found number 99, a plain building with a grey facade that could have been almost anything.

They were ushered down a long, empty corridor and into a cavernous, windowless room. Elizabeth had hoped to hear the laughter of young children but heard none; only silence. A bald man with a biro and clipboard and a lady with a thick folder of papers, beehive hair and false eyelashes sat at a solid wooden table. The room smelled of chalk and strong disinfectant. They asked Elizabeth a raft of questions that echoed in the room. The focus of their interrogation was plain:

What savings do you have?

How many properties do you own?

Do you have any other assets?

Do you have any inheritances?

Where do you work?

What do you do?

What money do you earn?

Is your job secure?

Same questions, but for your husband . . .

And so on.

The message was simple – no children for poor people.

Elizabeth cleared her throat and sat forward in her wooden chair. She had prepared for this moment. It was her chance to both become a mother and remain a wife.

'Now, Vasilios and I, we know we don't have much to offer by way of wealth,' she said in her best spokeswoman voice. 'But what we can offer are our hearts, overflowing. We come from good families and know we'll be the kindest and most loving parents. We feel that is ultimately more important than riches.'

The man with the biro glanced at Elizabeth over his black horn-rimmed glasses. They were so thick that Elizabeth saw her reflection twice. He could have been writing down everything she was saying, or furiously making his own judgement of her character, or writing his shopping list, his mind already made up. The woman fixed Elizabeth with a synthetic gaze.

'And your husband here . . .' the man said.

'Sorry?' Elizabeth said.

'This, your husband sitting here . . .'

'Oh no,' Elizabeth said. 'This isn't my husband. This is his cous . . . er, his brother.'

'So where is your husband? We'd obviously like to meet both potential parents and we thought the appointment today was with—'

'My husband, you see,' Elizabeth interjected, 'Vasilios, he couldn't make it today because he's working hard at his job in Australia. That's where we live, in Australia. He's a builder, you see. My husband works hard, very hard. There's a lot of work for builders in Australia, which is why he went there. And I've travelled all the way from there to see you today, from Australia. My family lives—'

'So,' the man interrupted, 'let me see if I understand you correctly. What you're saying is your husband isn't here today?'

'Yes,' said Elizabeth.

'And that you plan to take a child from here to the other side of the world to live with you in, where did you say? Australia? Is that correct?'

'Yes.'

'And this . . . this isn't even your husband sitting here?' He chose to repeat that.

'No.'

A protracted silence settled in the room. Elizabeth didn't know if they were waiting for her to extrapolate her one-word answer. The man coughed, glanced at the woman beside him, then back at Elizabeth who met him with a blank expression. Lefteris looked away, not wanting to get involved. It appeared as if the man was waiting for something extra out of Elizabeth, but she had no idea what else she could say or do. She eventually smiled politely.

Finally, the man clicked his biro and stood to thank Elizabeth and Lefteris for their time. The woman escorted them down the long corridor where their footsteps echoed on the cold parquetry. She showed Elizabeth and Lefteris out of the building, ensuring they left the premises. They saw no other people inside the orphanage, adults or children. A heavy wooden door of double thickness slammed behind them; Elizabeth heard it latch. She noticed it had been raining, making the concrete pavements streaked rivers of dirty brown dust.

After an hour and two *metrio* coffees in a nearby café, Elizabeth finished rationalising what had happened and thanked Lefteris for his support. She leaned over to return his now sodden handkerchief.

'Keep it,' he said.

Elizabeth returned to Florina that same evening on the next train. She was escorted the entire way by an image of her heartsick, dying mother. Crestfallen, there was no reason for Elizabeth to stay in Thessaloniki any longer. The city did not want her, and she now longed to have her loving family around her again. Deep down, Elizabeth knew she had effectively lost her final shot, that she and Bill had exhausted a blizzard of options. And now, she would await her fate at the hands of her husband.

'Let me explain it to him,' Elizabeth told Lefteris as she was boarding the carriage.

'Of course,' Lefteris said. 'May God protect you.'

CHAPTER 12

1973

'THERE HE IS!' A white-bearded Christos greeted Vasilios warmly. 'Where've you been, eh manga? We've missed you.'

The menu at Christos's *taverna* was dictated solely by the local produce available. Elizabeth liked that. On this particular evening, it was suckling lamb and *kokoretsi* on a spit, rabbit stew, *horta* greens with olive oil and lemon, and stuffed peppers, along with brandy and ouzo. Savvas ate so quickly that he couldn't distinguish between his grubby fingers and the meat he was eating. The air was saturated with the smells of herbs and spices. They dined beneath a walnut tree next to a garden of rosemary and oregano. Christos played his *bouzouki*, a rare treat, to serenade Elizabeth on her return to Florina after seventeen years. Vasilios couldn't stop smiling. Christos had been his friend since childhood.

The evening had been joyous, like so many in the past. But now, home again, Elizabeth's body ached. She sat in her family's kitchen with her brother and father, staring at nothing in particular and considering whether to mention what her sister had told her at the cemetery about Maria. It ate away at her. Elizabeth closed her eyes and pictured her mother smiling and leading a circle of dancers with a twirling handkerchief. Then she pictured her husband emptying his closet and filling his suitcase.

Savvas packed his briar pipe, a ritual he reserved solely for day's end. 'So,' he said to his sister, 'how'd your trip to Thessaloniki go?'

Elizabeth opened her eyes slowly, reluctantly.

'Eh, this that and the other,' she said, being brief. 'They wanted to know absolutely everything about us. What we earn, what jobs we do, what colour underwear we wear. And as soon as they heard where we lived, they made their minds up.'

Her father and brother sat quietly, gently nodding their heads, digesting Elizabeth's information. Soultana and Anna had already gone to bed.

'*Paithi mou*, did you offer a *fakelaki?*' Vasilios asked slowly.

Elizabeth's face went blank.

'What?' she said. 'When? Today, you mean?'

Savvas extinguished his pipe and rubbed the bridge of his nose with tawny yellow fingertips.

'Wait,' he said, 'you mean to say, you went all that way and didn't offer a *fakelaki?*'

Elizabeth was silent, speechless.

'An envelope, you know,' Savvas continued. 'It basically kept us alive during the war, eh Baba?'

Vasilios smiled knowingly, nodded.

'Oh,' Elizabeth said. 'Was I supposed to?'

Vasilios sighed. Savvas groaned. He couldn't quite comprehend how his baby sister had travelled all the way from Australia on such an important mission and yet somehow failed to follow the necessary local custom.

'I didn't realise you still did that here,' Elizabeth said. 'No one does it in Australia!'

The men stayed quiet now, speechless. They massaged their temples and lit fresh cigarettes.

'Would it really have made a difference?' Elizabeth added. 'I mean, I was asking to take a baby, not buy a bag of beans!'

Great plumes of silvery smoke glistened and choked the tiny room. Elizabeth found it hard to breathe. Her thoughts went to her husband. She feared what he may do on hearing his wife had failed to follow the requisite custom at the orphanage.

Savvas finally spoke.

'Tell me, dear sister. Do you really want a child?'

'Of course,' Elizabeth replied instinctively. 'My husband wants a baby more than anything in life. And so do I.'

Savvas dragged on his cigarette, a nebula of pale smoke above his head.

'Well, how about this. Would you like me to give you a child?'

Elizabeth wasn't sure she heard him properly. She was tired and thought this perhaps was the first of many nonsensical voices that would soon be ringing in her head.

'Savvas, my brother, what do you mean?'

'A child,' he repeated, 'you know, a baby. Would you like me to give you one?'

'But . . . how?'

'Anna and I. We'll have another.'

'You would do that?'

'And why not?'

Elizabeth couldn't answer that. 'Well,' she said, 'before you make any decisions, you'd better ask your wife.'

'Hm,' Savvas said, 'yes, of course I will.' And he left the room like a steam locomotive.

Elizabeth and her father were alone now. She looked at him for wisdom, guidance. He shrugged his shoulders and screwed up his gummy face.

'Eh, what do you want me to say, my child?' Vasilios said, scratching his grey whiskers. 'It would be very good if Savvas gave you a child so you could feel the same pain we do as parents. But I fear what may happen afterwards.'

'Afterwards?'

'Many things can happen. What if he offers you a child and then changes his mind? Or one day asks for the child back? Or Anna does those things? You'll have all sorts of trouble. And what will you one day say to the child about all this? This is a child we're talking about here, not a car or animal or pet. So many things could happen. You're playing with fire.'

Elizabeth paused. She wanted to believe her brother. 'I don't think so,' she said. 'I'll go to Australia with the baby and—'

'And . . .? And then what? "And" is the short-term view. Unfortunately, no one can give you the long-term one, not even me, with you both as my children. The potential consequences are immense and you're not in control. No one is, not even me. All you can do is discuss your brother's proposition carefully with your husband, and then again with your brother and his wife.'

Elizabeth considered what her sagacious father had said but

couldn't make any sense of it. Her longing for motherhood was too powerful and smothered her clarity of thought. Without even speaking with her husband, she knew precisely what he would say. He cared for the consequences even less than she.

Elizabeth hardly knew her sister-in-law, Anna. She had deep set brown eyes and a red wine stain birthmark on the right side of her face. 'Because my mother denied herself port when she was pregnant,' Anna had explained. 'So now I bear the mark.'

Savvas reappeared the next morning. Elizabeth had waited for an hour after he had shuffled off the previous night, expecting, hoping, that he may return.

'Ah,' Savvas said. 'Sleep there, did you? I left you in that same chair last night.'

'Good morning,' Elizabeth said slowly. 'No, I slept in bed, a little. How did you sleep?'

'Like a hibernating bear.'

'Tell me, last night, when you—'

'You mean my proposition?'

'Yes. What you said. Were you serious, did you mean it?'

'Tell you what,' Savvas said, 'before we go any further with this, perhaps you should write to your husband, and see what he thinks. If he says no, then we've nothing more to discuss.'

And with that, Savvas exited the kitchen to sit on the back stoop and roll his first cigarette of the day.

Elizabeth sat quietly, considering her feelings. Had her brother changed his mind? Had he already discussed it with his wife and she'd said no? She was being paranoid, and stopped herself. Instead, she took her brother at his word and imagined a newborn baby in her arms. One part of her wanted to take it for herself, to never breathe a word of this to her husband, to raise the baby alone. But where and how? It wasn't possible. She had only ever known two homes. And her husband's threat was just a reflection of his deep-held desire for a family. Elizabeth was sure of it, and convinced herself that he would be the world's best father. He loved her.

Blinking away her thoughts, Elizabeth stood and washed her face with cold water. She fetched her cardigan, and kissed her brother on the way out, saying nothing. Savvas watched her disappear down the hill towards the *plateia* and headed for the post office. Elizabeth rushed inside and scribbled a letter to her husband, which she sent via registered mail, the quickest service available.

Over the next two weeks, Elizabeth barely slept. She could no longer look either Savvas or Anna in the eye, let alone make proper conversation. She went for longer and longer walks, staying out later and later, trying to avoid them. No one said any more about the proposal.

Finally, a reply from Canberra arrived as a registered letter:

And you're even bothering to ask me? You already know the answer. Yes yes yes. Say yes. And say thank you from me.

There was no mention of anything further. Elizabeth was relieved. She would not end up tainted and have to carry the shame of a divorcee. She would remain a wife, and would hopefully soon be a mother.

Savvas read the letter and then handed it across the kitchen table to Anna.

'Well,' Savvas said, 'it's good to hear your husband's just a little enthusiastic! And from where we stand, we've decided that even with Billy in the picture, the extra work he is, we're happy to have another baby, to give to you to take and raise in Australia.'

Elizabeth's eyes opened wide. She looked straight over to Anna in the corner who was nodding gently.

'Anna, this is absolutely wonderful news,' Elizabeth said. 'I can't even begin to express my joy. Thank you from the very bottom of my heart! But first, I must say something because I've been thinking about it. You already have two sons. If the third child is a girl, I don't think you'll want to give her to me. Once she's in your arms, you'll want a daughter.'

Anna cleared her throat. 'Elizabeth,' she said calmly, 'now I've been thinking about this for some time, and let me tell you something . . .'

'Yes.'

'I know that it's possible the child will be a girl, and I must admit that it has also crossed my mind,' Anna said. 'But I can promise you, as I live and breathe by the Lord's good hand, the baby's sex is not relevant. Whether it's a boy or girl, the child will be yours. I promise that to you, today, before your family and Almighty God. Because I know that if I change my mind and don't give the baby to you after today, then God will find a way to take the child from me somehow.'

Anna, like Elizabeth, was a woman who believed in strong forces beyond mortal control. Torturous as it had been, the lengthy turnaround time with registered mail may have been a blessing and Anna had been able to think about the situation more deeply.

Elizabeth fixed her eyes again on her sister-in-law. Anna looked relaxed, almost joyous, as if a light shone through her.

'*Endaxi*,' Elizabeth said. '*Efharisto*.'

Embracing her brother and his wife, Elizabeth's eyes teemed with tears. That night, she finally slept soundly, like a kitten full of warm milk.

CHAPTER 13

2002

I WAS NOW more determined than ever to get to my family. The passing of my biological father had been a defining moment, and it made me work even harder in the lab. The perishable nature of my experiments meant I had to keep going, but I was hell-bent on finding my mutation and then getting on a plane bound for Greece. Conversations with the professor had also started me thinking about life after the PhD, which for many Australian graduates usually meant working overseas as a postdoctoral fellow. If you could prove yourself in the shark tank abroad, you could write your ticket home to a secure academic position.

With renewed vigour, I tried again to resequence the *Ikaros* gene from my cancerous mouse. I spent months grinding their bloated organs down to a thin syrup with a titanium-tipped electric homogeniser, then trying to extract the precious strands of DNA. I was never short of biological material – the malignant organs were huge. But the quality of DNA extracted was questionable because the mice were so sick. The sicker they were, the more genetic mutations they had, which made things complicated because I was searching for the very first mutation, the one that stirred the development of cancer.

'You may need to generate mice with two copies of the mutant gene,' the professor told me. 'All you've done so far has been using the heterozygous mutants with one copy.'

'Oh,' I said. 'So I should try breeding two carrier mice together, before they get sick?'

'Exactly. One in every four offspring will then have two copies of the mutant gene. They're the *homozygotes*. You should get cleaner, longer reads of DNA sequence. You can then check those for mutations against the published sequence in normal mice. The homozygous mutants will also give us a chance to see what happens when there are two copies of the mutant gene present. The female is the key. She needs to carry the gene, but has to stay healthy for long enough to produce pups.'

The Harvard lab had published an earlier *Cell* paper in 1994 showing that their homozygotes lacked an immune system. What were the chances that I would find the same?

I paired my carrier mice and waited a month before their progeny were born, and then another two months before I could sample and analyse their DNA. I carefully tested sixty DNA samples from sixty mice over the course of a week. And found . . . zero homozygotes.

I thought I'd ruined the experiment, paired the wrong mice, and ultimately wasted three precious months.

Before I spoke with the professor, I decided to retest the

samples, and burned another week. But the result was the same: zero homozygotes.

I was stumped. Finally, I scheduled an urgent meeting.

'I don't think you've done anything wrong,' the professor said. 'The homozygous phenotype is probably embryonic lethal.'

I sat back in my chair. I stared at the professor, then the data in front of me, then back to the professor. 'Embryonic lethal?'

'These results suggest that inheriting two copies of the mutant gene is deleterious to the organism,' the professor explained. 'It's too much for the animal to take so it dies during gestation. The mother then resorbs the foetuses. They're never born, which is why you don't see them scampering about in their cages, and why you didn't identify any here. They're there, but you have to look much earlier in time, to before they're born. It's like a spontaneous abortion due to genetic abnormalities.'

'Like a miscarriage?'

'Exactly.'

'So how do I analyse the foetuses?'

'You need to do timed matings,' the professor said. 'I actually haven't done them for a while, but I can show you how. Unfortunately, you're probably going to have to sacrifice a lot of females. And it's a lot more lab work.'

I felt the blood drain from my face.

The professor explained that it was certainly possible to anaesthetise a pregnant female, remove the embryonic brood from her swollen womb, stitch her back up, and hope she recovered. But the surgery was not worth the effort given the hundreds of experimental embryos that were likely needed to pinpoint the DNA mutation.

I set up my breeder pairs every afternoon. The animal wrangler told me to always add a female to a male's cage, not the other way around. Like his mammalian cousin *Homo sapiens*, the male mouse apparently preferred to perform his 'moves' on his own turf. It was where he felt more comfortable, more confident. The next morning, I returned early to check the female for a vaginal plug. This was a gelatinous secretion deposited by the male into the female's genital tract, which hardened into a plug and glued the tract together. It looked like a hole in the wall filled with putty, easily spotted on black mice, but if I waited too late in the day to check, the female would urinate out the plug. The vaginal plug was a carryover from the natural world where males would otherwise have actively guarded their mates rather than pursuing more.

The discovery of a vaginal plug signified copulation, and became experimental day zero. By day twenty, the pups would be born. The professor recommended we do our dissections on day fourteen, two-thirds of the way through gestation. Pregnant females were separated into their own cages; males that did their duty became prized stud bulls and had more females cycled past them. Sometimes it was two females at once in a rodent *ménage à trois*.

After fourteen days, I carefully carried a pregnant female in her cage to the pathology lab. I watched as the professor euthanised and pinned her body to a styrofoam dissecting board. He doused her distended abdomen with 70 per cent ethanol, deftly snipped open her lower abdomen and pulled up an overcrowded uterus with a pair of stainless steel tweezers.

'Whoa,' I whispered, 'incredible.' My surgical mask pulsed as I spoke.

The embryos were each encased within their own fragile yolk sac and fed through an intricate train network of fine blood vessels and chorionic villi leading to individual placentas. Together, the embryos appeared like red beads on a string. The professor rinsed the bloody necklace in a petri dish of saline and slowly detached each embryo one-by-one, puncturing their protective vacuum and removing the delicate unborns like the pits of sour cherries. I noticed how unsettled I suddenly felt by the embryos' appearance; they were eerily human-like, an aspect that reflected the high genetic similarity between man and mouse.

The professor lined up the first litter of embryos with his fine tweezers. Of the eight otherwise pink foetuses, two stood out. They were ghostly white, and slightly shrunken.

'That's them,' he said under his breath. 'Right there. See them? That's got to be the homozygotes.'

Examining the embryos, I saw it instantly. Exactly one quarter of the mice were anaemic, bloodless.

The result was clear. One mutated copy of the gene caused blood cancer. But two copies appeared to overload the blood system and obliterate its production completely. It was Mother Nature's dark power on display before my very eyes. Incredible. Exquisite. Humbling.

The professor's eyes grew large. He extended his gloved hand for the first time since the day we met. I shook it.

'This is incredible,' the professor said. 'You're back in business. To my knowledge, there's no published report of embryonic lethality due to anaemia for the *Ikaros* gene. Order some reverse transcriptase and resequence it again. But this time, don't use the

DNA you extracted from the cancerous tissues with all those secondary mutations. Use the clean DNA from the tails of these bloodless embryos. You'll get a much better read and we'll see once and for all if your mutant gene is *Ikaros*.'

He was right. In a week, I had a complete DNA sequence. And a week later, I had identified a mutation smack in the middle of the *Ikaros* gene. Changing a single letter of DNA had brought mammalian blood development crashing down; just a few atoms of carbon altering adenine to guanine. Given the complexity of the code for life, it was one in three billion possibilities. Three billion things that could go wrong every single time a cell replicated, and more than two hundred billion cells replicated each day. A microscopic change in the arrangement of a few atoms caused death when there would otherwise have been life. It was almost unfathomable if I hadn't seen it with my own eyes.

'It's a shame it's not a brand new gene,' the professor said. 'But what you've discovered is still very significant. What you've done is link a *known* gene with an *unknown* function. So we now know that in addition to causing cancer, this gene controls very early blood cell differentiation. Without it functioning properly, the blood system can't develop. This normally happens in the womb, when the stem cells are first forming. It's a great story that I think is going to end up published in a very good journal.'

It was times like those that I wished I could have explained to my parents what I had achieved. They didn't even know what DNA was.

My adopted mother – and my biological aunt – Elizabeth Papathanasiou, in the photo she sent to her future husband Bill in 1956.

My adopted father, Bill Papathanasiou, undertaking military service in the Hellenic Army in July 1953.

Mum and Dad, Elizabeth and Bill Papathanasiou, and their wedding party in October 1956 in Queanbeyan, Australia.

Mum and Dad at a social gathering in Canberra, Australia during the 1960s.

Mum working as a waitress at the Lolly House, an annex to a Canberra workers' hostel, in the 1960s.

Savvas and Anna Paraskevaidis, my biological parents, at their wedding in Florina, Greece, circa 1960. Also pictured are my paternal grandparents, Vasilios and Maria Paraskevaidis (left), and Aunt Soultana (right).

My biological father Savvas with his two sons – and my biological brothers – Georgios (left) and Vasilios (Billy) in Florina, Greece, circa 1965.

My biological mother, Anna Paraskevaidis, in Florina, Greece.

My paternal grandparents, Maria and Vasilios Paraskevaidis, were Orthodox Christian refugees who fled to northern Greece from Turkey during the 1923 population exchange.

My adopted mother, Elizabeth Papathanasiou, with her nephews Georgios (left) and Vasilios (Billy) in Florina, Greece, 1973.

My brothers Billy (left) and Georgios with their papou Vasilios in Florina, Greece, circa 1964.

The Australian Dream: Mum and Dad, Elizabeth and Bill Papathanasiou, outside their first home in the Canberra suburb of Narrabundah in 1959.

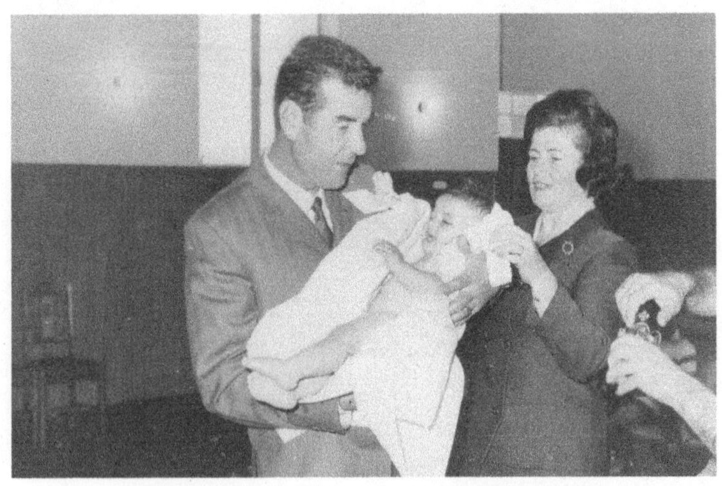

Mum and Dad as godparents at Saint Nicholas Greek Orthodox Church in Kingston, Canberra, Australia during the 1960s.

Three siblings in Florina, Greece, 1973: my aunt Soultana (left), biological father Savvas, and adopted mother Elizabeth.

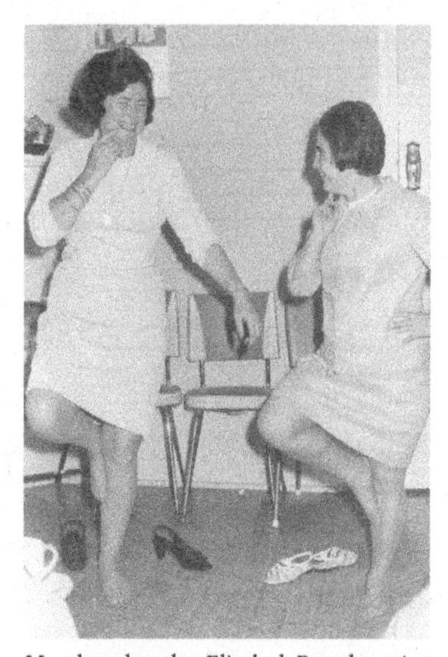

My adopted mother Elizabeth Papathanasiou (left) dancing with a friend in Queanbeyan, Australia during the 1960s.

A Turkish minaret overlooking the town of Florina in Greece, 1922, one year before what Greeks call 'the Disaster'.

CHAPTER 14

1973

ELIZABETH'S HOME TOWN had changed greatly during her absence. External walls and window shutters had been repainted, while broken bricks and bags of concrete lay dormant on every sidewalk alongside dangling wires, cavernous potholes and precarious scaffolding. Multi-storey buildings lacking their facades had the look of dollhouses. Unfinished, they were untouchable by the taxman.

Another novelty for Elizabeth was the backwardness of her former life. Certain local customs she had once performed without question started to grate, which made her feel both irritated and guilty. In Australia, she didn't need to chop and burn wood to heat water to take a shower. Nor did she have to wash everything by hand using a washboard, or be without a telephone. And she could flush away her used toilet paper down the S-bend.

'You still throw the paper in a bin?' she asked her sister from the doorway of the cramped bathroom when she had newly arrived back in the family home.

'It's the pipes,' Soultana replied. 'Not just the ones here at home but also the plumbing in the street. They're too narrow to handle clumps of paper, and they never got around to upgrading them. Our plumbing is still under Roman control.'

Elizabeth screwed up her face. 'But all that soiled paper in the bin is disgusting.'

'It never used to be, *princess* . . .'

From Vasilios's letters, Elizabeth worked out that her sister had once been married. Elizabeth cornered her in the kitchen one evening and asked what had happened.

'I'm not going to say anything about that time,' she replied. 'And I don't want to be reminded of it either.'

Elizabeth was suspicious. 'But why, weren't you married?' she asked. She contemplated mentioning her own marital troubles in order to gain her sister's trust.

'I was,' she said. 'But it didn't work out so I came back home.'

'No children?'

'Obviously not.'

'Did you try for any? What was his name? How long were you married?'

'Sister *mou*, please. Those things don't matter now. It didn't work out. There's no need to twist the knife.'

'I'm not twisting the knife. I'm interested in your life and what happened. You're my sister.'

Elizabeth was perhaps most interested in whether her family

harboured some common infertility. Of the four siblings, only Savvas had procreated.

'I live with Baba now,' Soultana said, quickly changing the topic. 'And he needs looking after, he's not well.'

Elizabeth thought for a moment. 'So what's wrong with him exactly?' she asked. 'He doesn't seem too bad to me. He complains a little about his joints, but who doesn't at his age?'

Vasilios had slowed in his advancing years. He no longer carried around freshly excavated rocks with his bare hands, like he did after he left the *foro* and worked at a quarry. Elizabeth wished he would stop smoking because he was constantly coughing.

'Can't you see?' Soultana said, pointing her index and middle fingers to her eyes.

Elizabeth could not. Soultana sat and crossed her legs.

'Ask yourself this,' she said, 'how often has Baba left the house since you got here?'

Elizabeth tried to recall her father's activities over the past week but she couldn't think straight anymore. After all that had happened, her nerves had worn to shreds, and her memory was shot.

'He *rarely* leaves the house,' Soultana continued. 'The night we all went out was a special occasion because you're here. Much as he loves Christos's *taverna*, he hasn't been there in months.'

'But why? What's wrong? Is he sick? Why doesn't he tell us?'

Soultana looked down at her hands, studied the veins beginning to appear on the back. 'My sister, have you ever seen what happens to a dog or cat when they're not long for this world?'

'No,' Elizabeth said.

Soultana looked up. 'They stay inside and wait for it.'

Elizabeth stood quietly, leaning against the door frame, her whole world focused on her sister's words.

'The brain starts sending signals to the body, and the body listens and starts shutting down,' Soultana explained. 'I saw this with Mama. Call me crazy, I hope I am. But I've sensed something here, a change. And Baba's not going to say anything until it's too late.'

Elizabeth felt a pain in the centre of her chest, like someone squeezing her heart.

'You would've missed these subtle changes because you're more focused on his more obvious physical ageing,' Soultana went on. 'That's normal. But I see how he looks at us and at the world. Admittedly, seeing you again has put a smile on his moustache. He's much more alert since you arrived. But this may be only temporary.'

'Does Savvas see the same changes you do?' Elizabeth asked.

'Yes and no,' Soultana said. 'But our brother's like that. He's a man. He needs a magnifying glass to see his own hand.'

Elizabeth shrugged. 'He's got his own family.'

Over the next week, Elizabeth paid much more careful attention to her father's behaviour. Whenever she returned home, she found him snoozing in his favourite armchair. When he wasn't sleeping, he was sitting up in bed or in the kitchen, reading the newspaper or listening to music, old *horiatiki* records, *zeibekiko*, *kalamatiano*. Sometimes he was smoking a cigarette or sipping a nip of whiskey. Soultana said that he'd spent so much time drinking to other people's health, he'd ruined his own.

When Elizabeth gently rapped on her father's door one afternoon, she found the watery summer sun streaming through the window across his exposed, white belly. Vasilios was snoring but had a small, discernible smile on his face. It was obvious he was dreaming, his pupils twitching beneath his eyelids. It was true that Elizabeth hadn't seen him visit his wife's grave. She just figured he went secretly and alone, to mourn quietly and privately. Soultana said he used to go, but he would return home broken, a wreck. So she had told him not to go, to protect him.

'And Baba's said nothing to you?' Elizabeth asked her sister. 'Have you asked him?'

'He says everything's fine, not a care in the world,' Soultana said. 'He doesn't want his children to worry. But he acts differently. That's why I wrote and asked you to come. Because I fear the next time you do, whenever that is, Baba might not be here.'

Elizabeth's prospect of a new, unknown life through Savvas and Anna and the happiness that came with it was suddenly dwarfed by the sorrow of the loss of another, known life, that itself once gave her life.

Soultana stood and walked over to her baby sister. She bent down and kissed her lightly on the forehead.

'All we can do is spend time with Baba and be his daughters,' Soultana said. 'We're the only two people in the world who can do that.'

Vasilios often asked Elizabeth about her new country. Usually at the end of the day when they sat together on the balcony, watching the mountain change colour from yellow to orange to purple. Vasilios now wanted to visit, his attitude had completely changed, and the great southern land intrigued him. Australia appeared baby new to his old eyes, with a freshness that hadn't been choked by officialdom, constitutional crises and coups d'état for nearly a century.

'The air is full of words, and the words are full of air,' Vasilios told his youngest child. 'And that's on a good day. On a bad day, the streets still run with blood like centuries ago.'

Vasilios wanted to know all about his son Vangelis. He seemed genuinely happy that he and Marika had made it work, despite being so far from home. Elizabeth wondered whether Soultana's shortcomings in this regard – whatever they were – helped change his tune.

'*Bravo tous*,' Vasilios said, trying to picture his grandchildren. True to form, Vangelis hadn't sent any photos. 'At least he did the right thing by passing on Mama's name. She would've loved it.'

'They've done well,' Elizabeth said. 'They just bought a second house.'

'If only he'd sent some money home, we may have fixed up this house a little as well.'

'The house is fine, Baba.'

'The house is not fine. It's old. Like me. I'm the house.'

'You're not old, Baba!'

'I am, dear child, I am. I can still remember a time before electricity, when we had no street lights. People go to bed later now. They have fewer babies.'

Elizabeth had noticed there were discernibly fewer children around town than she remembered. And a lot more stray dogs and cats.

'Do you remember when you were little, eh?' Vasilios said, smiling. 'At the table with your brothers and sisters, fighting over who would wipe clean the olive oil in the salad bowl with their chunk of bread? How Mama and I laughed. Yiayia too, may God rest their souls.'

❧

Elizabeth packed her suitcase in terror. Her time in Florina was at an end, and she was leaving behind what she might never see again.

'Nonsense,' said her sister. 'Your whole life's in Australia now. You've nothing left here.'

'But Baba . . .'

'Oh, who knows about him. I could be completely wrong. He could live to over a hundred like Yiayia did.'

Elizabeth hugged and kissed her small family as if it was the last time; especially her *baba*, who acted like he didn't know what the fuss was about.

'Next time,' Vasilios said. 'See you next time.'

'Next time,' Elizabeth repeated. In the back of her mind, she knew that 'next time' could be as soon as 'next year'.

She boarded the bus to Athens and took a seat towards the back. The bus was soon working its way up the gears for the long drive ahead. Elizabeth felt lightheaded and was unable to draw a full breath. Through the misshapen pane of moving glass, she watched her family growing ever smaller. Her sister was blowing kisses, her brother was blowing out a cigarette, her father was waving a handkerchief like a wet sail, and her mother was nowhere to be seen.

CHAPTER 15

2003

THE LAST YEAR of my PhD was spent trying to characterise precisely what my genetic mutation in the Ikaros gene was doing to derail blood development so catastrophically. It turned out that the corrupted protein was still assembling normally in large multi-molecular complexes but its presence prevented family member proteins from compensating for its loss of function. These experiments were done using the foetal livers from embryos, which was the site for all blood development before migrating to the bone marrow soon after birth. The professor claimed it was an elegant genetic study that deserved a wide audience, but the peer reviewers thought differently. My paper was met with rejection after rejection.

'This could take a while to get published,' the professor said. 'Some papers are just like that, especially the ones that report unexpected new findings, it takes a while for people to catch on. But you can stop doing experiments now, start writing your thesis and send out postdoctoral letters to prospective labs overseas.'

The postdoc loomed like a black swamp on the horizon. Formally, postdoctoral research was the limbo period between earning a doctorate and getting an academic appointment. Informally, it was academia's ugly underbelly, a winnowing-out period where the strongest scientists were selected according to intellectual fitness and sheer endurance, and the ability to withstand scathing criticism and tenuous job security.

My study of bloodless embryos had led me to examine more primitive cell types. Because they are still developing, embryos lack a complete repertoire of blood cells; only around birth do all the subsets of blood cells finally appear. This meant I had to delve further down the cellular family tree, to its very roots, to find the answers. From the fully mature immune cells which were cancerous, to the precursor cells from which they developed, and finally to the earliest stem cells from which the entire blood system sprouted.

These ancestral grandfather cells were rare – one in ten thousand. Without these extraordinary cells, no other blood cells could develop. Stem cells brought about tissue generation in embryos, and when there was disease or deficiency in adults, they brought about regeneration. This was the process by which bone marrow transplants worked, and it was the reason why parents now banked their baby's umbilical cord blood, which was replete with stem cells. When transplanted, the stem cells would divide and differentiate, and eventually replenish the entire blood system. The ability of stem cells to regenerate whole tissue systems was why there was such a growing interest in the field. Stem cell companies opened for business, promising 'potential' cures for everything from Alzheimer's disease to baldness. And with the isolation of human embryonic stem cells for the first time in 1998, an ethical minefield was about to open up.

Having been there himself, the professor always favoured going to work in America, and advised me accordingly. The Americans had the biggest journals and published the best papers. The professor also had an American father and Australian mother, and grew up in Washington DC before moving to Sydney as a teenager. But things were more complex for me. On the one hand were my brothers; working in Europe was a chance to be nearer to them for a few years and get to know them better. And on the other hand, an unjust war and search for invisible weapons of mass destruction was about to break out in Iraq, which meant that global anti-Americanism was at an all-time high. With each new day, our media outlets were saturated with more revealing satellite images churned out by an unrelenting propaganda machine. I knew I was being irrational if I let that impact my decision. And yet I did. The threat was real. Those who knew told us so.

In the end, I decided to check out Europe, and contacted labs that studied stem cells. With the hype of genome biology passing, it appeared that the next hot field of research would be stem cells. I soon had an exhausting itinerary drawn up of labs in England, Holland, Belgium and Austria, which I decided to end with a personal pilgrimage to northern Greece.

It was time. I needed to see myself up close, and find out who I could have been.

Given the significance of her role in the family and especially in my life, I insisted Mum be there to witness the reunion of three brothers. She was initially reluctant to travel, partly because of the distance, partly because of the culture shock, but mainly due to her husband. Dad had become very ill in late 2001; he passed out one morning following extensive rectal bleeding and was immediately hospitalised. Following scans, they found a large adenocarcinoma in his stomach. If the cancer hadn't spread to nearby lymph nodes, the prognosis was reasonable. But it was still a massive operation, especially for a man who was seventy-one years old and had smoked for more than half a century.

'How much longer do I expect to live?' Dad said to me from his hospital bed. 'Five years, ten years, fifteen? Ten would be nice. But now is still too soon, I'm not ready.'

'Let's just wait until after the operation,' I replied. 'But I'm sure it will all be fine.'

Of course, I wasn't sure; in fact, I was incredibly worried. Dad's illness was another reason why I delayed my travel to Greece. The surgeon had told me that the recovery period would be the hardest thing after such a major operation. Mum would need help with groceries, errands and emotional support. Given the nature of the tumour combined with Dad's age, the surgeon recommended against chemotherapy and radiation. Suddenly, within the space of six months, I had gone from having two fathers to the very real prospect of potentially having zero.

'What you don't understand is that this is *cancer*,' Dad told me. 'This can come back at any time and without warning. All it takes is one little piece to break loose and it can spread throughout the body. A heart problem would be better than this. With a heart attack, that's it, you're done, there's no worrying later.'

I eyed him crookedly. 'Are you serious?' I said. 'Come on now, that would be terrible. Do you really want to die?'

I knew he didn't. He wanted another chance.

Mum was sick with worry, to the point that we became concerned for her welfare.

'Look after your mother,' Dad told me. 'If she goes, then we're all done for.'

The gastroenterologist removed the tumour, which was basically a removal of Dad's entire stomach given its size – a gastrectomy. Fortunately, the lymph nodes were normal, but Dad still had to learn how to eat again without a stomach, or at least until the small intestine took over its functions. It meant smaller meals, digestive issues and constant complaining.

The monthly follow-up checks all went to plan. Eighteen months after the operation, Dad had almost completely recovered and found a new lease on life. He'd given up smoking and was eating better: Mum's honest Greek cuisine, slow-cooked, hearty, nutritiously olive oily food.

'I'm lucky,' he said, 'I escaped.'

But still, Mum worried. She had nursed him through the darkest days, prepared all of his meals, attended to his every need. Going to Greece for as little as two weeks was still two weeks too long.

'Go,' Dad kept telling her. 'I'm fine now.'

Eventually, Mum acquiesced after sensing it may be her last chance to see her homeland. Her sister was also fast approaching her ninth decade.

'I'm going for you, Panagiotis,' Mum said.

'I know, Mama. *Efharisto.*'

Mum phoned my brothers to share our travel plans. She would arrive a week before Easter by plane. Meanwhile, I would come four days later via overnight ferry from Italy and a bus north through Epirus and West Macedonia.

'Hee hee ha ha!' Billy squealed down the phone line. 'Bravo *theia*, bravo Panagiotis. I will show you off to everyone!'

And so, on the twentieth of March, the world held its breath. With the dropping of the first satellite-guided bombs over Baghdad, I strapped myself aboard a commercial airliner bound for Frankfurt via Singapore. With every jolt of the plane in flight, I pictured surface-to-air missiles whizzing past the wingtips. The pilot assured us that he would avoid the no-fly zone.

❧

By the time I boarded the ferry to Igoumenitsa five weeks later, I felt like I'd aged ten years. My scientific presentations went well, but the lab tour had been brutal and produced more questions than answers. The vast majority of the labs I visited studied stem cells, and most of the postdoctoral fellows curtly advised me to 'go to America if you have the chance'. This was the take-home message that I didn't want to hear. Subsisting on train station sandwiches and muesli bars, walking miles per day, I saw dark creases around my mouth in youth hostel mirrors, my cheeks sunken. I'd lost a considerable amount of weight and didn't look healthy. I looked stressed and tired, and was suddenly worried about what first impression I would make when I finally met my brothers.

The Greek sea captains aboard the overnight ferry from Brindisi appeared more enamoured with the European football match on TV than anything. It led me to question who was steering the ship across the Ionian. I went to bed and prayed I would wake up dry.

In the morning, I set foot on Greek soil for the first time in nearly thirty years. I inhaled and tasted the same air from which I'd drawn my very first breath. It settled in my lungs, and somehow felt right. Instantly, I felt comfortable hearing my first language all around me, spoken by strangers on the street as if they knew me. And the lady at the tourist bureau pronounced my full Greek name perfectly. I'd gotten so used to correcting people over the years. The sound of it was like beautiful music.

I found a payphone, rang the village, confirmed my arrival time with Georgios, and spoke with Mum.

'Things have changed here,' she said anxiously. 'They've changed a lot. Do me a favour: call your father, make sure he's okay.'

I hung up the receiver and punched in fifteen more digits. The phone rang for an eternity.

'Eh,' Dad said. 'I dropped your mum at the airport and came back and the house was empty, quiet. And for the rest of the day, the house was empty. And the next day, empty, quiet. But now it's better. Have a good time and look after Mama.'

CHAPTER 16

1974

ELIZABETH SQUIRMED IN her furry airline seat. Her clothes were suddenly scratchy and tight. The recirculated cabin air smelled musty, perfumed with deodorisers. They were only taxiing at Sydney's Kingsford Smith but she already felt jet-lagged. She closed her eyes and hoped the warm soupy air would quickly anaesthetise her into a long sleep.

Elizabeth was returning to Greece on a promise and nothing more; a few mere words and subsequent letters, solemn assurances. She went without a shred of paperwork. The legal work was all going to happen after-the-fact, via letters to her husband, who stayed in Australia to coordinate with the Greek embassy. He'd not mentioned divorce again. In fact, he'd been more amorous than ever since his wife had returned from Greece and especially in the lead-up to her latest departure. The letter that said 'Anna is pregnant' was like winning the lottery.

Despite all this, Elizabeth still felt incredible guilt and an immense shame at what she was about to do. Was she doing the right thing? Her husband had no doubt, but deep down, she wasn't sure. She questioned if she would be a good mother. She wondered whether her friends would see her as selfish. But above all, she worried about her sister-in-law. Anna had agreed to the proposition, but she wondered how much of it was willingly. Greece was very much a patriarchal society, and her brother was unequivocally the king of his castle. It was the same in Australia, even though things were slowly changing. Women were burning their bras, demanding equal pay, equal rights. This was something Bill would never understand. Would she forever be known as the barren, self-centred woman who stole her sister-in-law's baby to placate her demanding husband? What right did she have to a baby just because she was a woman?

Elizabeth's flight touched down in Athens two weeks before the baby was due, mid June. She found a payphone and some drachmas in the bottom of her purse. She always carried some, even in Australia, for luck. She dropped them into the coin slot and dialled her village. A telephone network had just been connected, but only for trunk calls. The phone rang through with no answer. She rang again. And again. Six times she called, her index finger tender from the rotary dial. No answer. The family knew her travel plans and that she would be arriving that day. *Had something happened?* Elizabeth started to panic.

With no other option, Elizabeth dialled the only other number she had – her sister's in Thessaloniki. The warmer weather regularly drove Soultana east for some time away from her claustrophobic village where she stayed in a friend's small, unoccupied flat.

Soultana answered on the fifth ring to hear her sobbing, frenzied sister's voice crackling on the other end.

'Calm down, calm down *agape mou*,' said Soultana. 'Now listen, the baby—'

The phone cut out.

Elizabeth couldn't redial the numbers quickly enough, which caused her to make mistakes, her fingers suddenly too big for the rotary dial. A lifetime appeared to pass before she finally had Soultana again.

'What's happened, what about the baby?' Elizabeth was shouting down the line, calling attention to herself in an otherwise quiet airport terminal.

'The baby came early, last week,' Soultana said. 'Because of this, the weight was only five and a half pounds, as light as a whisper. But don't worry, everything's fine. Anna and the baby had to stay at the clinic a while but they're home now. Oh, and it's another boy. Three boys!'

Elizabeth gasped and rolled her neck. She was drained from a combination of anticipation, excitement, worry and jet lag. But her baby had arrived, and arrived safely.

'Now listen,' Soultana continued, 'there's something else I need to tell you. It's about Baba. He died three weeks ago. As you know, I thought he'd entered the final phase a long time ago, which is why I asked you to come last year. But it was still sudden. In the past six months, Baba had stabilised, I think buoyed by your visit and the prospect of new life in the family. He was hanging on for that. He fell just short.'

The airport terminal appeared to melt away before Elizabeth's eyes; the sights, the sounds, all disappeared as the shock of the news hit her heart. But there was a difference this time. Compared to the details of her mother's death on a cold page that had travelled ten thousand miles, this was a message delivered with warmth by a familiar voice on an otherwise joyous day.

'Hello? Hello Elizabeth, are you there?' Soultana asked. 'Talk to me, *agape mou*. Don't be sad, don't cry.'

'No-oh,' Elizabeth's voice quivered. 'No, I . . . I know.'

'Today's a wonderful day. You're here to meet your new son!'

'I know.'

'Baba loved us and he knew we loved him. This is life, the old gives way to the new. It has to or the world would be a miserable place.'

'Yes, you're right . . . I'm just shocked.'

'Elizabeth, listen, let's end this now. I'll tell you more in person. But the last thing I need to tell you right now is no one's at the house today. They all went to Kozani for Billy to see a doctor. They should be back later tonight but you may be stuck waiting on the doorstep if you go there now. Since I have a house key with me, instead of catching a bus to Florina, catch a train to Thessaloniki and we'll travel home together. It's only two more hours and we can talk on the way so when you arrive home, you can meet the baby with a clear head. *Endaxi?* Okay, *filakia*, see you soon.'

Elizabeth replaced the receiver. One life enters, another departs. The universe's balance maintained.

She recalled a story her father once told her about her grandmother after whom she was named. When Elizabeth was born, her *yiayia* did not want the baby to be named after her for fear she would immediately drop dead. The superstition was that once there was a new Elizabeth in the world, another one had to go, to maintain the equilibrium. She reluctantly acquiesced on the name, and was proven wrong, living another twelve years to the ripe old age of one hundred and six.

Dog-tired, Elizabeth let out a light sigh and picked up her suitcase, shambling her ageing, aching bones to await an Athenian bus to take her to the train. An hour wait was not long enough to nap restfully. She had trouble getting out a complete yawn before it was interrupted by another yawn. Finally aboard the bus, Elizabeth dozed on and off the whole way. Her fatigue fought away the fragmentary faces of the dead in her dreams that she knew would visit her again soon.

❧

Soultana greeted her baby sister at the station with a tight embrace. She was dressed in black from head to toe. Wearing an emerald green blouse and tan skirt, Elizabeth felt suddenly self-conscious, as if she were wearing no clothes at all.

The warmth of her sister's arms and the familiarity of her perfume flicked a subconscious switch in Elizabeth's brain. She unexpectedly burst into tears.

'That's it. Let it out, *agape mou.*'

Elizabeth did. The exhaustion and the stress and the elation and the sorrow. Gallons of it, years of it, decades.

'Better now?' Soultana asked. '*Ela*, our train's leaving shortly.'

The sisters walked arm-in-arm in a slow military step. The country trains were on the furthest platform. They took their seats opposite each other in the last carriage. As they settled in, a young woman leaned across the aisle and proffered the contents of a small package wrapped in silver foil.

'Would you like some *tiropita?* Fresh baked this morning.'

Elizabeth's soul cried in appreciation of the kind gesture of *philoxenia*. How she missed the kindness of strangers that had once surrounded her. Perhaps her husband had been right: Australia's xenophobia, even if not always palpable, quietly burrowed away at the subconscious, only to be revealed at moments like these when a small gesture seemed remarkable.

'And not from a shop either,' the young woman added. 'My *mama* made these. But there's too much for me. Please. Have some.'

Elizabeth took a small delicate triangle, smiling her thanks. The fine layers of filo pastry were dripping with *graviera*, a melted hard cheese. The pastry crackled her dry mouth to life, while the sweet caramel flavour warmed her all over. It went down like vanilla ice cream.

'Mm,' Elizabeth hummed. 'Delicious! Please give my compliments to your *mama*.'

'I will. Where are you going today?'

The young woman struck up a conversation with the two old chooks on the train. Elizabeth was grateful for the distraction; it relieved her dark thoughts for an hour, pushed them away until the woman disembarked at Platy station in her home village. She had her hair cut short to fully expose her slender face and sharp jaw line. She wore pants and carried cigarettes and a backpack. She told them about how exciting she found studying at the polytechnic in Thessaloniki, her doubts surrounding her future with her boyfriend, a local farm boy, and how she was planning on travelling absolutely everywhere.

The tables had turned in her homeland. Elizabeth pondered how the women now left the men in the villages, flocking to the cities for education and excitement. She felt jealous. The society – the Greek women – whom Elizabeth had left behind had powered ahead. But the men who had emigrated had remained fixed in the century's first half, with the mindset of their fathers and their fathers before them.

'Now, I won't make this any more painful because today's not the day for tears,' Soultana told Elizabeth when they were alone. 'You've travelled a long distance and need to look forward, not back.'

Elizabeth nodded.

'*Endaxi*,' Soultana said. 'Baba was well, until he deteriorated rapidly one night. His heart was failing. We called the doctor who came to the house, but he couldn't do anything to help. By that stage, Baba was too frail.'

Soultana leaned forward and held her sister's hand. She told her their father had the best death possible. He died naturally, in his own home, with his family all around.

'So feel sad today Elizabeth, of course,' Soultana said. 'But don't wallow. Baba's life was long and graced with every blessing, including the promise of a final descendant.'

Elizabeth's cheeks were sodden by the time her sister finished.

Soultana had said everything right and Elizabeth was more grateful than ever for her sister's steadfast ways and traditional wisdom. She rose from her seat opposite Soultana and sat down next to her, resting her weary head on her sister's shoulder. For the rest of the journey home, they rode in silence with only the noise of the clattering train in their ears. Every now and then, Soultana stroked Elizabeth's hair as they stared out the window at acres of budding wildflowers and battleship-grey agave rosettes. It was summer, their father's favourite season.

❧

They arrived at the family home in the evening. The whitewashed house was still and silent but warm yellow light poured from every window.

'Wonderful,' Soultana said. 'Everyone's home. Enjoy the quiet while it lasts.'

Soultana pushed through the unlocked door first. Elizabeth's excitement combined with her terror to make her heart bulge in her chest. How long she had waited for this moment. The moment when she ceased being Elizabeth and finally became 'Mum'.

CHAPTER 17

1974

MUM FIRST SAW me in the front room of the same home where she had grown up, where she herself had once been a baby the same size. Anna held me in her arms as Savvas sat in an armchair, leafing through a newspaper. Mum was met with a warm but subdued welcome, air kisses all round. I was sleeping.

From across the room the first thing Mum spied was a black tuft of hair sticking out from a bundled white blanket. As she came around to kiss Anna, she saw my face appear, crinkled like crepe paper. My eyes were closed but a jet black shock of hair stood upright.

'His eyes too,' Anna said. 'As dark as the night. But they'll probably end up deep brown like his brothers.'

Mum's own eyes moistened. So did Soultana's and Anna's. Savvas sensed he was outnumbered and went outside for a cigarette. Billy and Georgios were already asleep in their bedroom.

'Here,' Anna said with no hesitation. 'Take him.'

Mum surprised herself by matching Anna's zeal. Her nerves had subsided, and the long dormant instinct of a mother kicked in. Anna's demeanour made Mum instantly believe that I was hers.

As she took me in her arms for the first time, Mum's whole face smiled. Anna beamed, too, as she watched us share our first moment. The whole room smelled of baby, of lavender and honeysuckle. Mum pondered the telegram she would send to her husband the next day, and how many different phrases she could conjure to describe how perfect his newborn son was.

But perfection didn't last long. Soultana was right – for such a small package, I had powerful lungs. Mum said that I cried so hard, she thought she felt the foundations of the stone house reverberate.

'Something's wrong with the baby,' she concluded. 'Or I'm doing something wrong.'

'This is just what babies do,' Anna said. 'And you're doing everything perfectly.'

Other times, I slept soundly. After gaining her confidence, Mum found herself half-wishing that I would wake up crying just so she could hold me close and comfort me back to sleep.

'How much do Billy and Georgios know?' Mum asked Soultana on the second day. They were alone in the kitchen, boiling lentils to make soup.

'They only know what their parents have told them,' she replied. 'I haven't involved myself. I haven't said anything. Really, I haven't.'

'Yes, but how much is that?'

'I'm pretty sure they know it all. They know their new baby brother isn't really their brother, at least, not like they are to each other. Well, Georgios knows. Billy just prefers to enjoy the moment. You'll see.'

Billy was now twelve-years-old and a mass of impulses that demanded immediate satisfaction. Georgios was quick to anger and argued for sport.

'I shouldn't be so harsh,' Soultana said. 'It's because of Billy that Georgios has had to grow up so quickly.'

Billy would approach the women like a cat without a bell, startling Mum as she turned around, his round face smiling broadly, eyes agog. Billy normally stared straight through Mum; she wasn't sure what he found so interesting. When he spoke, it was in short, sharp bursts punctuated by uproarious laughter, usually at things that weren't funny at all. He talked about the day he'd been kidnapped by wolves and kept hostage in a cave in the nearby mountains. He talked about the time he flew to the moon. Everyone laughed along, as if to keep him entertained, or calm. The arrival of the new baby had noticeably changed his approach.

'Baby,' Billy would say, pointing. 'Baby. Baby, baby!'

'Yes, *agape mou*, that's the baby,' Anna said.

'I want to hold him.'

'You do?'

'Yes. I want to hold him!'

'Of course, my love. But hold him with your *theia* helping. Here, put your arm around hers.'

Billy would watch his youngest brother intensely as if trying to work me out, communicating invisible messages with his big saucer eyes. I would blub and gurgle or scream and cry. All the while, Billy watched me like a movie, following every twist in a gripping plot. He would laugh at the top of his voice at what seemed like random moments.

'But watch him closely,' Soultana told Mum. 'Billy never laughs or makes any loud noises or wakes up the baby when he's sleeping.'

Mum watched. Her sister was right.

'Anna thinks Billy can communicate with the baby in ways that even she can't,' Soultana said. 'When Billy laughs, it's in response to something the baby has "said". Your little man is a comedian.'

Georgios was now ten-years-old and the polar opposite of his older brother. He was more like his father; barely a presence in his house. Not once did Mum see him show any interest in being an older brother.

'Don't worry about it,' said Soultana.

'But I do worry,' Mum said. She still had a fairytale image in her head of happy families. 'I mean, he'll always be his brother, no matter where he is. Is this some form of silent protest?'

'Maybe,' Soultana said. 'But if you know our brother, you know Georgios.'

From day one, my family made sure that I was purely bottle fed.

'I explained to the nurse this one was different,' Anna told Mum. 'That there would be absolutely no breastfeeding this one.'

For weeks, Mum waited for my first smile that wasn't gas. When it came, she felt a warmth burst through her heart like never before.

'Eye contact,' Anna told Mum. 'Always hold him up to look at your face. Chat with him. He might not respond but his little brain is absorbing it all like a sponge. He'll let you know when he's tired by looking away. Then hold him against your chest so he can hear your heart.'

Mum had never spent so much time with such a young baby, and looked to Anna for every reassurance. Anna was less introspective and simply guided her sister-in-law through each step, always insisting she take the lead.

Meanwhile, Soultana preyed on Mum's insecurities.

'What are you doing, are you crazy?' she hissed. 'For God's sake, don't let her handle the baby too much. She can always change her mind. Then you'll be going home alone to your husband . . . and his mother.'

Artemis had not approved of Mum's arrangement with her brother. She desperately wanted her son to become a father, but she wasn't convinced about Mum's family, including whether Anna would willingly give up the baby. But Mum saw nothing in Anna's or Savvas's behaviour to suggest there'd been any change to their agreement. And yet Soultana's whispers played on Mum's uncertainty. There was always the chance Soultana had heard something behind the scenes that Mum had not.

'I think you should have a word with them,' Soultana told her sister. 'Make sure it's all still as arranged. You've been carrying on like he's yours from the second you got here. And that's wonderful, that's how it should be, but you should have the conversation with Savvas again. Anna as well. Don't think he speaks on her behalf in matters maternal. Make sure you hear it from her too.'

Mum was confused. She thought she'd already had the conversation, including with Anna. Did they perhaps fear that she might *not* take the baby to Australia? That had never occurred to her, but she acknowledged it may have been on their minds, including throughout the pregnancy. What if she'd changed her mind? They would somehow need to raise another baby. It was no small undertaking, and especially with Billy's problems now in the frame. It would be like having four children.

'You don't think I'd be insulting them, to bring it up?' Mum asked her sister cautiously.

Soultana looked at her directly. 'Would you prefer to run the risk?' she replied.

Mum looked at the ground, then back up at her sister. 'No. When should I ask?'

'As soon as possible. Remember Vangelis arrives next week for a holiday, and that will open up a whole new dialogue around the dinner table.'

With the days getting longer, Savvas was spending more time at the *kafenion*. It was two more days before Mum finally corralled him in the kitchen while he was making coffee. Anna was sitting at the table feeding me a bottle.

'Savvas . . .'

Mum didn't know how to begin. Soultana's words were still rattling around inside her head.

'Umm . . . I wanted to check with you . . . about the baby . . . that we were still . . . ah . . .'

The words weren't coming out like she had rehearsed.

'The baby . . . that we were all . . . ah . . . that we were still all . . . of the same mind . . .'

Savvas and Anna looked at Mum blankly, then at each other.

'What do you mean?' Savvas said.

'You know. Your proposition . . . ?'

Savvas stopped making his coffee and put the copper *briki* pot to one side.

'What about it? Isn't that why we had the baby?' he said. 'Isn't that why my wife has been showing you the ropes? Didn't your husband already agree? What has all this been for?'

Mum held her hands up defensively. 'No no,' she said. 'I mean, yes yes! Yes. We still very much want the baby, absolutely. He's beautiful, nothing's changed. I just wanted to make sure it's the same for you.'

Savvas looked across at his wife and baby, before eyeing the kitchen ceiling a moment. He appeared to be trying to compose himself, processing. Eventually, he said:

'And why are you even asking? Isn't it obvious?'

He walked over to Mum and placed his rough hands lightly on her shoulders. He spoke as if reading a news bulletin.

'The baby is your son. We give him to you with all our hearts. Love him. Raise him well.'

With that, Savvas grabbed his cap and pipe and headed for the *kafenion*, leaving his coffee abandoned. The slamming of the back door startled me. I unlatched from the bottle and cried. Mum looked over at Anna, now busily trying to soothe me.

'I'm so, so sorry,' Mum said. 'I'm sorry for asking again. I was just . . . worried.'

Anna smiled gently, comforting me, rocking me. 'That's understandable,' she said. 'I would probably be asking the same.'

'My brother's just been so distant since I arrived, I've never seen him like this.'

'It's just his way of doing things,' she said. 'He doesn't want to get attached. Personally, I think he takes it too far.'

'What about you? How do you feel?'

Anna looked back down at me, her eyes softening. 'Eh,' she said, 'I'll survive.'

CHAPTER 18

2003

'LOOK AT THE crappy bus they gave us,' said a Greek voice behind me. 'I'm going to pop a tooth on this road like last time.'

The spherical bus driver had a thick black moustache, heavy gold chains, leather jacket and jeans. The only thing distinguishing him as our charioteer was his position behind the wheel. His workspace was decked out with a graveyard's worth of crucifixes and wallpapered with picture icons of the Virgin Mary. By his side rested a library of cheesy Greek disco CDs he rotated through at jukebox speed. He seemed more interested in the animated discussion he was having with a friend about another friend than whether our bus stayed on the rocky mountain road. The old clunker chugged precariously around the hairpin turns, spending more time in the oncoming lane than its own. It narrowly missed cars coming the other way, their horns blaring. We stopped twice for herds of goats. In between sentences, the driver's skinny friend ran up and down the aisle, sucking in lungfuls of air and collecting passengers' tickets.

It wasn't quite how I had pictured my triumphant return to Florina; aboard a clapped-out old banger crawling north through Epirus and West Macedonia. I stared out the window in the hope of a stinging bolt of clarity from the grey Greek sky. This was no longer a drill or a story Mum had told me or a muted voice on the other end of the phone. This was real. I felt nauseous.

After rattling for three hours, the emergency exit window worked itself loose, smashing on the road behind.

'Eh,' the driver said when it was brought to his attention, 'you can still get out if there's an emergency.'

Mum was the first person I saw standing at the bus terminal in Kozani. Beside her was Georgios in a crumpled shirt and jeans and hands in his pockets. He had a cigarette dangling from the side of his mouth that he tossed away as I disembarked.

'At last, you made it,' Mum said, embracing me warmly. 'Come meet your brother.'

'*Ela tho reh*,' Georgios said, grabbing my neck and pulling me in playfully. 'I'm your brother. Your brother!'

'And I'm *your* brother!' I said.

We were stuck on that one word, but it bore repeating as we hugged each other in a way only family could. Georgios reeked of nicotine and cologne. I smelled of fear.

We stood back and searched for ourselves in the other's face. Georgios's eyes were bigger than mine and pushed back deeper into his face. His hair was thick and lustrous, his nose long and straight. My hair was wiry and thinning, my nose shorter and flatter. But it was only when I got to the lower half of my brother's face that I saw what I couldn't discern from photos. Georgios had an identical mouth and chin. He even had a matching dimple in his chin, as though God had used the same chisel on both of us. I couldn't stop looking at it – the same mould from which I had been pressed. I grabbed Georgios's jaw playfully which made him laugh.

'But hang on,' I said, 'where's Billy? Mum promised me *two* brothers!'

'He's waiting at the house,' Georgios said. '*Pame*. Let's go.'

Mum and I got into Georgios's two-door hatchback. I couldn't distinguish the make or model.

'It's from Romania,' he said.

I applied my seatbelt. Georgios did not wear his. He looked at me blankly.

'What, you don't trust me?' he asked.

This was a test. Mum looked away; she wasn't wearing her seatbelt either, and I'd never seen her without one in Australia. Reluctantly, I undid my belt and white-knuckled it all the way to Florina.

Kozani is the capital and major city of the Greek region of West Macedonia. It was an hour drive north to Florina in the direction of the Albanian and former-Yugoslav borders. The rain started pouring as we drove. Georgios floored it along roads with the consistency of a metalwork file.

'I drive aggressively,' he explained. 'It's because I'm self-taught.'

I wanted to mention driving skills were taught while temperament was not, but figured it best I didn't.

'You're actually very lucky you didn't arrive yesterday,' Georgios added.

'How come?' I asked.

'Transport strike. Ferries stuck in ports, no trains and buses, flights grounded. Third general strike this year and it's only April. What a year awaits us.'

The landscape of northern Greece was a mixture of rural chic and industrial sludge. Rows of vines and green fields blurred past my window. Enormous power stations stood in the distance, their plumes of smoke erasing the sun and much of the sky. The side of the road was littered with discarded plastic bottles and stray dogs and wrecked cars.

'Eighty per cent of Greece's electricity comes from up here,' Georgios said. 'And we grow the best vegetables too. Red peppers are our specialty. *Pipairya Florinis*, sweet and rich, and all thanks to the soil.'

I was suddenly distracted from the views by the digital car stereo. 'Barry White?' I asked.

'You know Barry White?'

Georgios was immediately impressed that I recognised his taste in music, which pleased me. He punched the car horn lightly with his palm, in time with his laughter. Over time, I noticed it was what he did when he found something funny, as if tooting his joy to the world.

With the rain clearing, we pulled up outside a square house dwarfed by tower blocks. It was mid-afternoon and the whole town was quiet, deep in siesta.

'Billy's probably up by now,' Georgios said. 'He's been sleeping all day. Tell him he looks well.'

Georgios led me up the back stairs and into the kitchen. Sitting in an Italian suit at the table, Billy was smoking. There was an overflowing ashtray in front of him. When he saw me, he absently shunted the table out of the way as he got up. His eyes glazed over as he squeezed me harder than I ever thought possible without spinal surgery.

'Panagiotis!' he said. 'Panagiotis, Panagiotis! Where are you, *vreh yaithouraki?*'

I took Billy calling me a 'little donkey' as a term of endearment.

'Here I am!' I replied. 'How are you? Are you well? You look well.'

'I am well! Do you know who I am? Do you know who I am?' Billy boomed in case I was deaf. 'Who am I?'

'You're my brother.'

'Who am I?'

'My brother!'

'Who?'

'*My brother!*'

It was like a rousing chant building at a sporting event. Billy hugged me again, replacing the vertebrae he'd displaced the first time.

We squeezed in around the small table, Georgios offering coffees and sweet almond biscuits. He sparked a fresh cigarette and handed another to Billy. With its porthole windows and low ceiling, the kitchen was tiny and seemed impractical for both cooking and entertaining. When my Theia Soultana emerged, beaming, Mum was forced to shuffle into the doorway. Theia Soultana refused to let go of my hand and could not stop smiling, her two solid gold teeth catching my eye.

Together, the two sisters sat, staring at the three brothers, reunited for the first time. It was uncomfortable, all of us trying not to appear as if we were studying each other's faces, or were ourselves being studied.

'You've got the same hands as Vasilios,' Mum told me. 'The same ears too.'

'And his eyes,' Soultana said, 'their father's. Georgios has Anna's eyes.'

Billy eyeballed me blankly, as if his sibling was a puzzle he was trying to solve. I stared back but could not do it for as long or as intensely. I saw myself in Billy's features, which was both endlessly fascinating and profoundly eerie.

'How's he look to you, Billy?' asked Georgios.

'Fine!' Billy said. '*Palikari!*'

I hoped I would see something obvious in Billy's face or eyes that would help diagnose his condition. I didn't. As a present, I gave him a full set of Australian coins and he immediately set to studying the dodecagonal fifty-cent piece.

Georgios showed me through the house, the rooms through which our biological parents once moved, the walls on which my newborn eyes first focused. The front bedroom where I was conceived, physically, after 'the idea of you was conceived in the kitchen', Mum explained.

Cooking dinner in the kitchen was an arduous task requiring wood that first needed to be chopped and burnt in a combustion stove. The exception was a small gas burner powered by a portable bottle, only ever used to prepare coffee. There was no bench space and only a single sink the size of an ashtray. Two cartons of Marlboro high-tar cigarettes lived on top of the fridge.

'We should've updated this damn house long ago,' Georgios whispered. 'Papou said he'd do it, then Baba, then Theio Vangelis. It's basically as it was in the 1930s.'

Even the rugs appeared to be from the silent era.

'You can't live a modern life in a house like this,' Georgios told me. 'All my friends are in modern houses. It's not right for me to be forty years old and still be chopping wood to have a shower.'

'You're right, it's not,' I said. 'So why not fix it up?'

'Err, I'll tell you later,' said Georgios. 'Let me take you now to the hotel. It's right nearby. I've booked you a room for the week.'

'Oh, I'm not staying here?' I was genuinely disappointed.

'Trust me,' Georgios said. 'This is better for you and for me. Billy is everywhere, all the time. He'll bust into your room in the middle of the night as if it's his own and start having a conversation. He means no harm, but it can be uncomfortable, and you need your privacy and rest.'

Billy said goodbye by pinching my cheeks hard, nearly tearing them off. Georgios drove me to the nearby hotel owned by one of his friends. The décor had not evolved past the mid-1970s. Musky brown velour chairs, cigarette burns on sandpaper carpet, peeling strips of florid wallpaper. I reasoned they didn't see much tourist trade so far north.

I settled in, turned on the TV and began channel surfing. There were Greek folk singers on umpteen channels, Greek dancing to *bouzouki* music, and domestic football fixtures in empty stadia in response to crowd violence. The one news channel showed a squad of Athenian policemen in full battle regalia lobbing tear gas into T-shirted crowds armed with bottles and rocks. I fell asleep to the sound of Greek techno on a music channel, napping for a couple of hours.

When I woke, I showered and headed to a nearby bar. It was owned by another of Georgios's friends and wouldn't have looked out of place in a modern city. Leather ottomans, bright orange couches, boutique beers, glassy wooden floorboards. Looking around, I realised I was the only person in the room not smoking, which included the bartenders and DJ. It brought me unwanted attention.

My brothers were already there when I arrived. Georgios sipped a whiskey. I drank water. Billy hoovered three bowls of complimentary peanuts.

'This place is brand new,' Georgios said. 'Let's see how long it lasts.'

'Where is Papou?' Billy asked. 'You remember the lottery he won?'

'Of course I do,' said Georgios. 'But that was a long time ago.'

Billy leaned in close to my ear.

'Panagiotis,' he said with a smile, 'I got involved in a fight. I fought for you!'

'Fight?' I asked. 'What fight?'

'Because someone said we had a different *baba!*' Billy said. 'So I got into an argument with him, right there in the *kafenion!*'

'When did this happen?'

'About a month ago!'

'That's not nice. Nor is it true.'

'No. I did not like it!'

'Eh, it was just some drunk talking garbage,' said Georgios, diffusing the situation.

'Panagiotis,' Billy eyeballed me again, 'I'm going to say something to you and you're not allowed to get upset or annoyed.'

I gulped. '*Endaxi*,' I said.

'The mother who had us both, she's your first mother. My *theia*, your *mama*, she's your second.'

'Of course,' I said. 'I have two mothers.'

'And you also should know it was *me* who gave you away.'

'Really? It was you?'

'Yes. I was twelve-years-old and I gave you away. It was *my* idea!'

Georgios winked at me knowingly. I played along.

'Bravo! Thank you, Billy,' I said. 'You had a very good idea.'

'Of course it was a good idea,' Georgios interrupted. 'And you know, Billy, because he went to Australia, your brother is now going to be a doctor.'

'Really, a doctor?' Billy said. 'Maybe you can fix me . . .'

A steady stream of Georgios and Billy's friends and acquaintances, young and old, filed past over the course of the next hour. Georgios kept introducing me as '*o micros*' – the little one. Everyone seemed to know exactly what he was talking about. I felt like an instant celebrity.

Big brother Billy – '*o megalos*' – was unaccustomed to not being in the limelight. It was clear that he was the real star, the local luminary, as judged by all the people who said hello to him and who he regarded with a dismissive flick of the head. I quickly realised that people-watching was easy in Greece, with so many people dressed immaculately, the men in designer clothes and the women coiffured to within an inch. I felt positively underdressed alongside my village brothers, who looked like they'd just stepped off a Paris catwalk. But I decided I liked the older village residents most of all, their faces rich with character.

Eventually, Billy stood up from his barstool and informed his brethren he was 'going to buy cigarettes from Manolis'. He put on his cap and left the bar.

Georgios turned to me. 'Billy was worried what you'd be like,' he said. 'How he would see you, how you would see him. He doesn't have much to do with strangers, his world hasn't changed for years. He only invites in the people he wants to invite, and we're all locals. We love him with all our hearts, but unfortunately we've spoiled him.'

I realised then that I had a lot to learn about being a brother.

CHAPTER 19

1974

SOON AFTER HIS arrival in Florina, Vangelis was taken by his brother to the kafenion. They were not heard again until late that night, stumbling back into the house, and not seen again until the next morning, staggering into bed. They finally resurfaced in the evening, complaining of headaches and ordering the women around. Mum had to air out the kitchen, the smell of cigars and whiskey heavy and dolorous.

The next afternoon saw the family reunited for the first time in two decades when the four children visited their parents' graves. Vangelis and Savvas chain-smoked their way along the streets and across the bridge as the sisters followed in their smoky trail.

Vasilios's grave was a collection of white rounded stones, with some black ones in the shape of a cross. A wooden cross was staked into the earth as a makeshift headstone.

'It'll be some time before we get the proper one,' Soultana said, as she knelt down to pull out weeds and light her mother's candle. Savvas offered matches.

Mum signed her cross and knelt to pray. Vangelis also crossed himself and stood alongside Mum.

'*Ela* Vangelis!' Soultana snapped. 'Take your sunglasses off! Let Mama and Baba see your face for the first time in twenty years.'

'They *can't* see me!' Vangelis responded.

'You know what I mean. All this time, not so much as a letter . . .'

'And how's that my fault? Elizabeth wrote for us both.'

'Exactly. *She* wrote. *You* just left.'

'And what did you expect from me, lines of poetry? You know why I left.'

'Treated us like strangers.'

'Soultana . . .'

'Your own family, your blood . . .'

'Soultana, please, *parakalo*!'

Other mourners heard them. Mum's face went fire engine red. Savvas brought it to a head with a piercing wolf whistle.

'Easy *vreh*,' Vangelis said. 'You'll wake the dead.'

'Enough,' said Savvas. '*Ela* Vangelis, let's walk, *tsigaraki* . . .'

Savvas threw two cigarettes into his mouth, lit both, and gave one to Vangelis who started puffing away. Gone were the days when the two sons hid their habit from their father, coming home with holes burnt inside their pockets after he'd strolled past them on the street.

They set off on a lap of the cemetery. Soultana returned to her gardening with more fervour and determination than before. Out of the corner of her eye, she felt her sister's lingering gaze.

'Oh come on,' Soultana said. 'I mean, what was that? First

time he visits here and he wears his sunglasses to the cemetery like some hotshot Onassis.'

'I agree,' Mum whispered. 'But did you have to argue so loudly? People are watching.'

'And who are you to judge? It was Savvas and I who nursed our parents through their last days. Just remember who left and who stayed.'

Mum frowned. 'That's a bit much,' she said. 'You could've left, too. And I wrote letters all those years, every month, every chance. I even came back last year when you wrote to me that Baba was unwell.'

'True,' Soultana said. 'But,' she added, 'you had an ulterior motive.'

Mum paused. 'Wait, what did you say?'

She glared at her sister. She couldn't believe that Soultana had dragged me into the discussion. Did she feel she could get away with saying such hurtful things at the cemetery because it was where Mum was at her most vulnerable?

After a long, tense silence, Soultana finally spoke.

'All I'm saying is that you *did* also come for a baby,' she said. 'And you got what you wanted.'

Soultana finished her spring cleaning. Having not received the apology she was expecting, Mum tidied as best she could. They left together without speaking.

The sisters found their brothers under a large pine tree on a nearby street. They extinguished their cigarettes and lit fresh ones for the journey home. Vangelis's cheeks were moist with what Mum thought may have been tears, but she couldn't see his eyes for the sunglasses. Savvas said nothing and led the way.

When they returned home, Savvas again took Vangelis to the *kafenion* for another intensive session. At first, Mum reasoned these as innocuous moments, appropriate for the circumstances. Vangelis was, after all, on holiday, and the two brothers had much to catch up on. But it was her older sister who soon sat her down with coffee and told her the extent of their brother's illness.

'Savvas's drinking started well before Baba died,' Soultana said. 'But ever since then, it's gotten even worse. I try to cheer him up but he keeps bringing it back to the weight of Billy.'

'Billy . . .' Mum repeated, secretly relieved that it wasn't because of me. Her brother's behaviour seemed to explain his distance and potentially also Anna's reluctance to discuss the matter.

'For a long time, many people – and especially me – told our brother that Billy should have been institutionalised,' Soultana continued. 'It was with a view to our nephew potentially learning a skill or trade, and finding some purpose in life. But not only for his sake – also for the sake of the family. Billy now holds us all to ransom, and it's something that'll only get worse with time.'

Mum thought about what her sister was saying. 'Billy's still young,' she said, 'very young. It may still happen.'

'I don't see it. Not at this rate.'

'Why didn't Savvas want an institution?'

'He was distrustful and suspicious of the state. All he kept saying was, "How will I know they'll look after my child?" He didn't even consider the options. What Savvas wanted, Savvas got.'

'Would Billy have stayed in Florina?'

'That was the other issue,' said Soultana. 'He would've gone to either Athens or Thessaloniki. Our village is too small for that sort of thing.'

'Didn't they just take Billy to see a doctor in Kozani? What was that about?'

'It was a regularly scheduled appointment to restock his medication.'

'What kind of medication?'

'I think for his nerves. I wish I knew more but I don't ask too many questions these days. I've had my hand bitten off before, and learned my lesson.'

'Do you know what exactly happened to Billy when he was younger?' Mum asked.

Soultana sipped her cup of muddy coffee. 'Savvas told me that Billy fell off his highchair as a baby and landed hard on the floor headfirst. I wasn't home at the time. They took him to the nearby clinic and were relieved to hear he was fine. But over time, Billy's teachers noticed he wasn't developing like the other kids, he was lagging way behind. The doctors traced it back to that incident.'

'Has Savvas tried to find out what else is available to help Billy now?'

'Not really.'

'And Anna?'

'Has no say.'

'Have you said anything?'

'Till my face went blue but no one was listening. Like I said, I've learned my lesson. I don't speak about it anymore. I hold my tongue. And so should you. Focus on raising your child right, not his.'

The upshot was that Billy's brain stayed the same – unschooled, unguided – while his body continued to grow and take on more adult pastimes. It was a disastrous recipe producing the ultimate creature of leisure before their eyes. Mum was sad for Billy and annoyed with Savvas, but her sister was right: Mum's priorities were now elsewhere. And Soultana's thoughts were clear: she blamed Savvas completely for his plight. But there was an even bigger, more innocent victim in her eyes, from the gaze Soultana cast far into the future.

'What do you think is going to happen to young Georgios as the rest of us age, slow, and die?' she asked.

Mum did not answer. She slurped the remainder of her coffee and turned the cup upside-down on the saucer in order to see her future.

'He'll become his brother's keeper, that's what,' Soultana continued. 'His life won't be his own. If and when he marries, the woman will have to accept Billy too. Think about that a moment – she's effectively marrying two men. Could you do that? And Billy may even get upset if Georgios tries to marry. Billy is older and may think that if anyone marries first or is even with a woman first, it should be him.'

'At this rate he'll experience neither,' Mum said. She handed her cup to her sister who began studying the inky black patterns left in the sediment.

'Exactly,' she said. 'Had Savvas thought less with his heart and more with his head, he wouldn't have damned us all, but particularly his second son. It may have been a tough decision at the time, but this problem wasn't going to right itself with village herbs and Hail Marys. I think it's wonderful that you're taking this new baby and getting the hell out of here. He can have his own life in Australia and not have it ruined by his short-sighted father.'

CHAPTER 20

2003

'YOU'VE SEEN IT with your own eyes now, which is a better picture than my words could've ever painted,' Georgios said. 'To me, Billy is the alpha and the omega. He is my greatest love and most painful thorn.'

The bar was pumping with music and life. Hearing my brother say that was one of several moments I'd been dreading. It was probably something Georgios had wanted to say for thirty years. I didn't know how to reply and was suddenly unable to look my brother in the eye. Did Georgios want thanks? Did he want his load to be lightened? Or did he just want someone to sit and listen? He seemed to be asking for his life back. He seemed to be asking for mine.

'It was easier when we were younger,' Georgios said. 'Billy was less demanding and our parents were alive. I went on short trips to Athens and Crete, Italy and Bulgaria. It was enough.'

Georgios extinguished his cigarette and lit another. He ordered a fresh whiskey.

'But now even Theia Soultana's getting old, it's all on me,' he continued. 'Billy frets when I'm not around. He likes to create and amplify problems to feel normal, human. He gets stuck on little things. The ink on his shirt. How he nearly tripped over. And things from years ago.'

'I noticed.'

'We've all done something wrong in our lives, things we regret, that we're ashamed of. Not Billy. He is to us what we are to murderers, adulterers and thieves. He won't even swear. He fears God and knows right from wrong, so much so that he sees himself as a law enforcer, a protector.'

I nodded. 'That's important,' I said, 'to have a purpose.'

'Absolutely, it gets him out of bed in the afternoon. But for all his efforts, he's still a child. He worries, gets upset. There's no one in the world who can talk to Billy like me. I know what he's thinking before he does. I know what he wants before he knows. I know what to say and how to make him feel better, no matter his problem. I'm like, how you say, a psychotherapist. When I speak with Billy, hours and hours, let him get it out of his system, it's like psychotherapy. I don't want him taking drugs all the time.'

'So Billy takes no regular medication?' I asked.

Georgios said no. He was Billy's medication.

'He takes a short dose during winter, these little blue pills that keep him from becoming too sad.'

'What sort? I mean, what for? When no one knows what caused his condition. Or do they?'

'As I said, no one's sure. Winter's the worst time of year. The snow piles up and he can't go out as often, he's stuck at home all day. The doctor said to take them from December till March.'

'Can't the doctors do more? Is there someone I can talk to? There are so many drugs these days. I could search using a computer.'

Georgios sipped his drink. 'And what will that do? Where do you think we are, in Athens? Up here, clinics run on skeleton staff. We barely have vaccinations.'

I apologised, feeling my ignorance, and asked if we could take Billy to Athens.

'He won't travel. Plus he hates doctors.'

'But can't he see the strain he places on you and Theia Soultana?'

'Not really, no. Children are blind to such things.'

I paused, considering my next question. The music seemed to be getting louder.

'There were sanatoriums for Billy we could've taken him to, but they were in the city, and the stuff of nightmares. Electroshock therapy and heavily sedating medications. Baba thought that was cruel. In such a family-focused country as Greece, Baba would've been judged, and especially here in a small town.'

I nodded in agreement and swallowed a mouthful of water.

'What happened to Billy?' I asked. 'Do you know? Why did he turn out this way?'

'I was very young, so I can't tell you for sure,' Georgios said. 'When I asked Mama, she told me it was an illness that swept through the village and affected only the children. Some lost limbs, others went blind, some died. Billy got very, very sick. He survived, but his brain didn't develop. They were worried about me for a while there, too, in case I caught whatever was going round, a virus maybe.'

I thought a moment. 'Maybe meningitis,' I said.

'Theia Soultana said it was an accident. That Billy fell and hit his head. I don't know who to believe, but I do remember the illness.'

I looked across the bar and tried to picture Florina during the 1960s. The world still had diseases like polio. There was little known about mental disorders, the treatments were rudimentary, and the social stigma was strong.

'At the end of the day, it doesn't really matter what happened to Billy,' Georgios added.

I drummed my fingers pensively on the table. 'But there's got to be something we can do,' I said. 'What about I try to organise for a specialist to come here, to Florina? I know a few people. Maybe there's some new surgery available, something that wasn't around thirty years ago? Or what about . . .'

My brother shot down every single one of my suggestions. I stopped after a while. I didn't want to come across as patronising, questioning a process Georgios had probably already gone through many times before.

'This is all Billy knows of the world, all he'll ever know,' he said. 'He's not missing out on anything so he thinks we're not either. And, in many ways, we're not. Life's good up here. We're isolated, away from the ongoing headaches in the capital, and the world. We have fresh food, free time, and friends. I'm close to a pay rise at work, and will retire soon enough.'

Georgios worked for the state-owned Public Power

Corporation, which was the biggest electricity company in Greece. Western Macedonia was home to six power stations fuelled by lignite – brown coal. Parts of the region further outside Florina now had a post-apocalyptic landscape with sprawling black mines that spewed toxic air pollutants.

'I'm not unhappy,' he added. 'To be honest with you, Panagiotis, even if Billy was normal, I think my life would've turned out exactly the same. It's just the freedom I miss, and the opportunity to do things, even if I don't actually go and do them.'

Georgios's yearning was palpable, even amid the deafening, obnoxious Greek techno throbbing from the nearby speakers. Without warning, I felt an enormous wave of guilt wash over me. There I was with the academic world at my feet, tossing up between the highest institutions of learning in which to pursue my intellectual folly. And all that my brother wanted was to breathe his own air, even if it was much the same as what he already held in his lungs.

A memory cut across my mind. It was of a large aviary that Dad had built in the backyard when I was young, which stood opposite his infamous shed. As usual, he'd built the aviary with whatever scraps he could find, scavenged sheets of aluminium and steel and old window frames and wire. The aviary was full of bright yellow canaries; during summer, after the spring breeding, there were as many as forty birds flapping about inside. Dad had installed two doors with a small entry space; if a bird flew out as he entered, it couldn't get past the second door and escape into the wild. But occasionally, canaries did manage to find their way to freedom. Once out, there was no chance of catching them, so

Dad and I went inside the house. But it was surprising how often we returned an hour later to find the escapees flittering about the outside of the aviary, chirping at their colleagues through the wire and looking for a way back in. It was all they knew and all they wanted to know. But at least they had the opportunity to go out before they came back.

Georgios sighed and let out a dry cough, before refilling his lungs with tar. I anxiously sipped my water as if it were vodka and could soothe my senses.

'In many ways, I'm the only reason for Billy to be alive. It's taken me some time to accept that.'

'But you still love him,' I said.

'More than life itself,' Georgios said. 'From as young as I can remember, Mama told me children like Billy were a blessing from God. And you know, in as much as Billy tethers me to this town, to this life, I don't think I could cope without him. When work and worries and the weight of world sit heavy across my shoulders, I come home and Billy's there, just as I left him. His steadying presence strengthens me. His love is unconditional.'

I smiled and touched Georgios's shoulder. 'That's nice,' I said. 'I never had that.'

Georgios sighed lightly. 'I sometimes forget that,' he said. 'Even though we saw you go off into the world, you didn't have anyone waiting for you at home at the end of the day.'

'It's not so bad,' I said. 'I always had my own bedroom.'

Georgios laughed. 'And now you have two brothers anyway.'

'Mum always promised.'

Georgios grinned and flashed a wink.

'The biggest issue for me these days isn't Billy,' he said. 'It's the house. The lack of money is one thing, but the bigger factor is that Billy's become emotionally attached to an unhealthy extent. He won't let us tear it down. Because it's the only home he's ever known, and because he knows it was built by Papou.'

Georgios said Billy threw tantrums at the mere suggestion of renovating. 'He sometimes scares Theia Soultana. He's bigger than ever, and she's not young anymore.'

I was worried by this but Georgios reassured me that Billy's intentions were good. He was just a little careless, and sometimes didn't realise his own strength, which I'd already experienced first-hand.

'Theia is a problem too because she's lived in that house for close to seventy years,' Georgios said. 'She's used to doing things her way, as backward as they are. On the one hand, she's entertained the notion of letting Vangelis oversee the project. Ever since Theio Vangelis moved back to Florina twenty years ago, he became a property magnate and now takes in rent from dozens of tenants each week. I'm not exactly sure how, I don't see the full picture. So Theia has her reservations because she feels Vangelis will screw her over. Once upon a time, we even drew up plans for a multi-storey *polikatikeia*, one floor each. Good, yes?'

'Perfect,' I said.

Georgios exhaled. 'But who knows what will happen,' he said. 'Either way, I'm glad you've come now to see Papou's house in its original form.'

I told Georgios a little about my research and European tour, and where I potentially saw myself in ten years' time. It was partly by way of changing the topic but more as a means by which to ask my brother where he saw his life heading. He ignited his last cigarette and ordered a third shot.

'There's this Ionian island with monks, people who are close to God and live without temptation,' Georgios said. 'I had a friend who visited the island and a monk said to him: "You have three children." "No, I have two," my friend replied. "You have three," the monk repeated. My friend returned home to his wife. "I'm pregnant," she said. I later came across the same monk when he visited here. "You're a person who worries greatly," he told me, "but unnecessarily. You're going to one day see the arrival of children and grow old. There's no reason to lose sleep." From that day, my spirits have been lifted. I live with belief.'

In my mind, I took a step back and considered my brothers. They were a slight mess. Not one but two lives ruined. What had happened to Billy was tragic, but Georgios was suffering unnecessarily; a life sentence served by our biological father. Like Mum, who waited many years to tell me of my origins, it was done with the best intentions, with love. Misguided, smothering village love that came from village heart and village mind. I wasn't in a position to judge. I wasn't the parent of a disabled child and hadn't found myself infertile. But the lack of boundaries for Billy had reinforced Georgios's boundaries with the strongest tie of all: blood. I didn't completely believe Georgios when he said his life would've turned out the same if Billy had been normal. I was living proof of that.

Pity wasn't the right word for how I felt. Instead, I found myself developing the utmost admiration for my brother who was trying to make light of an eternally starless sky, with only an innate sense of love and family to guide the way. It was like a warm sensation washing over my skin.

A boisterous young group appeared and asked my brother where Billy was. And then the bar owner approached and insisted Billy could eat and drink any time for free.

'Billy,' Georgios laughed, 'my entire life, more popular than me!'

It was then that it dawned on me. It wasn't just my family who had raised Billy. The whole village had. Here, my family's rural location proved an advantage. Florina was small, so everyone knew everyone. Had my family lived in a big city, things would've been different. Perhaps Savvas knew this would happen. He trusted in his close-knit community.

Georgios fired me another cheeky wink. He looked cool, unruffled. He extinguished his last cigarette butt and downed his golden brown shot with one lift.

'*Pame?*' Georgios asked me. 'C'mon, let's go.'

We left the bar and found Billy leaning against a street lamp like some comic book detective. He was smoking and chatting with Takis, an old street vendor who made his living sitting in a tiny kiosk selling magazines, cigarettes and aspirin. Georgios told me that Billy often sat with Takis all night, keeping him company. Between them they would smoke a hundred cigarettes, drink twenty cups of coffee, and talk until the roosters crowed.

'Tell Billy he's doing a good job keeping the neighbourhood safe at night,' Georgios whispered to me as we approached. 'It's what he needs to believe.'

I walked straight up to Billy but didn't say a word. Instead, I wrapped my arms around his round shoulders and hugged him. He returned the favour, hugging me back with far too much force and love. But that's what made him so special, and everyone knew it.

CHAPTER 21

2003

I WOKE ON Good Friday to the sound of slow-ringing church bells and the sight of the Greek flag flying at half-mast on the hotel flagpole. I showered, brushed my teeth, and walked to the house. I entered through the kitchen and saw that Mum and Theia Soultana had been busy, boiling dozens of eggs and dyeing them crimson red for Easter Sunday. The once empty glass bowl on the table now resembled a colossal raspberry.

Georgios appeared, followed by his two aunts. They were on their way out and dressed in all black.

'Oh,' I said, looking down at my army pants and grey hoodie. 'I didn't realise . . .'

'That's okay,' Mum said. 'But at least your timing's right. We were just about to pass by the hotel to get you. Come on, we're walking.'

'Walking?'

I was genuinely surprised. From what I'd seen, Georgios

preferred to drive his Eastern Bloc jalopy two minutes to his destination than walk an arduous five. He'd told me that walking was for peasants.

'Where are we going?' I asked.

'Church,' Mum replied.

'Billy's not coming?'

'He's in his room, writing,' Georgios said. 'Leave him.'

For Billy, 'writing' meant sitting at a desk with a published book by his side and carefully transcribing the sentences into his own exercise book, line-by-line. With no knowledge of the alphabet, writing for Billy was more the copying of pictures that just so happened to be letters and words.

'He can do that for hours,' Georgios said. 'He thinks he's writing his own book. He'll later tell you, "I wrote a book today", and say it proudly.'

I walked in front alongside Georgios, with the older generation following behind. Mum carried a bunch of yellow daffodils. The stores were all closed but people were still out.

'I can already smell the wild lavender,' Mum told us, before recalling her Easters as a child.

'Early morning on Holy Saturday, we'd go up that mountain, right there, the one with the cross. The slopes would be covered with the tender new green of mulberry trees. Together with my brothers and sisters we'd pick the violet shoots of wild lavender needed for the Divine Liturgy later that night. The priest would scatter the lavender we'd collected across the floor so Christ could walk into the church. The streets would swell with people.'

We walked past a series of vine-covered terraces adorned with pink bougainvillea and crossed over a small ornate bridge. Arriving at the church, we found the *epitaphios* inside – a figure of Christ on a richly decorated bier covered with bright spring flowers and a carved wooden canopy. We approached the bier one at a time, crossed ourselves, and left a gentle kiss on Christ's body. The floral fragrance was overpowering, making my head swim.

'Go on,' Mum prompted me. 'You're not too old to crawl under it.'

I groaned. It was a ritual from childhood. Young children were blessed by crawling under the bier. Georgios chuckled and joined me, getting down on his aching knees.

'My *mama* made me do this too,' he said.

Leaving the church, we walked through a rusty gate that squealed as if in pain. Our shoes scrunched on loose white pebbles. Now the older generation led the way, through the crowded cemetery.

'It's so quiet here,' I said.

'The pine trees stand straight and make no noise when the wind passes through their needles,' said Mum. 'Out of respect.'

We were in an ancient burial ground, so old that I reasoned it might've even housed gods and goddesses. Most of the gravestones were faded, the inscriptions illegible. Theia Soultana said, 'This cemetery ran out of room years ago, filled with people born in the 1800s.'

I had suspected we might've been about to visit the graves of my biological parents. Instead, these belonged to my grandparents. Mum and Theia Soultana crouched down like angels, kissed the two headstones and began tending the graves, pulling out weeds, brushing away leaves and lighting lanterns behind small panes of glass. I stood back, unsure of what to do. Georgios lit a cigarette and looked to the sky. Mum emptied a small bottle of water into a vase on the grave and positioned her flowers. When she turned, her face glistened with tears. As Theia Soultana leaned in to kiss the headstones, I heard her say: 'If only you knew who'd come to see you. *If only you knew.*'

I put my arm around Mum. 'It's okay,' she said, retrieving a tissue from within her sleeve. 'I'm okay.'

'This church was originally a Turkish mosque that they converted to Orthodox in 1924,' Theia Soultana said. 'After the Disaster.'

I blinked confusedly. 'The Disaster?' I said. 'What's that?'

'You've never heard of the Disaster?' Theia Soultana's tone had turned incredulous. I looked over at Georgios and was genuinely dismayed to see that he, too, seemed disappointed in me.

Mum stepped in. 'Eh,' she said, 'I never really told him about all that. It was a world away from Australia, and it was well before even my time.'

'But he should know,' Theia Soultana said. 'I mean, he's now standing before his *papou* and *yiayia* who lived through it.'

CHAPTER 22

1938

IN THE LIVING room of their stone house, eight-year-old Elizabeth sat on her father's knee, listening to his stories of the past. It was late evening and past her bedtime, but she knew he seemed to forget the time when he got to talking, and especially when he got to remembering. His stories were complicated, he often repeated himself, and she could not always follow. But as the baby of the family, she simply liked sitting close to him and feeling his warmth.

Vasilios told her the year he was born – 1889 or thereabouts, even he wasn't sure – and of his two older sisters, who were Elizabeth's aunts. Elizabeth's mother Maria was also the youngest, but of six girls. Both Vasilios and Maria were Orthodox Christians who grew up in the Cappadocia region of Turkish Anatolia.

'So Baba, if you were in Turkey, how did you learn to speak Greek?' Elizabeth asked.

'I had to attend a special school in secret,' Vasilios replied. 'The Turks did not allow schools to operate so the only literate man in our village, an old priest, opened a secret school at night.'

Vasilios said he and the other boys were fearful as they went between their homes and school, and longed for a full moon to light their way. The priest would read to them in Greek from a great book until their necks turned to rubber in the flickering candlelight.

Elizabeth noticed her father never answered her questions about how he came to be in Florina. He was always careful with what he said about Turkey and then immediately switched to talking about Florina. The town's geography meant it was a microcosm of the country as a whole. Located within close proximity of the borders of Albania and Yugoslavia, Florina had been fought over by numerous conquerors: Romans, Slavs and Byzantines.

'Every single invading army has wanted the very dirt on which we built our house,' Vasilios told his youngest daughter.

Florina was only liberated from five hundred years of Ottoman rule after the First Balkan War of 1912–13. Vasilios settled his family in the region ten years later in 1923. It was during a tumultuous period when Greece's population swelled by a third and the country's economy collapsed. The Bulgarians were sent packing north and the Muslims driven east to Turkey. Mosques became churches, minarets were torn down, crosses erected. This, Vasilios told his daughter, was why he never felt secure in Florina, like a house built on muddy foundations.

'The Governor of Kozani didn't want the Muslims to leave the area. They were rich, educated and industrious. But the Greek army, the press, and the noise from a million pairs of dirty feet tramping their way west across the border meant there was no alternative. The governor was furious to see the rich people go east to Anatolia when all he got in return were barefoot peasants and idiots. Like us. The Turks ousted us like Greeks, and the Greeks greeted us like Turks.'

Elizabeth looked confused. 'Oh Baba,' she sighed, 'it must have been horrible.'

'It was terrible,' he said. 'Poverty and corruption were rife, the country had no money, it was even worse than it is today. That only eased when a path to America opened up.'

'So why didn't you go to America?' Elizabeth asked.

Her father could only laugh. Elizabeth crossed her arms and stared at him, waiting for a better explanation.

Vasilios sighed, wiping his eyes. 'Off you go then, little one,' he said. 'Bedtime.'

Under the quilt in their bedroom, Soultana spoke to her younger sister in whispers. Because she was older, she'd heard even more stories. She told her younger sister of the hand that had forced their parents' marriage. It belonged to the Ottoman army.

'Baba was told to go to the army,' Soultana said. 'But our *yiayia* didn't want him to go and fight. He was her only son and might die.'

'So what happened?' Elizabeth whispered back.

'Yiayia had to work fast. The only thing that could save Baba was if he was married.'

Vasilios's mother was fortunate that a wedding had taken place that very same week in their Anatolian village. It was there that she met Maria's mother. Maria was only eleven years old.

'Eleven?' Elizabeth said. 'I'm not even eleven!'

'Mama was still playing with dolls at the time,' Soultana said.

Maria was often in the cellar playing with her 'dolls' – a few nondescript rags – when her husband would arrive to visit. Her mother would stamp down on the wooden floorboards with a leather boot and yell: 'Maria! Leave your dolls and come upstairs, your husband's here!'

Maria was too young to fully comprehend the situation but she had no choice. Her mother had five other daughters she was raising on her own after her husband had died of tuberculosis. If there had been a prized son, things might have been different. Girls were, at best, a burden.

'Is that why Baba talks about us like that?' Elizabeth asked her sister.

'Yes,' Soultana replied.

Elizabeth had heard Vasilios introducing his four children by saying: 'I have two children and two girls.'

He sometimes even referred to his daughters as his 'two guests' to signify that Soultana and Elizabeth's permanent homes were actually those of their future husbands.

The more daughters Maria's mother could marry off, the lighter her load. Being the youngest, Maria was the first taken, as the most eligible and pure.

'All this happened in Turkey before what they called "the Disaster" in 1923,' Soultana said.

Elizabeth hid her face in the blankets, and only revealed it slowly. 'That's before I was born,' she said. 'What happened?'

'I don't know exactly,' Soultana replied.

She said that the family was forced out of Turkey and west, finally settling in Florina, a snug village surrounded by a dense forest of beech and oak in the northern mountains. It had not been possible for them to go to a Greek island – they were full of mosquitoes and disease and open to attack from all sides. By contrast, the air in Florina was clean, and the geography protected.

'But what I do know is that Baba came here first,' Soultana told her younger sister. 'He made the journey on his own before us, and then sent for Mama and the rest of us to come later.'

CHAPTER 23

1923

VASILIOS DUSTED OFF his flat cap and placed it on his head. He adjusted it, making sure it was sitting straight. He had just kissed his children goodbye, from oldest to youngest, whispering to each to be good for their mother. Vasilios's final kiss was bound for the lips of his wife.

'You will come once I've got a foothold in the new world,' Vasilios told her. 'In a few months time.'

'Yes,' Maria replied.

She handed Vasilios a glass jar of soil. He rested it in his leather bag alongside a golden bottle of olive oil and some warm clothes. He slung a woollen scarf Maria had knitted over his head and wrapped it tightly around his neck. Vasilios took one last look at his four children – Despina, Savvas, Soultana and Vangelis – as if inhaling his last lungful of oxygen before a marathon.

'See you soon,' Vasilios said to his wife in Greek, before adding in Turkish: 'Trust no one.'

Sparking a cigarette in his gloved hands, he turned away into the icy February morning. He needed to hurry. The vast, writhing chain of human misery was already snaking its way out of Anatolia, heading west to the coast. It started raining as he walked. He turned up his jacket collar and pressed down on his cap.

'Don't cry,' Maria told her children as she wiped their red faces. 'Don't cry. We'll see Baba again soon.'

Vasilios was a Christian running for his life; a fugitive mourning the loss of his ancestral land in Cappadocia. By virtue of both his faith and gender, he was forced to leave before his family.

The Greco-Turkish War ended in 1922. It had been a bloody three-year conflict between revolutionaries seeking to divide the Ottoman Empire. The result was a decisive Turkish victory, the loss of Greece's territorial gains, and the establishment of a new republic. With the return of the triumphant Turkish army in autumn, the Turks had started taking all able-bodied Orthodox Christian men into labour camps. If the Greeks dared return to march on Ankara, the Turks' prisoners would be executed in retaliation.

Vasilios was not interested in being human collateral. All he needed to do was get to the port with his forged papers that said his family had already left and his passage west to Greece was guaranteed.

It would be a long march: a trek of several hundred miles across treacherous terrain to reach the Turkish coast, before a perilous sea crossing to Greece. Vasilios was told it would take at least three months, depending on the person. It required courage, strength, and smarts. If you were old, weak or invalid, you probably wouldn't make it at all. With a strong back and young legs, Vasilios thought he was in good shape for the journey; at least, physically.

Striding down a hill, Vasilios saw the vast train of humanity disappearing into the distance. He joined the line and started walking. He quickly realised there was no talking. Vital reserves of energy were best saved for walking, and this was a 500-mile-long funeral procession.

The first few days brought both bitter cold and stifling heat. Vasilios wrapped the scarf across his face in the mornings, only the thin slits of his eyes exposed to the elements. Walking west to the sea, the afternoons meant the sun burning their faces. The refugees only stopped when the light had disappeared completely. They bedded down under trees or in caves or on the smoothest earth they could find, or simply collapsed where they stood.

Horses, their heads bowed with exhaustion, carried crying babies in baskets on either side of their saddles. Old women dressed in black walked with a cane in one hand and a caged chicken in the other. There was constant weeping. If someone could not keep up or fell over or collapsed through exhaustion, the crowd kept going. No one helped them. The faces of Vasilios's four young children urged him forward, one aching foot after the other.

With the end of fighting in 1922, Europe's leaders had met to discuss the region known as 'the Near East'. Tired of conflict, of bloodshed and instability, the terms of a divorce were laid down. The decree went out for the two populations to be unmixed. It was to be a compulsory exchange of Orthodox Christians in Turkish territory with Muslims living on Greek land. At least one million people would be displaced.

The population exchange was a bold exercise in racial purification that ultimately sought to minimise the risk of future war. Flooding the unpopulated and uncultivated northern mountains with Christian refugees was also a way for Greece to ward off any future invasions by Slavs. Greece was an exhausted country ravaged by war; it was making the best of a bad situation by ethnically shoring up its borders. Whatever short-term refugee crisis it suffered would supposedly be outweighed by long-term stability in the region and future economic gains.

But it wasn't just the journey to Greece that concerned Vasilios. The destination did, too. He was bound for the north, the region which had been newly-annexed and which needed populating. In the south, the Peloponnese and even in Thessaly, nationhood or character was unquestioned. But in the unpredictable north, the land's identity wavered according to the strongest army of the day. Vasilios worried about this instability and the safety of his young family in a tiny border town. But what choice did he have?

After two weeks, Vasilios's belt tightened a notch. His battered boots struggled to contain his throbbing feet. It took his final droplets of energy to remove them at dusk. He rubbed his blisters with the olive oil he carried. His bag and shoes became his pillow; it was the only way to stop thieves. Closing his eyes with exhaustion each night, Vasilios crossed himself three times and recited a prayer that his mother had taught him when he was young. He knew the stars above the Turkish countryside might be the last thing he would ever see when he closed his eyes.

After a month, Vasilios's belt tightened a second notch.

The mountain town of Afyonkarahisar marked the halfway

point. Vasilios saw it as a mental landmark – he was now closer to the sea than he was to home. He thanked God for protecting him and prayed for his family. But Afyonkarahisar also represented something more ominous. In Turkish, *afyon* meant 'opium'. The poppies that grew across acres of fields in Afyon Province made Vasilios's nostrils twinge with trepidation. The abundance of raw opium brought with it an undesirable element and only made the journey harder.

Every day, Vasilios saw more bodies as the road took its toll. A young boy he had walked alongside for several days and occasionally smiled at suddenly disappeared, only to be seen again face-down in a trench. In step with the body count, increasing numbers of birds began to circle. Those family members who could spare the energy dug shallow graves and buried their loved ones. Most didn't, and the birds saw to their removal.

Vasilios eyed the predatory birds with apprehension as they circled and dive-bombed from the sky. Their actions were innate, involuntary. He didn't question them or judge them. Instead, Vasilios reserved his hatred for the gangs of opium-fuelled Turks that dogged the second half of the trek. They were cruel and inhuman. They abducted and raped in broad daylight, making off with young girls and women as they kicked and screamed and thrashed. Some were snatched from Vasilios's very side. If Vasilios had the strength, he would've retaliated. But his priorities lay elsewhere. High on opium and the recent military victory, the swaggering Turks knew this. Vasilios hid his eyes beneath his flat cap and kept walking.

In the back of his mind was the thought his family would soon be following in his footsteps. Conditions could have improved by then, or be much worse. Some of the girls taken by gangs were not much older than his own Despina.

Dear God, thought Vasilios, *what have I done?*

Could he have protected his family had they all gone together?

Should he have married off his daughters to local Turks and given them an Islamic life of security?

Vasilios knew that if he hadn't left, he was no use to his family. As a fit Christian man, he was a prime candidate for the labour camps. His only hope were the forged papers he slept with down the front of his trousers.

With corpses littering the route, swarms of disease were the next wave to hit. The smell was overpowering, even in the open landscape. Malarial mosquitoes and vermin massed in plague proportions. Vasilios walked faster. He was running out of time to reach the coast and out of *fakelakia* with which to bribe the Turkish guards. The tang of salt in his lungs could not come fast enough. He kept asking others how much further, how much further. A day, two days, a week, a month . . . ?

The seasons changed. Winter had given way to spring which turned into summer and the countryside was carpeted with wildflowers and new grass. Vasilios collected orange seeds from the road and stored them safely in his jar of Anatolian soil.

Suddenly, one day, there was screaming in the distance. It was a sound familiar to Vasilios's sunburnt ears. After four months on the road, it was also a sound he'd grown immune to. But there was something about this scream. The timbre was higher and lighter, the duration longer. It wasn't a wail in agony or distress. It almost sounded happy. Vasilios tried to remember the feeling.

Climbing to the top of a lush green ridge, he saw the Aegean Sea. It was the bluest, sweetest sight. People threw their hands in the air and ran the final mile to the water. Vasilios sprinted.

A sea of humanity saturated the waterfront. Emaciated, diseased Christians clogged every dirty corner. They turned potato sacks into makeshift clothes and old rubber tyres into shoes. Shanty towns had sprung up, refugees sheltering in oil drums and beneath metal sheeting, boiling fish heads and wild grass. Diseased cats were everywhere, all bones and patchy fur.

Vasilios arrived at the port breathless. His clothes were rags, his skin black. The stench of human filth made him retch. There was no space to lie down and sleep, and no toilets. He was given a bread ration, which he could barely hold down for hunger. Having run out of notches on his belt, he'd started constructing his own with a rusty nail.

Vasilios's hollow eyes saw a large tent at the southern end of the port. The tent had the Turkish Red Crescent symbol. He fought his way through the crowd and walked inside the tent to ask for bandages. Unlike the exodus of Christians from Turkey, the influx of Muslims from Greece was supervised by envoys. The Red Crescent supplied new arrivals with wood and coal to keep them warm and offered vaccinations. The Greeks saw no such luxuries. To the victor went the spoils. Vasilios walked out.

Boats bound for Thessaloniki were left floating off the Turkish coast to prevent the spread of smallpox, typhus and cholera. After two nights on the docks, Vasilios was herded onto an overcrowded boat that looked like it could sink at any moment. He was quarantined for a week on a remote island whose name he did not know. It was there that he got his first taste of what it meant to be 'coming home'. Bowed with despair, he was spat upon by the native Greeks from their upper windows as he shambled past. '*Tourkosporoi!*' they jeered at him; 'Seed of Turk!' The mere fact that he had lived in the Turkish state made his loyalty to Christianity suspicious. He did not fight back, or even plead his case. He had neither the energy nor the spirit.

The same welcome greeted Vasilios in his new village of Florina. The native Greeks were suspicious of the refugees and their odd dialect. They went to different churches and *kafenions* and even used different water pumps fearing some kind of contamination. The Muslims who had left were a known quantity. Vasilios's kind, though Christian, were still alien.

Vasilios was billeted to live with an outgoing Muslim family. It was meant to be a means for integration, but merely reflected the delay in executing the population exchange. The Turks in Greece resented their houses being requisitioned, and were blind to the fact that Vasilios's own home would suffer the same fate. As they left, they tore down doors and shutters and painted ethnic epithets on the walls.

This is it, thought Vasilios. *This is now home.*

CHAPTER 24

1974

IT WAS THE height of summer, mid-July. Mum and her family were all huddled around the radio in the kitchen, listening to a morning news bulletin. She was holding me in her arms while I slept.

'What's going on? Are we fighting with the Turks again?' Mum's voice was tired.

'Eh,' said Savvas, 'some might say we never stopped.'

Overnight, a military coup by Greek-Cypriots wanting to fold the island into the Greek state had overthrown the archbishop president and replaced him with a puppet regime. In response, the Turks sent thirty ships carrying as many tanks to Cyprus, and were now advancing towards the capital, Nicosia. The Hellenic fleet complete with submarines had been deployed. All of Greece's airports and borders immediately closed. The country was fearful, and Mum and I were now stuck. Her tension rose. A country in lockdown was of no use to her or her new baby.

The news bulletin cast her mind back thirty years. Having locked themselves in their house for days, Mum's family was almost relieved by the time the Germans finally appeared on motorcycles flying their bright red pennants through Florina's tight streets. Due to its northern geography, Florina was the very first Greek town to see the German invaders. Two weeks later, they took the capital, driving straight to the Acropolis to raise the *Reichskriegsflagge.*

For the rest of the day, garbled news bulletins poured through. War cries called on the Greek army to turn the Turkish invaders into mincemeat. In the late afternoon, an announcement was made that all unbaptised infants should be baptised immediately. Dying unbaptised was a ticket to Hell. The high priest would be opening the local church for two hours.

Mum didn't hesitate.

'Let's go,' she told her family. 'I'm not risking the baby.'

Baptism and baby names were topics that Mum had long discussed with her husband.

'Bring him home unbaptised,' his telegram had said. 'At least then I can be involved in one family occasion.'

After fighting off a raft of suggestions from Artemis, Mum finally settled on a name for the baby: 'Panagiotis'. It was a way of honouring her own mother, since Maria and Panagiotis shared the same saint's day, the fifteenth of August. Coincidentally, it had also been the date when Mum first arrived in Australia.

Anna agreed the name was perfect for me.

The two mothers carried me to the nearby church in a fruit

box. By the time they arrived, the line of people spilled out the front door and snaked around the corner.

'*Parakalo*, please!' The bearded, myopic priest appeared with a raised index finger. 'Only one person inside at a time, just the godfather or godmother. There's no room inside and we need to get through this quickly. Remember, only one.'

Anna and Mum looked at each other.

'You go,' Anna said.

'Don't be silly,' Mum said. 'You go.'

'Elizabeth, please, I've already had two sons baptised. This is your only chance.'

'No, it's not. I'll be there in Australia. You won't be.'

'You'll baptise him twice?'

'Is that wrong?'

'To be honest, I don't know,' Anna said. 'I don't think so. So long as the name's the same.'

'It's my husband, he had his heart set on a big celebration with our friends. And I didn't foresee this, what has happened today.'

'No one did.'

'So you should go,' said Mum. 'As his godmother.'

'I can't be his *koumbara*. That's not right.'

'Anna, I insist.'

'I'm still not going in without you.'

'Fine, we'll both go.'

'But the priest said—'

'Said what? So what?' Mum said. 'He'll make an exception. Even if we have to explain it all to him over the font and hold up the line for a few minutes.'

So we stood there: two proud, determined women, avoiding the looks from others in the queue, and me, cradled, in an otherwise sombre single file. A few people gently sobbed as they stood holding their young. Like Mum, they would not have woken that morning expecting a sudden baptism for their precious newborns. They would have planned big celebrations, joyous occasions with food, music and dancing to welcome their newest family member. Instead, the tone of such a significant day was one of mourning.

The priest's stovepipe brimless hat appeared at the door again.

'Boys to the left, girls to the right!'

Even with such pandemonium, the good father still remembered to prepare two fonts. In the eyes of the church, baptism creates blood relations. Should all the babies have been baptised in the same font on the same day, they would have been brother and sister before God, and unable to marry each other. In a small village like Florina, that could one day pose problems.

Anna and Mum approached the altar. Straw-coloured light flickered against the walls of the church, wax dripping onto the candle followers. The priest raised a bushy eyebrow above his thick eyeglass frames when he saw them. He wrinkled his forehead and tugged at his iron grey beard.

'Ladies, please, I asked for only one person at a time,' he said. 'Who is the mother?'

'She is,' Mum and Anna said in unison, pointing at each other.

The priest looked confused, and even more displeased.

Mum leaned in. 'It's a long story,' she whispered. 'And we don't want to hold up the queue any longer.'

Running out of time, the priest was in no mood for a round

table discussion, especially with me smeared in olive oil, wriggling like an eel through his ageing fingers. He turned me eastwards, blew in my face three times to chase away evil spirits, made a sign of the cross, uttered four exorcisms against temptation, and dunked me three times into the tepid water.

'The servant of God Panagiotis is baptised in the name of the Father, and of the Son, and of the Holy Spirit!'

I screamed like I was being dipped in acid. Mum exhaled, job done. Her son finally had a name, he would not be going to Hell. Mum relaxed and smiled for the first time all day.

We returned home. In our absence, the family had marshalled forces. Soultana had prepared a celebration dinner. Through connections, Savvas had organised for a lamb to be slaughtered and delivered. Soultana baked it with garden rosemary and oregano. She chargrilled eggplants and drizzled them with fresh honey. Vangelis sourced walnuts preserved in syrup and farm yoghurt. The radio stayed on all night as my family ate and talked; occasionally, they even laughed. There were no further announcements, only martial music.

Over the next month, Cypriot churches were gradually transformed into mosques. Refugees from the eastern side of the island poured west in their thousands, just as they had in 1923. A quarter of a million souls, one third of the country, were driven from their homes. Mass rapes and shootings of unarmed civilians were reported, moments after being told they would not be harmed. Bodies were found burned in village kilns.

Other victims were disabled or pregnant. Prisoners had their heads cracked against walls and cigarettes stubbed out on their skin. They were beaten with electrified clubs and given urine to drink. The countryside was scalded with napalm.

Returning home from the *kafenion* one evening, Vangelis looked distraught. 'I heard that a ninety-year-old Greek woman was raped by a Turkish soldier as he wore her wedding ring,' he told the family.

Soultana looked skyward, did her cross. 'I'm so glad Baba isn't alive to see this,' was all she said.

In August, important men met. On the final day, the conference lasted all night, and ended unresolved. Military conflict resumed ninety minutes later.

Mum knew that she and her baby must leave.

CHAPTER 25

1974

WITH THE ARRIVAL of the final paperwork making the adoption official, Mum's black leather handbag with Bakelite handle was now replete with priceless items. The birth certificate noted Elizabeth and Bill as my parents; there was no mention of Savvas or Anna. Also included were a silver chain with cross and Evil Eye that Anna had given for when I was older. After six months, Mum finally felt like my carer and protector.

Vangelis had organised a friend with a big Volkswagen van for the drive to Athens. The morning of our departure, Mum once again found herself at the top of her family's front steps. Maria's wisteria vine ushered her down to the bottom where yet another assortment of family was waiting to bid her another tearful goodbye.

Billy leaned forward and carefully kissed the top of my head, now thick with woolly black hair.

'Bravo, Billy!' said Soultana. 'A nice kiss for your brother.'

'My *brother*,' Billy said, as if wanting me to hear it.

Georgios also offered a kiss. It was less tender.

Soultana held me high. 'See you soon, little man. Return to us a handsome *palikari!*'

Mum looked over to Anna with both elation and sadness. Anna tried to hide her tears as Savvas whispered in her ear. Soultana handed me to Savvas. His eyes were bloodshot. Holding me in his arms, caressing my face, he spoke softly, words that Mum could not hear. That sixty seconds was more attention than Mum had seen him give me in six months. With a light kiss, he passed me to his wife, who repeated the ritual, wiping away streams of tears from her chin and my cheeks. Mum came closer and put her arm around us both.

'*Signomi*,' Anna apologised. 'Elizabeth, I'm so sorry. The baby's face is all wet.'

'That's fine, Anna. I don't know when we'll return so don't feel as if you have to hold back.'

'Elizabeth, let me say one thing,' Anna stammered. 'I may become depressed and I may worry and I may lose sleep. But I'm ready for it all. I've given him to you freely and I know he's going to a good home, as if my own. I can see you're ready. I made a pact with Almighty God, and may He always protect your son. Your joy is my joy.'

It was only then that Mum finally began to cry. After she had sobbed for a minute, Vangelis spoke.

'C'mon kids,' he said. 'We'll miss our plane.'

As the van worked its way up through the gears, from the rear window Mum saw Anna drop to her knees. Billy ran into her arms and Savvas knelt down to comfort her. Mum's final family snapshot was of her brother holding his wife, whose back was to the car, limply shaking a white handkerchief as he wiped his own face and nose. Billy and Georgios stood a foot behind; only Billy waved. The lone figure smiling brightly and gesturing with gusto was Soultana, relieved at the sight of her baby sister and baby nephew finally on their way. The scene reminded Mum of when she said goodbye to her parents nearly twenty years ago.

This time, though, Mum smiled at the thought of shortening the distance home with each passing minute. Having seen their hurt up close, her family's pain lingered. It would for years. Arrangements and agreements aside, Mum knew that her son came from an act of love and from someone else's body. The deepest connection would always be there. Sitting comfortably and kicking my strong new grasshopper legs in my carrier, I looked up and around at my strange surroundings inside the van, oblivious to the enormity of the moment.

❧

At the Kingsford Smith arrivals gate in Sydney, a pensive new father had been pacing the floor a good hour, cremating an entire pack of cigarettes. It was as if Bill was waiting outside the delivery room of a maternity ward. By the time his wife appeared, Bill's whole body was convulsing with excitement. She was not confident her husband was in any state to take a firm hold of his new son.

Her determination lasted no longer than it took for Bill to spot the baby carrier. He rushed over and knelt before it, wrapping his big workman hands around my back and pulling me out. It was at that moment that Bill finally became 'Dad'. Hoisting me high into the air, Dad wanted to admire his son, to believe he was real, flawless, his. He kept asking his wife, 'Is this him? This is him, right?' and spinning the soft bundle around.

'Look at you, look at you! Hey! Big boy!'

My lungs opened, I started to cry. Dad didn't care. His excitement and joy could not be contained.

Dad's babbling continued into the car park. As for his world-weary wife, Mum shambled along, dragging her suitcase, trying not to think of her despairing sister-in-law and family, and hoping for at least some form of acknowledgement of her presence from her husband. A hug hello, welcome back, thanks for all you did, love you.

It was a rare instance for Dad to be motivated enough to venture up the highway to Sydney. He'd seen very little of Australia since arriving, and only ever holidayed on the South Coast of New South Wales where one of his four brothers lived. It was as if he had used up all his desire to travel through the mere act of immigrating. Mum even had a domestic ticket to fly back to Canberra but Dad insisted on escorting his gift home personally, unable to wait three more agonising hours. As we drove back to the capital, the vibrato of the asphalt highway proved suitably tranquilising for mother and son alike.

Dad was still buzzing when we arrived home. Mum took a seat on her suitcase in the hallway and sat the carrier down on the floor. Dad propped his new son up a little, a trophy to admire.

My eyes, the size of full moons, promptly started scanning the long empty corridor.

'He's trying to figure out where he is,' Mum said.

Dad rested his hands on his hips, smiled. 'He's home. Eh mate. You're home.'

Then, after a moment, he added: 'He has very big ears.'

'He'll grow into them.'

CHAPTER 26

2003

AFTER WALKING BACK to the house from the old cemetery, Theia Soultana needed to rest. Georgios jangled his car keys at me and Mum and said we were all going for a drive.

We headed north. The newer cemetery was on the outskirts of town, a coliseum of glistening white marble and gold lettering. Georgios led the way to a single slab. Here lay our parents, one buried on top of the other; it was less expensive that way. He didn't make a big deal of it, just showed me where they were and started his chores, going in search of matches from the office. I got the impression that my brother wanted me to be alone with them, without him as a buffer, perhaps to explain myself. For why I hadn't come sooner, for why I'd been so scared. A pair of crows in their black executioners' hoods squawked from a nearby tree. Clouds rolled in from the west, their underbellies dark and bruised.

Behind a sliding glass window on my father's grave, there was a decolourised photo fading in the Mediterranean sun. It was of him sitting in a chair with a drink in his hand. His other arm was thrust into the air, as if he was dancing a *tsifteteli* with the photographer. He was old and thin but his spirit looked young. Anna's grave had a black and white photo of her and Savvas sitting at a table and staring down the camera. I couldn't look them in the eyes; it was as if they were asking me questions I was unable to answer. That they weren't talking back, that they weren't looking away only made it harder. But I had nothing.

'I'm sorry,' I said. 'I should've come earlier.'

I scrambled to manufacture an emotion other than guilt. Regret loomed large but was almost as bad, if not worse. Guilt at least offered an opportunity to make amends. Instead, all I could offer them was the man I'd become, who had studied his guts out to add a few letters after his name. The problem was that short of having cured cancer or fronted with offspring, I felt my achievements counted for nothing. Letters meant nothing to them. I thanked my biological parents for their spectacular sacrifice and generosity; especially my mother. In spite of all that happened, I still had no doubt that giving away a baby would have been absolutely devastating for her.

Mum and Georgios arrived with candles and matches. As one mother leaned in to gently kiss the other's headstone, I heard her sobbing: 'If only you could've seen him,' she was repeating, 'if only . . .'

Mum was doubly emotional for seeing her brother's grave. The last time she saw him, I was in a baby carrier. I wondered how she felt seeing me and my biological parents, essentially reunited. I'd heard that the moment an adopted child met their birth parents, it returned the adopted parents to a time of infertility. The blood was reunited, and I am now an outsider. I approached Mum and lightly touched her shoulder in reassurance.

Georgios saw my ashen face staring down at the grave.

'Eh,' he said. 'You look like you've seen a ghost.'

I looked up at him solemnly. He winked at me.

'Listen,' he said coolly, 'don't make this more than it is. Mama and Baba were proud of you. That's all you need to know, all you should ever think about. You weren't theirs. Deep down, they knew.'

Looking around, I saw groups of people – families – sitting around graves, talking, eating sandwiches, sharing drinks. Georgios explained that some of the villagers spent all day in the cemetery to again be with loved ones and reunited as a family. At dusk, the groundskeeper had to ask them to leave.

I asked if I could walk back to the hotel. I needed the air, the space, the time. I could tell that Georgios knew I wanted to think, to ruminate and analyse, which was precisely what he didn't want me to do. But he let me walk anyway. Mum told me not to get lost. In the distance, the dull rumble of thunder was heard.

I was hot and sweaty by the time I reached town. Within sight of the hotel, a stranger stopped me as I climbed a long hill. He had short cropped hair, wore a thick gold chain, and carried a folded newspaper. He claimed to recognise me from an earlier introduction with my brothers. I couldn't remember every face I'd met. There had been so many.

'Thank God you're finally here,' the man said. 'Georgios needs help with Billy.'

'I'm sorry? He hasn't said anything to me.'

'Of course he hasn't. And nor will he. In fact, no one will. Sorry to be the one to tell you this but it's for your own good.'

I took a step back. The man's grey eyes were fixed on me.

'How long are you here?' he asked.

I took a moment to respond, and then spoke cautiously. 'One week.'

'A week? Is that all? You've had a lifetime of opportunity in Australia. Remember that Billy is just as much your brother as he is Georgios's.'

I stayed silent, scratched my chin. On my head, I felt the first drops of rain.

'What happens when Soultana dies, and then maybe Georgios? Have you thought about that? You need to be ready to step in. To know what you're doing. To be prepared.'

The man felt the same rain and held the newspaper over his head. He said goodbye and hurried on down the hill. I ran the final stretch. I couldn't remember when I last ran so fast.

Back at the hotel, watching the rain through an open window, I replayed the day's events in my head. I felt guilt, and a little anger. I didn't want to admit it, but there was truth in what the stranger had told me.

I considered the Billy situation. Mum and Dad knew of it before they entered into the arrangement with my biological parents. Didn't they consider the long-term impact? Perhaps this was why Mum waited so long to tell me. She knew the longer she waited, the weaker the bond between brothers would be.

It was an ultimately cruel arrangement. Cruel on Georgios who knew he had a normal brother but who didn't know he existed, and cruel on Anna and Savvas who had to give away one of their children. And cruel on me, too, who now had to live with such thoughts and feelings, which had only amplified since arriving in Greece. And for what? All so Mum and Dad could become parents. And yet, without them, and their desire to be parents, I would never have existed. I should've been thanking them, not angry with them. Perhaps I was only angry at myself.

There was a knock at my door. It was Mum with an umbrella, coming to visit, worried about me.

'I'm okay,' I said. 'Really, I'm fine.'

Mum looked at me with her gentle brown eyes. 'I'm glad,' she said. 'That mustn't have been easy.'

'It wasn't.'

She paused. 'Georgios told me that my brother was asking about you all the time, and especially before he died. All he wanted to do was see you once. You should have come over.'

I sighed. 'Gee,' I said wearily, 'thanks.'

'Sorry,' Mum said. 'I was just trying to say that he loved you and that it would've been nice if you'd seen him.'

'Look, I know what I did. I can't justify not coming earlier. There's nothing I can say other than sorry.'

'Georgios also told me he thought many times to come to Australia to tell you what happened when you were born. He was going to just turn up one day and surprise you. But he knew that doing that would annoy both his parents and your dad and me, and probably scare you. What I'm trying to say is that he loves you too.'

'Thanks. I know.'

Mum sat on the bed and studied the falling rain. 'He told me he still remembers how quiet the house was when you left. "They took my baby away," is what he told me.'

I felt a sharp pain in the middle of my chest.

'No one spoke for three days after you left. It was like they were mourning. And for that, I'm solely to blame. I was selfish. Coming back here has made me realise that.'

'No you're not, Mum. It was all agreed to.'

'It was, but it was also harder on Savvas and Anna than I think anyone realised. Except maybe my father.'

'Your father?'

Mum adjusted her weight, making the bed springs squeak. 'I remember him telling me that he feared what may happen afterwards. He thought I was playing with fire.'

I nodded thoughtfully and ran my fingers through my thinning hair. Outside the window, the wet blue and white striped flag flapped lazily on the pole.

'But all these people are gone now,' Mum sighed. 'They're the voices of the dead.'

I reflected on what had happened so long ago, trying to make sense of it. In spite of all that I'd heard since arriving in Florina, my biological parents knew from the start that I wasn't theirs. There was no way they could've developed the same bond with me as they had with their other two children. It was completely understandable that they mourned my departure and missed me, but we were never close. They loved me, but had more imagination than reality with me.

I joined Mum on the polyester bedspread and placed my hand near hers.

'Georgios seems like a reasonable soul,' I said. 'He's old enough to know that regrets are a part of life. He regrets not coming to Australia, the family regrets how they've treated Billy. My biological parents regretted giving me away, you regret not telling me earlier. And I regret not coming sooner to see my father. But I don't think many people would swap shoes with our family. These were all difficult situations, and none of us are bad people.'

Mum smiled. She pulled me closer and hugged me in a way she never had before; warmer, wiser, and perhaps even with a newfound respect for the son who had finally grown up.

It was all over now. There was only one more thing I wanted to say, but I dared not say it out loud in front of Mum. And that was: 'When my adoptive parents die, I know I'll feel a loss and pain that my brothers would never feel.'

CHAPTER 27

2003

ON FRIDAY EVENING, three separate epitaphios from three different churches congregated in Florina's central square, before making their way to Saint Panteleimon. Billy wore a tight suit that made him look like a burst sausage. He stood transfixed by the rhythmic motion of the swinging censers, smoking and dancing at the front of the procession like the heads of dragons. A high priest used a two-dollar microphone that gave more static than speech to deliver a sermon condemning the evils of war and advocating peace. The expectant crowd clogged the tight village streets for Saturday night's Resurrection service to wait for the Easter flame. Without the flame on the dinner table, there was no breaking the fast.

At midnight, the church was hushed, darkened. The bells rang and silenced the gossiping crowd. The head priest appeared at the doors, chanting and carrying a white candle bearing the Light of the Resurrection. It worked its way through the throng like a swarm of friendly fireflies. When the flame finally reached my family, we wished one another '*Christos Anesti*' with light kisses. We then stood to bask in the buttery glowing faces of the relieved crowd, each already thinking about the food on their dinner table. Pyromaniacs were soon active, living up to the tradition of setting off firecrackers at midnight mass. We walked home to the sound of deafening car alarms.

On our return, Billy wolfed down three steaming bowls of *mayeiritsa*. He only paused as his soup bowl was re-filled. He stared at me blankly as he chewed.

'What's wrong? You don't eat *mayeiritsa?*' he asked, mouth full.

'No thanks,' I said, making a face.

'Why not?' asked Georgios. Crossing himself as he sat down to his bowl, he sounded offended.

'I don't like it,' I replied.

Mayeiritsa had all the visceral organs from whatever dead livestock had been roasted for the Sunday feast, all boiled together, then fried. The liver, intestines, even the lungs and heart – nothing was wasted. After forty days fasting during Lent, *mayeiritsa's* main purpose was to prepare the body for the feast by introducing meat protein. Billy, on the other hand, seemed to gulp it down like a vanilla milkshake.

On the Sunday, I finally demonstrated my Easter spirit by eating more roast lamb than I could have possibly imagined. It had been slowly roasted on a spit since the early morning, and I'd never tasted anything so delicious. The meat melted on my tongue. Georgios explained that it was the quality of the local produce combined with ancient herbs and a 'special reserve' extra virgin olive oil that was retained for major occasions. I retired to my hotel room to digest and sleep away the afternoon.

When I finally returned to the house, I heard raised voices inside. Male voices only, but mainly Billy's. As I pushed open the back door, Billy stormed past me, nearly knocking me over.

'Easy there, boss,' I said. Billy loved it when I called him that. 'Where are you going?'

'*Volta!*' Billy replied, not looking back.

I found Georgios in the kitchen, picking up a broken plate. What was once an oily salad was strewn across the floor.

'What happened? Are you okay?' I asked.

'I'm fine,' said Georgios. 'Billy, he was upset. Theia Soultana and Theia Eliso have gone out.'

'Upset? Over what, did you have a fight?'

'Billy accidentally broke Papou's watch,' Georgios said. 'He dropped it and broke the glass face.'

'So?'

'Billy loved his *papou* so his watch was sacred. Billy got upset, scared, he thought he was going to be in trouble, from me, from Papou. I'm tired, I didn't sleep well and so didn't handle the situation. Billy threw the food I prepared for him on the floor.'

I bent down and helped my brother pick up the last few slippery chunks of tomato and cucumber.

'Thanks,' Georgios said.

'Will Billy be alright?'

'He'll be out all night now. Someone will give him some food, he'll be fine. We'll patch things up when he gets back tomorrow.' He sighed. 'Anyway, I could do with the break. To sleep.'

Georgios's eyes were bloodshot, the skin on his face creased like an unironed shirt. He hadn't shaved since my arrival.

The next morning as I walked up to the house, I heard a voice in the kitchen singing a soft tune. I poked the back door open and through the crack saw Georgios sitting with his arm around Billy, stroking his thick grey hair and gently singing what I recognised as the Greek national anthem. Billy's eyes were closed and he was breathing deeply. Georgios saw me through the gap and gestured to me to not approach. I nodded obediently and went back to the hotel.

Witnessing the altercation between my brothers was the final push I needed. Sensing a spare hour at my disposal, I sought out the nearest doctors' surgery. It was closed. A passer-by who saw me bashing on the door directed me to another clinic two streets away. This one was open. There was no receptionist in the waiting room, nor were there any magazines, pot plants or waiting patients. I tiptoed through and knocked on what I thought was the surgery door. There was a young man behind a desk, reading a thick file and smoking a cigarette. The window was open a crack.

'Excuse me but I was wondering if you could help me.'

'I'm sorry. Do you have an appointment?'

'I don't, but I was wondering if you perhaps knew my brother.'

Unsurprisingly, the doctor said he knew Billy, but not in any professional capacity. He'd only arrived in Florina six months earlier. He kept referring to Billy as having 'a mental retardation' even though I called it 'an intellectual disability'. He could not equivocally say what had caused Billy's condition.

'I wasn't here forty years ago.'

'Of course,' I said. 'But is there a chance there would be any medical records documenting what happened?'

The doctor extinguished his butt in a dirty ashtray. 'Not in this office,' he said. 'And given the bureaucracy I've had to wade through, I doubt there are any anywhere.'

The doctor rattled off a range of possibilities for what might have happened to Billy.

'Problems during pregnancy or birth, whooping cough, measles, meningitis, toxins, iodine deficiency, head trauma, something genetic . . .'

It was nothing I didn't already know.

'Could Billy get his chromosomes tested, make sure his karyotype is normal?' I asked.

The doctor looked surprised.

'I'm a geneticist,' I quickly added.

'Well of course he could,' the doctor said. 'But not in this office. He'd have to go to Thessaloniki or Athens.'

I hung my head.

'Are you worried in case you might have inherited something?' the doctor asked. 'If so, then I would recommend getting yourself tested.'

This had been in the back of my mind, but it wasn't why I was asking about Billy. I thanked the doctor for his time and left.

The other two clinics I visited were equally fruitless. I swore one of the doctors was fishing for a bribe. He kept leaving long pauses in the conversation and clearing his throat. I kept my wallet in my pocket and left, walking back to the hotel. On my way, I encountered Theia Soultana carrying her canvas shopping bag. She was heading to the market for groceries. She asked where I had been. I used it as an opportunity to ask about Billy.

'Don't go wasting your time chasing doctors,' she said. 'They know nothing. Billy fell off his highchair as a baby.'

'Were you there *theia*, did you see it happen?'

'No. Only your mother was home at the time, she told us what happened later at the clinic when we all arrived. We were all terribly worried.'

'Georgios said there was an illness, a disease, which swept through the village and infected Billy's brain . . .'

'An illness?'

'Yes. He said a lot of kids got off worse and died. Do you remember an illness?'

Theia Soultana narrowed her eyes and stared into the middle distance. Her eyes glazed over as she cast her mind back years, decades. With a snap of her eyelids, she returned to the present.

'You know, I don't remember any illness,' she said flatly. 'I don't remember any children dying.'

'No? Are you sure?'

She returned her gaze to me. Her eyes were dispassionate.

'A big thing like that, in a small place like this, lots of people would definitely remember it. And I don't.'

I was surprised at her tone. It was blunt, almost gruff. I wasn't entirely convinced but didn't know what else to do or say. I decided to change topic and ask about the other issue on my mind. It had gnawed at me from the moment Mum had told me about the adoption.

'My mother Anna,' I said, 'did she really agree to her husband's proposition?'

I had asked Georgios this same question, but he said he was too young and couldn't remember. But my aunt wasn't. She looked at me crookedly.

'Didn't my sister explain it to you?' she asked. 'I thought she had. She told me she had.'

'Yes, she did,' I said, 'but you were the one who was here at the time, you know what happened.'

Theia Soultana's bottom lip quivered. 'Panagiotis, I can only tell you what I know. What goes on between a husband and wife in a marriage is private, it's up to them.'

'Of course,' I said, 'but what do you know, what did you see? Did you hear arguments? Did they fight?'

My aunt paused, studying my face. Eventually, she said, 'Panagiotis, it was so long ago . . .'

'But surely you would remember something so significant?'

She checked her watch then looked at me impatiently. 'What I remember was that the proposition was my brother's idea, and that his word was absolute. That's all I can tell you, and that's more from knowing my brother over many years than anything specific. Now, do you want anything from the supermarket? I'm making *pastitsio* tonight. It's one of Billy's favourites and I've run out of butter for the béchamel sauce.'

I paused, eyeing her carefully. 'No, *theia*. Nothing for me, thanks.'

Before leaving Greece: My aunt Soultana (left) and her sister, my mum Elizabeth, with me, baby Panagiotis (Peter), in Florina on 4 October 1974.

Now in Australia: me in Canberra in 1975.

The family home in Florina, Greece, October 2013. This was my first home before I left for Australia with my adopted mother in late 1974.

Growing up as an only child: me at home in Canberra, Australia on 10 February 1976.

A happy family: with my adopted parents in Canberra, Australia, 1982. At the time this department store photo was taken, I thought these were my biological parents.

Reunited for the first time: with my brothers Vasilios (Billy, left), me, and Georgios (right) in Florina, Greece, April 2003.

A return visit: with my brothers Georgios (left), Vasilios (Billy, centre), and me in Florina, Greece, October 2013.

Graduating university with a PhD in biomedical science from the Australian National University, Canberra, Australia, December 2005. At this time, I was living in Palo Alto, California, USA, and working at Stanford University, but returned to Australia to holiday and graduate.

Celebrating Dad's 80th birthday in Canberra, Australia, March 2010.

CHAPTER 28

2003

THE REST OF my week in Florina was crammed with social events and sightseeing. Georgios dragged me to meet seemingly every person he'd ever met and every attraction he'd ever seen. We weaved recklessly through tight streets and around mountain bends. From my unsteady seat in the front of his labouring Romanian jalopy, I eventually began to protest. I told my brother I was exhausted after my European adventure and asked him to ease off. But Georgios wasn't listening, and proceeded to merely gun the accelerator harder to show me more, faster, which made me feel even more car sick. He was clearly excited to have me around after so long and understandably wanted to both show me off and show me around. I felt bad trying to curtail my brother's enthusiasm, but it was only because I was so nauseous and overwhelmed.

In the nearby village of Nympheo, located on a high plateau overlooking a checkerboard plain, we wandered the cobbled streets admiring the stone houses. We saw bears in the wildlife sanctuary, and got lost in the surrounding forests of beech woods. At the Prespa Lakes shared by Greece, Albania and the Former Yugoslav Republic of Macedonia, we walked over quaint bridges and saw century-old juniper trees. Pods of enormous Dalmatian pelicans floated past the long yellow reeds, their placid nature broken only by sudden and violent plunges of their orange beaks into the icy grey water. We crossed a long floating bridge to light candles and admire the interior of a thousand-year-old church. The faded frescoes were both spooky and magical in the watery light. It took us longer to find the crumbling Byzantine monuments, and we had built up a sweat by the time we reached the *askitaria* – the isolated hermitage caves, once sought for their physical solitude, and now preserved for their rock paintings. Georgios told me there were brown bears and horseshoe bats hibernating in other caves nearby. Above us, a variety of raptors circled the sky, hawks and eagles and falcons, their talons poised to strike at the sight of a tiny scurrying rodent or scuttling amphibian.

Taking a shortcut back to the car, we came across a shorthorn cow on a rocky road. It studied us intently, refusing to move for the strange interlopers. A local farmer and his wife eventually appeared and shooed it away. Stopping at a small café, Georgios ordered a double espresso. I drank mountain tea served with honey and lemon. Georgios called it 'shepherd's tea' because shepherds once prepared it while herding their flocks on the steep hillsides.

'Our mother used to make the best shepherd's tea,' he sighed. 'She ruined me, I can't drink anyone else's now.'

He eyed me watchfully as I sipped the rest of my tea, which I decided to leave half-finished.

Georgios inhaled deeply, filling his lungs with fresh mountain air. 'Ah,' he said, 'clean and crisp.'

He then reached for his pocket and helped himself to a cigarette.

'You know, Papou never came to see the Prespes.'

'Really?' I asked. 'How come? They're so beautiful.'

'The borders are sensitive and visitors were only recently allowed to the area. There was fierce fighting during the civil war. The locals left, the people who once lived in all the little villages up here. To visit the lakes required permission and you needed to be accompanied by a soldier.'

A stray calico cat appeared from behind a rock wall and slowly pattered up to our table. It was stringy and underweight, but its eyes were clear. It sniffed warily at my feet before it finally plucked up the courage to leap into my lap. I patted it, watched it curl and extend its front paws in pleasure, heard it purr, felt its warmth as it sat. It got frightened and ran away when two scruffy dogs approached the table. They sniffed around and before I knew what was happening, they started having sex right next to Georgios's leg. He paid them no mind and continued sipping his espresso. The dogs were stuck together for some time after they finished, facing away from each other.

'This is called "the tie",' said the waiter who came to see what was happening. He crouched and patted the dogs gently. 'The male's got a gland that swells, locking it into the female. It takes some time for the gland to shrink.'

I screwed up my face. 'Don't they desex animals here?' I asked my brother. 'I see stray animals roaming along every street.'

He took a long drag on his cigarette. 'Greece has bigger problems,' he replied coolly.

I thought about the coffin lids I had seen standing erect outside numerous residential front doors in town. Georgios explained it signified that there had been a death in the household, with the deceased being kept inside until the funeral. It told the world that the family was in mourning; the equivalent of a flag being flown at half-mast. The local hospital lacked adequate refrigeration resources.

'We did the same with Baba two years ago,' he added. 'People visited and said goodbye.'

As the week passed, Mum started appearing in my hotel room with increasing frequency. She complained of a burning pain in her stomach that refused to go away.

'I'm here to avoid my sister,' she eventually confessed. 'I need a break from her. She won't so much as let me breathe at home without a disparaging remark. She made me wash my clothes with a washboard earlier, scrubbing the stains clean. I hadn't used, or even seen, a washboard in decades.'

I also sought a moment's respite from family and went in search of the town's only internet café. It was a single dark room full of young men wearing brand names and designer logos, all chain-smoking in front of bulky computer screens. I was the only customer not playing an online first-person shooter game. I logged on and checked my email – the professor had written with news. After five attempts, my paper on my new *Ikaros* mouse mutant had finally been accepted for publication in *Immunity*, one of the best international journals of immunology. Relief washed over me, my shoulders instantly lighter. The major hurdle was overcome; now, only the thesis remained.

On the morning of my departure, Mum stood at the bottom of the steps of the family home. She wore a forced smile; she still had a week to stay. The family walked me to the bus station.

I approached Georgios. 'So,' I said tentatively, 'what happens now?'

A week earlier, part of me might have expected Georgios to handcuff Billy to my arm and hop the next train out of town, or demand that I write him a cheque for reparations. Instead, Georgios presented me with a delicate gold chain and a shirt of the local football club, PAOK F.C. He explained that the logo of a double-headed eagle faced east and west in honour of the club's refugee roots in Constantinople and the players who had fled to northern Greece during the 1923 population exchange.

The eagle's wings were folded as a sign of long-term bereavement for the displacement from home. The club's colours were also symbolic: black mourning for the lost homeland, and white for the hope of a better tomorrow.

'I love it,' I said, and immediately slipped it on over my T-shirt.

Georgios smiled and put his hands reassuringly on my shoulders.

'What happens now is you go back to your life and your work,' he said. 'You make us proud. You visit more often.'

'I will,' I said.

'We'll only start worrying about you if we hear your work's

not going well,' he added. 'Look back from time to time, but make sure you always look forward. Like the eagle.'

I looked down, admiring my new shirt. '*Endaxi*,' I said. 'And you, the house?'

'We're fine,' Georgios said. 'Slowly slowly.'

Billy pushed in front of Georgios. 'When are you coming back?' he asked.

'Soon, boss,' I replied.

'When?' he repeated, unsatisfied with my answer.

'Soon, if I end up working in Europe.'

'What's your feeling?' Georgios asked.

I scratched my chin. 'I'm a bit numb,' I replied. 'We'll see.'

'When are you coming back?' Billy insisted.

'Soon, *yaithouraki*!'

Seeing me impersonate him made Billy laugh uproariously. He momentarily cut off my oxygen in an almighty bear hug.

'I love you, *yaithouraki*!' Billy squealed. 'I love you!'

I reached into my pocket and pulled out something for Billy – a new wristwatch. I presented it to my eldest brother and gave another identical one to my middle brother. I had slipped out that morning and bought two hefty diving watches, haggling with the jeweller to sell me the second at a discounted price.

'This way,' I told my brothers, 'whenever you check the time, you can think of me.'

Another bear hug from Billy. Georgios slapped my back playfully. 'You didn't have to,' he said.

'I wanted to,' I smiled.

Then it was Theia Soultana embracing me and handing me a

new spring rose, dark and red, its stem trimmed of thorns and wrapped tightly in foil.

'May God protect you,' she said, 'now and always.'

We asked a passer-by to snap a few final family photos, which I promised to print and post. Billy loved being photographed. He stood with a wide smile for several seconds after the flash, as if not realising the photo had been taken.

I stored my suitcase in the baggage compartment and boarded the coach. The engine rumbled. I waved to Billy from the bus window until my arm was a sandbag. He stood flapping back with both arms, as if trying to fly after the bus. Mum did the sign of the cross, Theia Soultana blew kisses. Georgios cupped his hands and turned away to light a cigarette.

The week hadn't been easy. It had been challenging, but it had also been incredibly life-affirming. These people were now in my life. Meeting them had made me realise how lucky I was. Perhaps not as lucky as those born into wealth or privilege or connections; my family had none of those. But they had love, which ultimately mattered most.

The longer I'd stayed in Florina, spent time with my brothers, heard them talk, watched them eat, saw them socialise and laugh and argue, the more I realised how little we had in common. My brothers could chew away entire afternoons, and sometimes also the subsequent evenings, sitting in a local café or bar, chain-smoking and drinking enough caffeine to raise the dead. By contrast, I was itchy after an hour, disinterested, looking for focus and direction and fresh air. I didn't feel like my pace was fast, but it certainly wasn't slow either, while my brothers felt theirs was just right. It left me thinking that they would be bored stupid if they ever came to Australia. We locked ourselves in our suburban spaces once the sun went down, watched TV or surfed the internet. My brothers did just as little, but they still went out and socialised in clothes that made my wardrobe look like a collection of potato sacks.

I admired how they spoke passionately, openly, with their whole hearts, while I was more guarded with my opinions and comments, constantly mindful of ramifications; a few real but mostly imagined. They lived for today, for now, not tomorrow, later. If they argued, they did the same – fervently, vigorously, until they cleared their minds, vented their spleens, and then got back to business. There was no lingering animosity or intrusive thoughts of self-doubt, and no bitterness with the world.

The wasteland countryside of car wrecks and hungry stray dogs and dilapidated churches blurred past my bus window. As the late afternoon light hit my face, I saw my transparent reflection in the glass. It felt like I'd just met my two reflections, the two versions of myself that I could've been. And although I admired both their spirits, each was fundamentally different. Rather than a sharp reflection in a bathroom mirror, meeting my brothers was more like the bus window: with the right light, a dull likeness was cast. I saw only hints of myself in Billy and Georgios, aspects that were only skin deep. Perhaps if I smoked I would hold my cigarette like Billy, or if I drank I would have a penchant for whiskey like Georgios.

Beyond blood, my brothers and I shared little. But that was enough. We were family.

As the bus drove on, I eased into my seat and exhaled the last of my tension, making the rose's petals droop just a little.

CHAPTER 29

1977–1980

'DIZZY,' DAD SAID, slumping in his recliner. It was the third time that week he'd returned from the building site early.

'Again?' said Mum.

'Yes *again*. Fix me food, quickly. And shut the boy up.'

I was busy playing with my space Lego in the living room, oblivious to what had started happening to Dad every afternoon. The symptoms drove him home from the worksite, complaining of headaches and a world that refused to stop spinning. Mum's cooking, magically, worked like a tonic. It was only when my *yiayia* had her blood sugar tested that Dad realised the genetic slot machine had spun him the same diabetic lemons. He then unleashed a bitter world of scorn onto the raft of doctors who had failed to identify his diabetes earlier or, according to Dad, who had kept it from him.

'Dirty crooks, they've damned me. I was blind, my sugar was

up, down, all over the place, I couldn't even speak properly. Those quacks knew what was wrong with me all along, bloody Saxon bastards.'

Dad's contempt for the medical fraternity knew no limits. He would complain for hours at a time until poor Mum's head throbbed like a bruise. Still working on building sites, Dad had ruined his body to provide for his family, but he retained a fertile mind. Mum prayed for something to occupy it. Fatherhood wasn't quite the panacea she had hoped it would be, with Dad always ready to hand me back to his wife when the reality of parenting a boisterous toddler became too much.

In an extended family where Mum was one of four and Dad one of six, my solitude stuck out like a smudge on a masterpiece. On the other side of my bedroom door, I knew that Mum and Dad could hear me 'talking' with my toys, and often witnessed me playing the parts of multiple characters in a game. Mum later admitted that those were the moments when she felt most ashamed for tearing me away from my biological family, and especially my brothers. I had been brought into the world to enrich *their* lives, to give *their* lives meaning. Mum suspected this was why Dad monsooned me with so many presents – to assuage his guilt. My *yiayia* flat out ignored me, which disappointed Mum greatly. Mum and Dad tried to play games with me, to adopt the roles of my absent siblings. But they were now pushing fifty years old, and simply getting down on the floor was hard work.

'What if he grows up to become some maladjusted loner?'

Dad was whispering to Mum. He did not want to interrupt the tea party that I was hosting on the other side of the bedroom door.

'Or his creativity and imagination could run wild,' Mum said.

School brought with it a combination of both. Being the only ethnic kid in class, I often found myself left out of playground activities. The other kids thought I looked funny with my dark hair and darker eyes. The pre-school teacher had summoned Mum to class one day to show her the results of a drawing exercise. It was times like those when Mum felt most like a fraud, surrounded by other mothers, real mothers and their biological offspring. The teacher held up the other kids' pictures to show Mum: objects and shapes mainly, Picassoesque animals, surrealist houses, stick figures, scribbles. Then she held up mine.

'I've *never* seen anything like this,' she said.

Mum struggled to focus on the crumpled page. Instead of shapes, she saw the words 'WET PAINT' and 'WALK' written, with all their letters the right way round.

'I've seen so many children pass through here,' the teacher said. 'But this is the first time I've ever seen one write letters, let alone entire words.'

Every vertical surface at home fast became wallpapered with drawings on canvases of tractor-feed computer paper.

'Don't tear them,' I would tell Mum, as if they were the culmination of a lifetime's artistic sufferance. 'Careful Mama, don't tear them.'

Dad just stood back and grinned like a champion, his house transformed into the Louvre.

Mum's only complaint was when she saw me drawing. Her otherwise perfect son was using his nefarious left hand. She cured me of that ailment with continual whacks of her hard ruler. Finally, everything was perfect.

Until one day towards the end of kindergarten. Mum stood in the kitchen peeling potatoes. I came home from school, storming in through the back door and slamming it hard like a shotgun blast. I dumped my schoolbag against the base of the fridge and said, 'One of the kids at school today told me I was adopted.'

Mum looked across at Dad, who was sitting at the table and reading the form guide. His startled glare matched hers.

They had feared this day would come; but not so soon. They had not properly discussed it. They were not ready. And their boy was nowhere near old enough to know the truth. He was six.

'Ha!' Mum laughed.

Dad followed her lead and joined in the chorus, smiling broadly. I looked up from my untied shoelaces, my eyes beginning to moisten.

'Is that why you're upset?' Mum said. 'Don't be silly, of course you're not adopted! Who told you that, sweetie?'

I looked back down at my shoes. 'One of the kids,' I muttered.

'Darling, I'm sure whoever said it was just teasing you. Kids tease, I know they do. I once went to school, too, you know. All you need to know is that you're our son and we're your mum and dad, and your *only* mum and dad. There are no others.'

Dad lifted the last few drops of his gluey coffee to his lips and let out a final chortle. He ruffled my thick, fairy-floss hair and went outside to seek refuge in his homemade shed.

My glare remained on the vinyl kitchen tiles for a long time.

'Mm,' I said slowly, ' . . .yeah.'

Mum sighed and smiled, relieved.

'Of course,' she said. 'And listen, when you go to school tomorrow, tell whoever said that to stop saying such awful things about our family. They're not true. In fact, they're very bad accusations.'

'Okay,' I said.

'Promise me!' said Mum. 'Or else I'll come down there myself and—'

'Okay Mum, okay!' I feared embarrassment more than adoption. '*Endaxi*.'

Mum was glad she had pushed me to the point of annoyance. It meant the doubt was crammed further back into the recesses of my young brain, until it hopefully disappeared altogether.

She watched me trudge to my bedroom to dump my black Darth Vader schoolbag and change into play clothes. And then, when I wasn't looking, she slipped out to the shed where she found Dad methodically filing away at a squeaky metal pipe he had clamped into his work vice. She almost stepped on a rusty nail when she entered the shed, and accidentally stubbed her toe against a paint can.

'So?' Mum said.

'Eh?' Dad replied, not looking back.

'So? What do you think about all that?'

Mum quickly glanced over her shoulder to make sure I hadn't silently crept up behind her.

'Pah,' Dad said, 's'nothing. Kids.'

'For now.'

'So?'

'So?' Mum said. 'So we need to talk about this. We need to

work out a plan for when the time is right. It's now probably just kids teasing, no one who knows the truth would've said anything. But one day they might. And even if they don't, one day I'd like to tell Panagiotis the truth myself. He should know. He deserves to know, both for his mind and his body. Like the blood sugar you inherited from your mother. Secrets fester, and I have no secrets from God. Panagiotis needs to know. I think about it every time I see him, and when I see him upset, I think he knows and is angry with me. He—'

'Listen,' Dad said, hearing enough, 'I'm with you, all the way. Whatever you decide. You know I'm no good at these sorts of things. Whatever you want, just let me know. Whatever you decide, whatever . . .'

And with that, he blew away his filings, brushed away his burrs, and continued with his labour.

CHAPTER 30

2004–2006

I RETURNED TO Australia to write my thesis and lodge fellowship applications. Having had enough fellow scientists tell me to go to America, including the professor, I made a second trip abroad to scout labs at only two locations: Stanford and Harvard. On the advice of the professor, who provided glowing reviews, I opted for the sunshine, scenery and liberal political outlook of California. The lofty gum trees on the lush Stanford campus also reminded me of home.

My new professor – which the Americans called your postdoctoral 'mentor' – was an equally accomplished scientist. He was some thirty years older than my Australian professor and had published six times as many papers. He was also the first scientist anywhere in the world to have isolated a purified population of stem cells in any species; these were blood forming stem cells from the mouse in 1988. The discovery opened the field of stem cell research and positioned him as a potential future Nobel Laureate.

It also positioned me nicely for a future academic position; to conduct research on blood stem cells in the lab of the man who had first discovered blood stem cells was incredible training. He'd already mentored three of my compatriots who all went on to start their own labs in Australia. He said he 'liked Aussies', and especially 'liked their wine'.

With a major paper published in *Immunity*, a four-hundred page thesis that won a national genetics prize, and enthusiastic letters of support, I secured a five-year research fellowship. It was the same fellowship my friend from Melbourne had secured, and he'd also published a paper in *Immunity* and went to California a year earlier, albeit the southern part in San Diego. Funding half my time abroad and half back in Australia, it was designed to stop the 'brain drain' that occurred when so many Antipodeans left the sunburnt land and never returned. I was ecstatic with the outcome. I didn't really want to leave my homeland, so the prospect of a return ticket with research funding was ideal. I also wanted to give back to the nation that had done so much to both educate me and welcome my immigrant parents.

Despite her promise, Mum cried at the airport. Dad was more reserved, with his only advice to 'look after yourself'. I told him to do the same. It had now been three years since his stomach cancer had been removed and while the signs were good, he wasn't out of the woods yet.

The Iraq War was now in full swing. A larger-than-life-sized portrait photo of the Commander-in-Chief welcomed me at San Francisco International Airport with a reassuring smile. I was biometrically fingerprinted and asked my business by a stony-faced immigration officer. The official had trouble understanding what kind of biologist I was and the nature of my research. I leaned closer in to the bulletproof glass.

'Don't worry,' I said, 'it's not biochemical weapons.' Smile.

The officer's face didn't move. He narrowed his eyes, slowly typed a few lines into his computer, and stamped my passport.

With its white picket fences, the master-planned residential community that was my new Palo Alto home looked more like a 1950s television set. It was the great American Dream: the birds sang on cue, squirrels scurried through the lush grass, the sky was forever blue. The ladies in the leasing office wore pearl necklaces and designer suits, sat behind big oak desks under exposed wooden beams, and offered cool bottled water and fresh baked cookies. I was chauffeured by golf buggy past gleaming luxury cars to my brand new, empty apartment. Without any furniture, I sat on the carpet and ate heart attack pizza the first night, then curled up in my sleeping bag on the living room floor. I used a 25-pound bag of rice as a pillow. Listening to the unfamiliar noises of night, I felt like I'd lost everything, and prayed this was worth all the effort.

I turned thirty the week after I arrived in California and celebrated with a Mexican feast of burritos and fish tacos at a local taqueria. My parents called to wish me well and were soon calling almost daily. They didn't say a lot and nor did I. It was enough to hear each other's voices; it was the closest thing to touching. Mum sounded constantly nasal, claiming to 'have a cold'. Dad shouted down the international phone line like it was 1979. He repeated one-way, generic statements of encouragement before handing over the phone to Mum as quickly as possible.

Stem cell isolation was a laborious sorting process that took all day in the lab and all night on a rumbling machine that dwelled in the bowels of my new institute. It was the same technology I'd used in Australia, but this machine didn't just analyse cells – it physically sorted them into separate populations which could then be used for experiments, like transplants and molecular assays. Part of the interest in stem cells was to understand why they possessed such incredible regenerative properties, which required an analysis of their active genes. Perhaps it was possible to re-activate these genes in other cells and turn them into cells with newfound regenerative potential. Salamanders did this when they regrew limbs. It meant the possibility of engineering tissues in the lab, which could then be transplanted in instances of injury or illness. Stem cells had the potential to transform medicine and humankind. The field was hot and the prize was lucrative.

Naturally, I threw myself at my work. I spent all day in the lab preparing my cell suspensions for sorting. Blood stem cells were rare – one in ten thousand – but were most abundant in the bone marrow. Bone marrow extraction from mice involved cleaning the legs of skin and fur and then snapping the bone at the hip with heavy tweezers. By flushing the marrow from the femurs and tibiae into a petri dish with a syringe, it was possible to then label the subsequent cell suspension with fluorescent markers specific for stem cells. It was the same principle I'd used to analyse my *Ikaros* mouse mutant, only ten times more complicated. With my bone marrow stem cells finally labelled, I grabbed a stale sandwich for dinner from the hospital cafeteria before it closed, and then holed up in the darkened basement for the evening. The multi-laser cell sorter was an enormous leviathan of a machine that was normally run by a specialist technician with years of training. But because these technicians didn't work through the night, it meant we had to learn how to sort stem cells ourselves. It was a baffling process that required the fine-tuning skills of a safe-cracker and the patience of a saint. A blockage in the cell sorter was catastrophic; all it took was for a microscopic shard of bone to be shot through a pressurised nozzle the width of a human hair for an entire day's work to be ruined. That this could happen at any moment had me constantly on edge.

I'd read about an emerging theory that linked cancer back to stem cells. Because cancers developed from multiple gene mutations in a single cell, the only cells that actually lived long enough to accumulate enough of these mutations were stem cells. Cancer cells and stem cells, because they continually copied themselves, also had the same genes active. But it only took a single misspelling in the DNA code to tip the balance from the right amount of blood cells to too many, or not enough. I'd already seen this with my *Ikaros* mutants, who both developed cancer as heterozygous adults and lacked blood stem cells as homozygous embryos.

Clinicians often wandered into the lab with their foam coolers full of precious human tissue samples. Some were from surgeries – usually cancerous tissues – while others were from autopsies – often motor vehicle accidents – and were undiseased samples used as controls. Their powder-blue ice boxes were like scientific treasure chests. They held gold-standard samples, clinically relevant human tissue, with immediate application to disease. I couldn't help but regard them with envy. I would've loved to have done experiments with human cancer stem cells. My mouse blood stem cells were pretty cool, but they weren't human cancer stem cells. And I wasn't a future surgeon who had trained in Germany or Japan – I was a lab jockey from the wrong side of the equator. I thought about my dad and his stomach cancer and what happened to his invaluable tissue sample. In the right hands, using the right combination of fluorescent markers, it could've shed a light on its cancerous origins. But instead, it probably just ended up in the hospital incinerator.

I went to a conference in San Diego, and caught up with my old friend from Melbourne. He was loving life in America; his research was going well, and he spent many enjoyable weekends scuba-diving off the coast. He was also organising fundraisers for cancer research, and volunteering his time at camps for children affected by HIV and AIDS. He showed me San Diego's famous zoo and its best taquerias. As we ate fish tacos and looked out over the blue Pacific Ocean, I asked if he was thinking about going back to Australia for the second half of his fellowship.

'No,' he replied.

'No?' I was shocked.

'I plan to skip out, abscond, if you will. The fellowship was my ticket out and, quite frankly, I think I can do more to help people if I continue my research here in the States. There's just too much on offer: funding, facilities and findings.'

At the same conference, I saw a snappily-dressed and well-spoken scientist from Seoul report on his groundbreaking human embryonic stem cell experiments. I watched him with his entourage of minders hobnobbing alongside America's top scientific brass, shaking hands and slapping backs. Little did anyone realise that he would have the most spectacular fall from grace by year's end when it was revealed his results were all fabricated. 'I was blinded by work and my drive for achievement,' his mea culpa stated.

Meetings with my mentor were brief but to the point. It was not unexpected for a man advising the US Congress on proposed bans limiting federal funding for stem cell research and fielding urgent calls from the president. But he was generous with his knowledge and guidance whenever we met to discuss data. He was also a generous host who took his entire lab staff to his ranch in Montana for the annual lab retreat. My mentor was the son of a hardware store owner and grandson of a fur trader, his grandfather having emigrated from Russia to avoid being drafted by the czar during the First World War. In that respect, we had something in common. Arriving as an immigrant at Ellis Island, his grandfather made his way west, eventually settling in Big Sky Country.

Lab retreats were a chance to unwind, to eat barbeque and drink beer around a campfire. Montana was also home to the biggest mountain ranges and pickup trucks I'd ever seen, while department stores sold the unique combination of guns and guitars. It was rugged cowboy territory, terrain for game-hunting and songwriting. Hiking to the top of a snowy peak in the Bitterroot Range, I saw views that were sweeping and spectacular. Above me, raptors circled majestically, grand, exotic birds with broad wings that I was only familiar with as national symbols, bald eagles and hawks and falcons. It was an unexpectedly awe-inspiring sight. For a brief moment, America made a little more sense to me.

But the feeling didn't last. The breakneck pace of American

academic life, the pressure to succeed, and the ultra-competitive environment caused me to burn out after only two years. I was no longer the hardest-working person in the lab; far from it, in fact. I couldn't keep up with the Chinese scientists who worked around the clock. I didn't have pharmaceutical assistance like the clinicians who prescribed themselves stimulants to increase mental focus and productivity. I overheard them bragging about how little sleep they needed, and how they even worked on Christmas Day. It sounded like a race to the bottom.

I met my mentor and explained how I felt.

'I've seen this before in many people,' he said. 'I can recognise the symptoms. You feel helpless, hopeless, worthless.'

He rallied his team of specialist medical associates. The next morning, the Chair of Psychiatry – an expert on unipolar depression – contacted me to make an appointment with one of his senior intake staff for what he called a 'clinical evaluation'. I went along and was deemed to be an excellent candidate for antidepressants.

'No thanks,' I said. 'I think I just need some balance back in my life.'

Instead, I made an appointment with the university's counselling service. The counsellor was a kindly middle-aged woman with curly grey hair and red-framed glasses. She advised the expected treatments – good food, exercise, mindfulness – and ultimately apologised to me.

'What for?' I asked, confused.

'For what this place does to people,' she replied. 'It's not wrong, but it's not right either. And it's certainly not healthy.'

I considered myself lucky. I stepped away from the flame before I got burnt.

'I'm actually fairly homesick,' I said. 'I miss my family.'

'Then do what you have to do.'

I hadn't seen enough of the Bay Area so I decided to get out more and explore. I irregularly caught the train to San Francisco for a day out, saw the bridge and prison and ate sushi and burritos. I went mountain biking at Skeggs Point, saw banana slugs and got caked in mud. I marvelled at thousand-year-old giant sequoias in Muir Woods. There was so much more. But I wasn't interested.

I rang my village and spoke with Georgios for hours. His steady disposition became a soothing balm. 'Your mum is really worried about you,' he said. 'She tells me all the time.'

'Tell her I worry about her,' I replied.

Mum offered to fly over and stay with me a while. I said that wasn't necessary and that I would see her soon. I still wanted to help people who were sick, but no longer thought I could. So instead, I volunteered a couple of nights a week at the local soup kitchen in East Palo Alto. Even with all the money and brainpower in Silicon Valley, there was still widespread homelessness and poverty. It made me realise who the real saints were.

Mum and Dad's abiding voices transported me back to simpler days when everything worked out as they had promised. I passed every school exam, just like they said. I woke up after surgery. God gave me siblings.

'You're always welcome to come and stay here with me and Billy,' Georgios said.

It was a kind offer. And I did consider it. Perhaps three slow months in Florina were just the tonic my tired soul needed. I could sit for hours in cafés with Georgios and drink espressos from a bottomless *flitzani* cup. I could stay out all night with Billy playing backgammon and become close friends with every street merchant and tavern owner in town. I'd often wondered what life would've been like had I stayed in Florina. Would I have been hardworking and bookish, would I have left for better opportunities, or would I just have slipped into the same comfortable groove as my brothers? Suddenly, I had an unexpected chance to find out. It was tempting. But there was something else I had in mind.

I met again with my mentor and told him my plans. He leaned back in his chair and stroked his furrowed brow. 'Are you sure?' he asked. 'There's nothing I can do to change your mind?'

'You've been incredible,' I said. 'I'll never forget my time here.'

I reached into my backpack and presented him with a bottle of robust Australian red.

'Thank you,' he said, eyeing the unfamiliar label. 'I'll drink it in a few years. Are you sure you won't reconsider?'

'Thank you, no,' I said.

And with that, I shook my mentor's hand for the last time, grateful for the chance to have studied at the feet of both a great scientist and man.

'I'm proud of you,' he said. 'Stay in touch.'

'I will.'

I arranged for all my household items to go to Goodwill. I broke my lease and packed everything I had left into two large suitcases and one big cardboard box. I took a backpack with me and shipped the rest to Australia.

CHAPTER 31

2006

DURING MY FINAL week in California, I decided to enroll in a writing course at The New School in Greenwich Village. I had loved to write creatively when I was at primary school, but ditched the practice during high school when I realised that everything boiled down to grades and tertiary entrance scores if you wanted to go to university. In those days to score high marks, you needed to do subjects like chemistry and biology and mathematics; certainly not English. There was some magical process of 'standardisation' that took place, and creative writing was viewed poorly. Before this realisation dawned on me, I used to sit at home for hours and churn through page after page of a tattered exercise book. I let my imagination freewheel and told stories that only a child's mind could conjure. It was wonderful. It was freedom.

As an eleven-year-old in 1985, I was briefly the most popular kid in school when I wrote a story that featured my friends as characters and put them in all manner of crazy situations. My fifth grade teacher was so impressed that she made me read out the entire story to the class over several days during our daily story time. To this day, I can still remember the expectant faces of my classmates, waiting to hear mention of their name, and to then hear what I'd made them do or say. I didn't realise it at the time, but it was also the first time my classmates had ever appeared in a book. They felt famous; that someone had deemed them important enough to write about. I just saw it as inspiration.

Singed with scientific burnout, I had decided that it was time to reconnect with the other hemisphere of my brain, the artistic half, and see if my love for writing was still there. And the Big Apple seemed like the most logical destination given its literary reputation. It was also a familiar city following my time working at New York University before I started my PhD.

Over three glorious months, I slept on a friend's couch on the Upper East Side of Manhattan and tested myself against a class of budding New York literary types. We wrote short exercises, gave criticism and praise, with a published novelist as our tutor. Most of the pieces featured neurotic female protagonists or drug-fuelled businessmen, while I wrote about a dry, desolate land where my heart belonged. Interestingly, of all the pieces I wrote, the one that struck the biggest chord was about the day I found out I was adopted. At home, I sat on a beanbag while writing at a coffee table and ate pizza slices that needed two hands. I caught up with old friends, pleased to see me after ten years. By the time I flew out, my soul was renewed.

The second leg of my academic detox involved a return visit

to Florina. It wasn't like the first time I had visited my brothers, and in many ways, it was much better. The novelty was gone, but so was the pressure. We studied each other less and got to know each other more.

I arrived from Athens at midnight. Georgios met me at the bus station with a warm embrace. We drove away in his Romanian hatchback, speeding down the dead centre of the road on top of the double yellow line. My brother only veered into his lane at the sight of an oncoming vehicle. He still wasn't wearing his seatbelt.

In Florina, Georgios parked on a bus stop and took me into a *kafenion*. Billy sat smoking under a colossal plasma screen. He stood when he saw me, a glazed expression on his face, and squeezed me until my spine crunched. He introduced me to everyone as '*o micros*' like he did the first time, but I imagined he'd probably do that every time I visited. Georgios ordered me a toasted sandwich with melted *kasseri* cheese that was like velvet across my lips. My village brothers were boisterous, reaching their prime in the night. I was fading. Over the course of the next hour, I watched them inhale their body weight in tar as I inhaled mine in secondhand smoke. After my umpteenth yawn, Georgios finally acquiesced and took me home, leaving Billy to witness the new dawn. The sight of my two brothers was a little kiss on each of my weary eyes.

It took a while to fall asleep, my restless brain accustomed to the interminable snarling of Manhattan traffic, not tranquility and silence. But in the end, I slept soundly under three generations of quilts. In the morning, Georgios gave me some fresh clothes to change into. The clothes were his, and they fitted me as if they were my own. Hand-me-downs were something I'd never had. The feeling made me smile, wearing something pre-loved by my own blood.

'Theia said to leave your clothes,' Georgios said. 'She'll wash them later.'

'But I can—'

'No. Leave them.'

Georgios explained that Theia Soultana still insisted on washing everyone's clothes by hand with a corrugated washboard, despite her advancing years and declining health.

'I've tried stopping her but it only causes arguments,' he said. 'I even bought a new washing machine a year ago. She refuses to use it. She says it ruins the clothes. The machine sits idle.'

Breakfast was freshly baked *spanakopita* with crunchy filo pastry and local feta cheese. I ate two big bowls of farm yoghurt drizzled with preserved *vissino* cherries. The yoghurt was so thick it almost needed a knife. The sight of old women wearing headscarves and beating rugs with large paddles was like a welcoming embrace. I watched a man water his lawn with a hose for half an hour. Theia Soultana appeared, kissed me warmly on both cheeks and immediately asked for my dirty clothes. I was glad I couldn't pack much in my backpack.

Georgios woke at noon. I listened to my brother cough his way through the day's first half hour. Wheeze and hack and sputter and spit. He then had his usual Greek breakfast of a jet black coffee and two cigarettes.

He took me out walking through narrow streets, down to the

centre of town. We ended up at a boutique in the *plateia* where Georgios proceeded to buy Billy a Zegna suit and matching shoes. He knew all his measurements by heart. As we walked home, Georgios whispered in my ear: 'Tell Billy these are from you. He'll like them more. He'll wear them all the time and tell people that you bought them for him.'

The suit wasn't cheap. I felt guilty taking the credit for such an expensive gift, but I knew Georgios's ploy. It was the gesture, not the cost.

'Okay,' I said.

We walked on. After a while, Georgios put a loving arm around my shoulder.

'I like it when we walk,' he said, 'but at first, you scared me.'

I looked at him sideways. 'Scared you?' I said. 'From walking? How?'

Georgios lit a smoke. 'The first time you were here, we were out walking one night in the darkness. You were walking a few metres behind me, and at the time I swore I was being followed by my father. Your footfalls are identical to his. "How could it be," I asked myself, "that this person who never saw my father walk somehow walks just like him?" I felt as if I was walking with a ghost.'

Billy was asleep when we got home. I left the suit for him to find, along with a handwritten note in the most basic of Greek, and snuck away back down to the *plateia*. Relocating the barber shop I'd seen earlier that morning, I took a seat in the first chair.

'All of it,' I said to the barber. 'Take all of it off.'

The barber looked at me quizzically a moment. He examined

my thinning hair, most of it disappearing from the top and front, before offering me a seat and reaching for his unforgiving zero blade clippers.

As he sheared and shaved, I made sure to look down at my thighs, and away from the mirror. I didn't want to look at myself until he'd completely finished. I just looked down at my legs and watched the dark clumps of hair fall.

After about ten minutes, the electric buzzing stopped. It was only then that I finally looked up. As the barber brushed away the strands that had fallen around my neck and shoulders, I saw my face smile. I liked what I saw. It was a perfectly shaped skull that had been hiding beneath the feeble coverage; not too big and bulbous, and without any major dents and deformities. I may have missed out on inheriting good hair genes, but I won the lottery when it came to head shape. It was a bit pale, white and unkissed by the sun, but I imagined that would soon be corrected in Australia. I paid and tipped the barber, and even kissed him on both cheeks. Shaving my head was both symbolic and a revelation. I regretted not doing it earlier.

Billy slept like a hibernating bear until late afternoon. As I waited for him on the stone steps of our family home, I rubbed my hands all over my head. I couldn't stop feeling it, the newly exposed hair follicles, it was like the gentlest electric massage. Gazing down at the matching terracotta rooftops of our town, I could hear it slowly returning to life after siesta. Voices echoed from the tight streets below, car horns, dogs barking. The air in my lungs was cool, felt right. I imagined part of that feeling came from staying in the family home, which hadn't happened the first time I'd visited. Behind the rooftops was the mountain in which the rebel *andartes* had hidden during the Second World War. The mountain was now home to roe deer and grey wolves and the ruins of an old hotel casino; a 1970s business deal gone sour, according to my brother. And at the top of the mountain was the big white cross that was illuminated each night and protected Florina from harm.

The sun was setting, the mountain changing colour, deep orange and maroon and purple. I felt a heavy tap on my shoulder and turned to see my reflection in Billy's shiny new brogues, ready for their world premiere.

'*Yaithouraki!* Stand up!' he said, giggling.

I stood and let Billy squeeze me with so much love that I swore he cracked a rib.

'Okay, okay,' I said. '*Endaxi. Parakalo*, Billy.'

He saw my skull. 'What did you do to your hair?'

'Do you like it, boss?'

He paused, examined my bald head, leaned in and kissed it.

'I do!'

Even though Billy's hair was as ashen as a winter sky, it was still wonderfully thick.

'And thank you for my new brown suit and brown shoes!' he boomed. 'They're very nice!' He talked half to me and half to a mirror on the wall, to his reflection, like a proud budgerigar.

'You're welcome,' I repeated.

'I'm going to Dimitrios's now, then to Takis's shop!' Billy told the mirror. 'You come down later with Georgios.'

'Okay, boss,' I said. 'We will.'

'And later tonight I have to work,' Billy added. 'I need to make some money so I can buy milk for the orphans.'

Billy started telling me about the previous night, how he'd worked as a security guard for a friend's business. He'd walked the streets until dawn to ensure there was no trouble; which, of course, there never was in Florina. I asked Billy whether his patrol was at the request of the mayor. Billy smiled broadly and said it was.

'Good luck tonight, boss,' I said. 'I hope you make lots of money.'

'So do I. The orphans need milk. Bye!'

Billy lit a cigarette and trotted down the hill to the *plateia*, shooing two stray cats out of his way. He passed Georgios underneath an old olive tree, its trunk as thick as an oak. They spoke briefly and continued on.

Georgios smiled as he approached me. I could tell he'd seen my new hair, or lack thereof.

'I like it!' he said. 'It suits you.'

'Thanks,' I said. 'I'd thought about doing it for a while, and in the end thought it would be good to do here in Florina.'

He came and sat next to me and kissed me lovingly on the top of my new head. It tickled. A new family ritual had suddenly begun.

'I used to kiss Baba like that on his bald head too,' Georgios said.

So it was an old ritual after all.

Georgios explained that he'd had his head shaved both at school and during military service using manual clippers. Head shaving with manual clippers was used as punishment for young criminals during the 1950s and 1960s, and later extended to hippies and leftist youths during the 1967–74 military regime. The practice of shaving students' heads with manual clippers finally ended in 1982.

'Billy loves the suit,' he added.

'You chose well.'

'He needed a new one. And here, come inside, I have something for you.'

Georgios walked me to his room and rummaged around inside an old closet. When his hands finally emerged, they were holding a light grey Armani suit.

'Take it,' he said. 'It doesn't fit me anymore.'

I tried it on immediately. It fitted perfectly. The cut was superb, the fabric exquisite. Georgios closed his bedroom door, made me stand in front of the full-length mirror which hung on the back. I admired myself. The suit was bold across the shoulders, with gentle lines around the waist. I thought I'd never looked so incredible in a suit, or any clothing, for that matter. I credited my new haircut, which gave me the appearance of a mannequin, and made the suit look even better than it was.

'Make sure you wear it,' Georgios said. 'Our *theia* has all these nice clothes she never wears, which is such a waste. This is why I'm giving it to you, because it's just sitting in my closet.'

I smiled and hugged my brother. 'I will,' I said. 'I love it, thank you.'

'Can't have one of my brothers in a new suit and the other one miss out . . .'

'Guess we need to take Billy to get a haircut now.'

Georgios laughed. 'Sure,' he said, 'just not like that. He shaved his head a few years ago and looked ridiculous.'

We returned to the balcony to watch the daylight disappear. A gentle breeze made the leaves flicker on our grandfather's three orange trees in the front yard. Georgios asked me how I felt and what was next.

'Much better now,' I said, 'and home is next.'

CHAPTER 32

2006–2011

MY PARENTS' FIFTIETH wedding anniversary in October 2006 was a joyous but small occasion where I invited what few friends they still had alive. Dad's gift was five years cancer-free, which he celebrated with an overdose of chocolate cake. Mum insisted Dad rein in his consumption to prevent his blood sugar rocketing out of control. Meanwhile, I gifted Mum a diamond ring from Tiffany's; she was overjoyed and slipped it on her finger alongside her wedding ring and the ruby ring I'd bought for her fortieth anniversary in 1996. I'd sent my parents to the Melbourne Cup that year as well, which Dad loved apart from the flights. He hadn't set foot on a plane before that day, and never did again.

'Our lives have been blessed,' Mum told me as she smiled at Tiffany. 'From here on in, only illnesses await us.'

'Don't say that, Mum,' I said.

'It is what it is,' she replied. 'But I've no regrets. For better or worse, your dad's stuck with me for fifty years. I'm blessed.'

With research funding in my pocket, I could go anywhere in the country. But I had an idea in mind that sought to bring together my genetics and stem cell knowledge. Many mouse mutagenesis screens had been conducted around the world for cancer, developmental disorders, autoimmune diseases, etc. But no one had yet tried a screen that was specific for stem cell defects. So I decided to combine my genetics experience with the assays I'd learned to quantify different subsets of blood stem and progenitor cells at Stanford. The screen was to be run using livers from embryos, which was the major site of blood development before moving to the bone marrow, and counted using fluorescent activated cell sorting. The choice of embryos was designed to leverage my expertise and keep animal housing costs to a minimum. I knew it would again be long days in the lab preparing cells and longer nights in the basement counting them. But the project was both ambitious and exciting, and was also uniquely mine. Given the facilities already in place at the Australian National University, I returned to my old stomping ground, ordered a new suite of stem cell-specific markers, and began to optimise my screening assay. I also started to write up the data from Stanford into papers and submit them to scientific journals. Unlike the one paper that came out of my PhD, there would be three papers from my time as a postdoc, although none would likely be as impactful.

I met a girl. It was on a summer mixed soccer team. I'd known numerous girls throughout the years, since my late teens, with relationships varying from one night to several years. But this girl felt different. Jayne was older, and so was I.

Georgios irregularly rang my phone. I was often surprised

by the times he called, at lunchtime and early afternoon. A quick mental calculation revealed it was the middle of the night in Florina, sometimes three or four in the morning.

'I love you,' he said. 'I love you, Panagiotis.'

His voice was sloppy. He was drunk. He claimed he was 'just tired', but I could tell it was more.

'I love you,' he repeated. 'You know that, right?'

'I do,' I replied. 'And I love you too.'

'What did you do today? What are you doing now? What are you doing later?'

He just wanted to talk; to go around and around in circles, and be transported to another world. It was rather cute, really, to know that I was in his thoughts when he was tired and emotional. I entertained him for as long as I could until I was too tired and suggested he call my mum. She would later tell me: 'Your brother called, he'd been drinking. I had to pretend I was busy just to get him off the phone, he wouldn't let me go. And I'm too old for drunk talk.'

Georgios asked me about my writing, which we'd discussed when I was in Greece. He liked my idea of becoming a writer. 'Writing comes from the heart,' he slurred. 'It's a worthwhile pursuit.'

I wasn't so sure. Was my New York writing sojourn merely a scratch I needed to itch, or was it something more permanent? Needing to find out, I spent hours writing short stories and articles. Writing felt natural, it was freedom and fun, but it also felt fanciful alongside scientific research which remained my primary focus. Unfortunately, I'd been unable to secure a grant to continue my experiments. Despite publishing three papers from my post-doctoral research – two in the journal *Stem Cells* and one in the *Proceedings of the National Academy of Sciences of the USA* – and starting to identify stem cell mutants in my screen of mutagenised embryos, my grant applications ranked highly but always fell short. By the end of 2009, having received another negative outcome, I knew I had one final chance to secure funding or be unable to continue my project. I would probably also have to leave science and consider work in another field. For someone who had been at the bench for more than a decade, and had only ever thought of becoming a scientist, it was a possibility I didn't even want to entertain.

The year 2010 brought major challenges. It started in January when I was hit with two devastating pieces of news.

The first concerned my friend from Melbourne who had stayed in San Diego to continue his research. He was returning home from the lab at ten o'clock on a Sunday night when his car was slammed from behind by a drunk driver. The other driver was a bartender leaving a work Christmas party at a hotel. The impact ruptured the petrol tank and both cars burst into flames, spinning in opposite directions. A passing motorist rescued the drunk and his passenger but was unable to reach my friend, who died at the scene. He was thirty-three years old. More than three hundred people attended his memorial in America; double that number in Australia. When I heard the news, which wasn't until January, I had to sit down. It shook me to the core. The number of times I had driven home from the lab at obscene hours, in both Australia and America, was incalculable. Dad always used to warn me to be wary of other motorists at those hours. And when I finally made my way to Melbourne to pay my respects to my friends' parents, all they wanted to know was: 'What in the world was our son doing at work so late on a Sunday night?'

I knew what he was doing. He was trying to help people.

The drunk driver, who had a hipflask in his pocket at the time of the crash, was convicted of vehicular manslaughter and sentenced to six years in prison.

My friend's parents would eventually establish an award in his honour for young Australian immunologists who, like their son, wanted to devote their lives to finding cures for debilitating diseases. This was after they sued the hotel for wrongful death under the legal doctrine of *respondeat superior*: that a party is responsible for the acts of their agents.

The second piece of news hit even closer to home. Just like my biological mother had seen some twenty years earlier, Mum noticed a lump in her breast and was diagnosed with breast cancer. Fortunately, Mum acted. Deciding against chemotherapy and radiation, she had a single mastectomy of the right breast. 'It's not like I need it anymore,' she said.

During the appointment, the oncologist asked Mum how many children she had. She looked over at me blankly and replied, 'One.'

'Wait,' I said, 'I know where this is going. I'm adopted. Mum didn't have children, she didn't breastfeed.'

The oncologist smiled, nodded, wrote his notes.

I explained the situation to Mum. During my studies, I'd read that being exposed to oestrogen over time increased the risk of breast cancer, and that oestrogen levels increased in women who had never been pregnant. By contrast, hormones produced during pregnancy and breastfeeding kept oestrogen levels low, which reduced cell growth and the risk of breast cancer.

'Ah sorry,' Mum said. She thought the oncologist was just being polite by asking how many children she had. 'Yes, my son is right, I didn't have children. He is actually my brother's child.'

It was the first time that Mum had been under general anaesthetic in her eighty years. She admitted she was more worried about that than anything else. I had already been under general three times: for the removal of two wisdom teeth when I was nineteen, for a circumcision when I was twenty-three, and to repair a torn anterior cruciate ligament in my knee when I was thirty-three. I assured Mum that everything would be fine but I could still see the worry in her glassy brown eyes. Her operation was a success, anaesthesia and otherwise. The breast tissue was removed without incident and the draining lymph nodes were unaffected. Mum didn't like the breast prosthesis she was eventually given to wear but it was a small price to pay. Dad was especially relieved – he would have someone to keep looking after him. As loath as I was to admit it, I knew that Dad would struggle without Mum around. If one of them had to die first, it couldn't be her.

I worked for six months without a salary in order to complete my initial stem cell screen and publish my findings. This was a particularly difficult period given that my girlfriend and I had just bought a house, which came with a sizeable mortgage that needed continual repayments. My stem cells paper was published in *Blood*, a respected international journal of haematology, just before Christmas. After screening more than a thousand embryos from nearly fifty pedigrees, I isolated six strains with defects in blood cell production. I even identified one of the mutant genes as *c-Myb*; like *Ikaros*, it was known to play a role in both blood production and cancer, and demonstrated proof of principal in my screen. As a final touch, I dedicated my paper to my friend from Melbourne. Despite such promising findings, and the prospect of the five yet-to-be-identified genes, my last grant application was unsuccessful. With the mortgage on my mind, I made the heartbreaking but inevitable decision to leave science. I was gravely disappointed with myself, and felt like a failure. I had worked hard on complex projects, trained with exceptional people, conceived original ideas, published in strong journals, and it still wasn't enough.

But now, I had a new passion: writing. Combining this with my technical knowhow, I moved into scientific writing to pay the bills, but continued my creative writing outside of work hours. I often wrote late into the night, which was soon causing chaos in other areas of my life. Night-time was when I felt most productive, when it was quiet and it felt like the whole world was asleep. It was agonising at times, trying to find the words. But I soon realised that writing was therapy; it grounded me when I felt anxious, and helped channel and order my thoughts. Staying disciplined, I wrote every day. Even if it was just a sentence, the words piled up over time. Sometimes inspiration didn't strike until two in the morning. But then, as my head hit the pillow at dawn, I slept with a smile on my face.

CHAPTER 33

2012–2013

HAVING NAVIGATED HER way through cancer, Mum soon had another test of her mortality. Within eight months, she lost her two remaining siblings. The first was her other brother Vangelis in February. He was eighty-four.

'I was never as close with him as I was with Savvas,' she told me when she shared the news. We were again in her bedroom, her calloused feet resting on her thick blue rug.

'Of course,' I said, 'I was the connection there.'

'Definitely,' she replied. 'At times, I wondered whether Vangelis was envious of that. But he still had his own children, and he couldn't help me like Savvas could.'

Mum acknowledged that without Vangelis, our lives in Australia would not have transpired. 'He was the first in the family to emigrate. It was through Vangelis that I met your dad here. Vangelis was the only one brave enough to see the possibility of a better life. For that, we all owe him an enormous gratitude.'

Vangelis was a character. I remembered him a little from my childhood, visiting us occasionally, and also seeing him again in Florina when I met my brothers. He was cheeky and had a zest for life.

'Why did he go back to Greece, Mum?' I asked.

Vangelis had packed up his family and returned to Florina during the early 1980s. He'd laid down roots in Canberra over thirty and owned several houses, so his move seemed strange to me.

Mum shrugged. 'I think he was just homesick,' she replied. 'He'd made a better life for himself here, but the call of one's homeland gets louder as the years pass. You think about the soil where you'll be buried, and where you'll lie for all eternity. It's a yearning.'

Her voice sounded faraway, almost wistful. Her gaze was distant.

'Your home is always your home. If you were born there and have all your early memories there, it's natural to want to die there too.'

I considered what she was saying. Was she referring to her and Dad as well?

'Ugh, your father . . .' she moaned. 'He's different. Once he got out of Greece, he was never looking back.'

This was resonant of something Dad often said to me. His life advice was minimal but included: 'Always look forward; never back. Forward is where you're going, and all you can control.'

The second death was Mum's sister, Soultana, in October, aged eighty-seven. Mum felt her passing acutely. Perhaps that was because she was her only sister, or perhaps it was because she was Mum's only remaining sibling.

'She drove me crazy at times,' Mum told me. 'But deep down I knew it was because she loved me. Sisters have a special bond, it's hard to explain.'

Mum acknowledged that Soultana became the surrogate parent for my brothers for more than a decade after our parents died. This was a role assumed voluntarily, but ultimately out of love for Billy.

'My sister never agreed with our brother's decision to leave Billy unschooled, untamed. Perhaps that was because she knew she would one day be taking over his care. Vangelis was never going to do it, and I was here in Australia. Now, the duty has been passed to Georgios.'

That hadn't occurred to me. Georgios was now sole carer. I vowed to help in any way I could, which I imagined meant sending financial support. I suggested it to Mum.

'Save your money,' she said curtly, 'you have responsibilities, too, and will hopefully one day have your own family. Georgios has a job, Billy has a pension, and the house is theirs now. Wait until they ask. And then, come and talk to me first.'

Theia Soultana had been on my mind before she died. Georgios rang my mum irregularly and told her that her sister wasn't well, only for my aunt to call a week later and say she was fine. Then one day, she stopped calling. Georgios said she took to her bed without a fuss and gradually deteriorated. She refused medical treatment, and just slipped away one night.

'She knew it was her time,' Mum said. 'She didn't fight it.'

Mum made it sound so peaceful, so natural. We spend our

whole lives avoiding death. To hear someone embrace it came across as liberating.

Mum wasn't going to travel for the funeral. I wasn't surprised. I asked whether I should. 'What's the point?' Mum said. 'You saw her when she was alive. That was enough. Go for your brothers if you want to see them. But not for her. How long has it been now, six years?'

'Too long,' I replied.

❧

A year later, in the spring of 2013, my girlfriend finally became my wife. It took me and Jayne nearly seven years to walk down the aisle. This came from a combination of the intensity of my work, the insecurity of my work, outrageous house prices, and general laziness and distraction. We always knew we would be together, and often wondered whether marriage was even necessary. It wasn't of course, but in the end we decided to stick with tradition. With only fourteen guests at the wedding, we married at the same Greek Orthodox church where I was baptised, Saint Nicholas. Jayne wore a secondhand dress she bought online, and I wore something equally pre-loved: my brother's grey Armani suit.

We honeymooned on the Greek islands, which were just as idyllic as I had imagined. The water was warm, the light crisp. I felt like I could see further, it was impossible to take a bad photo. We rode a quad bike and avoided being killed by it. The Greeks who rented it to us snickered when we requested helmets. We ate seafood straight out of the Aegean and salad vegetables plucked straight from the ground. Unsurprisingly, the food was even tastier on the less touristy islands, and the locals friendlier. Lured by the prospect of fresh fish, stray cats roamed along every street, emaciated and cunning. I regretted not visiting sooner; the islands were everything they promised.

After the islands, we made our way north through Athens to Thessaloniki, and then west to my home town of Florina. I was eager to introduce Jayne to my brothers, and vice versa. It was my first visit to Greece in seven years and the country had undergone major changes. The economic party was over, and the austerity hangover was in full effect. The era of two sets of tax books and envelopes stuffed with money was seemingly over. It was an eerie feeling in Athens. Tourists still strolled around the ancient sites during the day while police in smart blue uniforms with crisp white gloves controlled traffic. But at night, it became a ghost town as people wrapped in blankets waited in the shadows for Red Cross dispatch teams. It was like two different cities in one: one rich and carefree, the other poor and wounded.

We passed through Thessaloniki as quickly as possible. I was anxious to reach Florina, and feared what I may find on arrival.

CHAPTER 34

2013–2014

THE TRAIN FROM Thessaloniki to Florina stopped so the drivers could have a smoke break. Worried about what awaited me in Florina, I wanted to have one too. Jayne was equally anxious. It was enough that she was meeting her two new brothers-in-law for the first time. Across the aisle from us, an Orthodox priest with a thick iron-grey tapped away on his smartphone.

I eventually exhaled my tension, relieved when we arrived and I saw that Florina was much the same. Having not experienced the same dizzying highs as the cities during the influx of European cash, the rural areas avoided the accompanying lows.

Georgios showed me around the house like it was my first time. I was surprised to see that he'd somehow had it renovated during the midst of an economic crisis. The kitchen had been upgraded, the bathroom retiled and the shower finally had its own hot water system. He wouldn't have to chop wood anymore.

'We started it years ago,' he explained. 'Billy finally acquiesced, and it's good to have it done. All this will be yours one day . . . your children's.'

I smiled knowingly at my new wife. 'Let's see,' I told Georgios.

Much to my relief, the brothers adored Jayne. For the first time in their lives, they had 'a sister', as Billy put it. Although he did ask if she happened to also have a sister, and was disappointed to hear she only had a brother.

'Feel my muscles,' Billy asked me. He was wearing a white singlet, as if trying to show off.

I squeezed a meaty bicep. 'Strong,' I said.

He felt my arms, thin and weak like overcooked spaghetti. 'I'll take you to the gymnasium,' he said. 'Two, three hours workout. Then I'll come to Australia and train you there. You need some weight on your bones. You need vitamins.'

'C'mon, Billy,' Georgios said, 'put a shirt on, we're taking our brother out.'

Crossing the border into the Former Yugoslav Republic of Macedonia, there was no need for passports; my brothers were familiar faces to all the border guards. Georgios presented them with homemade preserves and thick blocks of farm cheese. From the backseat of the car, I watched them all laughing together, patting each other heartily on the back, telling jokes and stories. My brothers were escorted into a small department store and returned soon after with cartons of duty-free cigarettes and bottles of top-shelf spirits; Russian vodkas, French cognacs and Scottish whiskeys. Georgios bought Jayne a pair of knee-high Italian leather boots.

'All girls like shoes,' he told me.

Georgios took me to the cemetery again. My uncle Vangelis's

grave was enormous, a tall marble obelisk, white and gleaming and new. His wife lay beside him; she had died a year earlier, her grave more modest.

'Our uncle only cared for money,' Georgios said. 'He thought the Grim Reaper would come for him and that he'd be able to show his wallet and be spared. Our cousins are now fighting over inheritances.'

I visited my biological parents, told them I'd gotten married and introduced Jayne who stood next to me awkwardly. I asked my brother where our aunt Soultana's grave was. I wanted to pay my respects.

'You're looking at it,' Georgios replied.

It turned out they just lifted the marble slab to my parents' grave and placed her inside. No expense, no fuss.

'It's what she would've wanted,' my brother added.

He reached for his packet of tobacco. I fired him a disapproving look. Georgios had started rolling his own cigarettes, which was his way of cutting down. Because it now took time to prepare a smoke, he smoked less. Billy, on the other hand, appeared to be smoking more than ever. His lips barely touched one cigarette before it was replaced by another. Georgios estimated our older brother was having three packs a day. Billy's weight had also ballooned, which had come from not having our *theia* around to look after him. Georgios now bought most of their meals out.

'I do worry about Billy's health,' he told me. 'I tell him to go easy. His knees have started to hurt now – they have to work harder to carry the extra weight. But at least he walks all over town each day. And the meals we eat are mainly from *tavernas* which source local produce.'

As he rolled his smoke, Georgios recounted an argument he'd recently had with Billy. Billy was complaining about a sore tooth early one morning. Georgios hadn't slept well and told him to go away. Billy ended up breaking a mirror. It was his way of expressing his frustration and also solving his problem – by breaking a reflection of himself in pain, he believed it would also end his pain. Billy then spent the rest of the day anxious to buy a new mirror, reminding Georgios of it every few minutes.

'I apologised to Billy,' Georgios told me. 'I had been working hard that week and was tired. We bought a new mirror.'

We started on a meditative lap of the cemetery so that Georgios could enjoy his smoke. As we walked, he stared into the distance.

'I'm seeing more how things fit together now. I never used to.'

'What do you mean?' I asked.

'I mean I used to get really frustrated with Billy when I was younger, and always asked why it was me in this situation, and why things weren't different. But now I'm older, and also since I've gotten to know you, I see very clearly how you're the antithesis of Billy. With that in mind, it's clear where I should fit on the spectrum, and it's exactly where I am.'

'You mean . . . in the middle?'

'Exactly. It's where I feel comfortable. You and Billy help me appreciate the richness of life. Many people don't get to see such a tapestry. Since meeting you, I've actually been quite comforted by it all, to see that there's a synchronicity in the universe, and an overall harmony. I feel a deep peace. Everything happens for a reason, I firmly believe that. There's a reason why you went where you went, and I can see that now. And because of this, I'm eagerly looking forward to the future. In light of all that's happened, there simply must be a few more twists in the tale. Someone has been pulling the strings all this time and I doubt they'll stop now.'

Georgios's words were measured, soothing. It made me admire him even more.

My brothers were now both in their fifties and still unmarried. Or they were married to each other, as I'd often heard locals say. It appeared their lives were much the same in the absence of a parental figure. I worried about Billy's health as well, but about Georgios's more. He seemed content, but he was showing physical signs of stress, his face more gaunt, perhaps from now being Billy's one-and-only source of family and care. Georgios's health was ultimately the more important since he carried the wellbeing of not one, but two individuals on his shoulders. Without Georgios, there was no Billy. With that in mind, I decided to ignore my mum's advice.

'If you ever need anything,' I told my brother, 'any assistance or money, call.'

He grinned appreciatively and lovingly rubbed the spiky new stubble on top of my head.

'And next time I come to visit, you can greet me as what you'll be,' I added, 'which is an uncle.'

Georgios smiled with mild embarrassment. 'That would be wonderful!' he said, eyes wide. 'But you can't say that. Those things are beyond your control. I pray that God blesses you and your lovely new wife.'

He hugged Jayne warmly the day we left, returning on the train to Thessaloniki. She loved the shoes. We then continued on to Paris and England. The former was sightseeing, the City of Light, kissing in front of the Eiffel Tower and exhausting ourselves touring the Louvre. In England, I attended a creative writing course in West Yorkshire, staying for a week in a forbidding eighteenth-century granite farmhouse. It was more intense than my course in New York, with tutorials and exercises across five days. My fellow students were all friendly and spent much of the week on the sauce. Combined with the lack of television, radio and internet, the isolation of the soggy Yorkshire countryside helped clear my mind. I spent several afternoons wandering through steep forests, soaking in the Pennine landscape of woods and rivers, weavers' cottages, packhorse trails and ruins of old mills.

London was the antidote to relaxation. Traffic, pollution, people, but also energy, excitement, life. The visit was partly professional. I submitted my writing to literary agents and enrolled in a master's degree in arts at City University. I signed upon a whim; it was meant to be the carrot leading the horse, something I could work towards, and which included the potential for another international adventure. I had more life experience now and was convinced I could experience an overseas destination better. To that end, I also met with a researcher at Imperial College with a view to a future job as an in-house scientific writer. The lab was enormous and focused on stem cells, tissue engineering, and new biomaterials. It employed bioengineers, material scientists, chemists, surgeons and biologists. The lab head didn't have enough time to deal with all the papers they were writing and publishing, so needed another pair of scientific eyes.

We returned to Australia and the everyday. Married life was much the same as unmarried life. Only now, there was something missing.

Jayne and I tried for two years to fall pregnant. Infertility is defined as not being able to conceive after one year of unprotected sex. Suddenly, we were thrust into a world of multivitamins and mineral supplements, oestrogen modulators, injections, fertility specialists, acupuncturists, and ovulation blood tests. Jayne cut caffeine and alcohol. I did too. But still, our hopes were dashed when her period came. Every month, it was like a red cross next to our names.

Jayne was stricken, and so was I. Our house was suddenly infuriatingly quiet. We had two spare bedrooms we had filled with junk. We tried not to take it personally, but each blamed ourselves. I took the failure especially hard. Jayne had the pressure of possessing the bulk of the necessary equipment, but I had the weight of history. It was my family who had a track record of infertility. In addition to my parents, many of my aunts and uncles had failed to have children, and on both sides of the family. By contrast, Jayne's family was largely unaffected. She once had a younger brother who died very soon after birth with a genetic condition known as Edwards syndrome. Babies with Edwards syndrome have trisomy: three copies of a chromosome instead of two. In the case of Edwards syndrome, which occurs in about 1 in 5000 live births, this is an extra chromosome 18. Babies born with Edwards syndrome are small, have heart defects and severe intellectual disability, and rarely survive beyond the first year of life.

But rare genetic conditions and developmental defects were one thing, while recurring infertility as adults was another. The infertility was firmly on my side of the family, and affected multiple members. Neither of my brothers had procreated. What if it was me, and what if I could do nothing to fix it?

CHAPTER 35

2014

FITTED OUT WITH black leather upholstery, darkly appointed with painted walls and fixtures, the small room used for sperm collection at the fertility clinic was everything I had both imagined and dreaded. There was even a small pile of flesh-toned publications for 'assistance'. It was perhaps the single most underwhelming experience of my life.

Fortunately, my numbers were normal – total count, motility, morphology. I was relieved. But Jayne was less enthusiastic. She was pleased to have her worries halved. But unfortunately, the problem was now squarely hers.

'I heard about a couple who found out that her eggs were incompatible with his sperm. They ended up having to wash the sperm and then she got pregnant with artificial insemination.'

The theories swirled around our dinner table; most made my head hurt, and all focused around medical science. It seemed our only hope. There was no discussion of orphanages or adoptions or the generosity of siblings in the same way there was no talk of incubators or microscopes or petri dishes by immigrants during the 1970s.

And so, the discussion about in vitro fertilisation opened up. This would involve financial and emotional preparation. We were both up for the challenge. I felt for Jayne. I cuddled her and told her to not blame herself, that it was just bad luck. Above all, I admired her bravery since we both knew the bulk of the work would fall to her.

I was soon receiving two-word text messages that put the fear of God into me: 'Sex tonight'. Having daily blood tests for ovulation, Jayne was on the clock, and I struggled to force something that normally came so naturally. It wasn't at all pleasurable or fun, and felt like another chore at the end of a long day. Later, I turned forty, which was a decidedly empty feeling. I'd always pictured myself having a big party with children at my side, or at least in my arms. Instead, Jayne and I went out to dinner.

'I think my cycles are short, they're just a bit over three weeks,' she told me over cheesecake dessert. 'Early ovulation means the follicles are the wrong size, and the eggs are unviable.'

Following an internal examination, a fertility specialist concluded that Jayne had polycystic ovary syndrome. She had blood tests to check her egg supply, and had her fallopian tubes flushed. An internal ultrasound showed which ovary was ovulating, with the right consistently outperforming the left. Jayne said the specialists' waiting rooms were the most depressing of all, full of downcast women with unfulfilled dreams, the mood sombre and funereal. She was now thirty-five-years-old and fast approaching the tipping point. Fertility was falling and risks were rising.

After yet another referral, Jayne saw a specialist gynaecologist in Sydney. He conducted another internal examination and then a laparoscopy before he delivered a diagnosis of endometriosis. We were both surprised. Jayne had never shown any symptoms of pelvic pain associated with the condition, or had issues during menstruation or sex. We travelled back to Sydney for the surgery and hoped it would provide the answer, but were realistic. In many cases, it didn't. The timing of the surgery was fortunate – we were due to leave for London a month later. I had accepted the scientific writer job at Imperial College and they desperately wanted me to start.

We were told the surgery was a success. It was encouraging news, but we put it out of our heads for a while. We had other more immediate priorities to attend to, and Jayne needed time to recover. Packing away the house, and packing up two suitcases, we boarded a commercial airliner. A day later, we arrived at Heathrow, jet lagged, overfed and under-slept.

I started my job almost immediately, boarding the Piccadilly line in the morning, and after work catching the Northern line to my Master's writing course at City University. Meanwhile, Jayne tried to find us a place to live beyond our temporary accommodation. High street real estate agents were soon calling her, showing her rentals, basement flats with no light and even less air. A brass upstart spoke to us in a squeaky voice, leaning back in his chair with legs spread wide. Another wanted to know how much I earned and doubted we had the income to rent in the area. A petite young female had the firmest and most direct handshake of all the agents.

A month later, we moved into our West Hampstead rental. It was the size of a broom cupboard and cost an absolute bomb. We met a friendly neighbourhood cat, grey and white, big paws, matted fur, dirty with London pollution. Strangely, our shower faced the street; we were forced to hang a black garbage bag over the window, much to the landlord's annoyance. We bought budget sheets, towels, pillows, and quilt, along with cutlery, crockery, and a clothes rack. We carried them all home on the overcrowded Jubilee line in cumbersome piles, receiving dirty looks the entire way.

Throughout all this, we sought recommendations for IVF clinics and booked appointments. They made me recall a time soon after I left science when I applied for a job as an embryologist at a private fertility clinic. Jayne saw gloriously round pregnant bellies on the street everywhere, and sobbed when she got home. She confided in me that she'd even considered keeping a daily belly tally and then seeing if she could exceed it, but that 'that would've been the most depressing game'. On the tube, she thought that some women wore 'Baby on Board' badges to secure priority seating even though they didn't look pregnant – which to her was a further slap in the face. I tried to keep her spirits up, taking her out to enjoy the city. We saw plays at the Old Vic and ate delicacies at the local street market, Venezuelan *arepas*, Caribbean curries and Sri Lankan *kottus*.

Being born in Greece but raised in Australia meant I was a dual citizen. Greek citizenship was conferred at birth in 1974, while the Australian didn't come until 1988. In the thirty years since, the world had changed, grown more wary and suspicious.

Countries were now busily shoring up their borders. Looking back, Australian citizenship was perhaps the greatest gift my adoptive parents could've given me after life itself.

Jayne had not been so fortunate. She had Danish and Croatian heritage but it was distant. She needed a visa to work in London. Filling out the necessary application forms, she mailed her precious Australian passport to the Home Office. Six weeks later, a letter arrived that said they'd never received it, which meant her passport had been either lost or stolen. They had no record of the Royal Mail reference number. Jayne reported it to the police, and fell into a deep depression. I made her buttermilk pancakes with honey and chamomile tea.

The seasons changed, autumn became winter. Sunset was at four o'clock in the afternoon, and it was pitch black by four-thirty. There were days with wild wind, then sunshine, then dark clouds, then sunshine again, then rain, then chilling wind. I bought snow boots; Jayne bought a puffer jacket. She filled her days with galleries, cafés and parks, was inspired by architecture, art and cinema. My days were taken up with writing and editing scientific papers and grants and PhD theses. But when I got home, I wrote creatively, further and further into the night, sending out my work to literary agents, rejection after rejection. All the while, the grey and white cat lay outstretched on our rug. Sometimes, I even took him to bed with us, before returning him to the street in the cold, grey morning.

Jayne slept restlessly and dreamt constantly of home. She carried immense negativity from what had happened with her passport. She dwelled on its loss and thought that if she had just done this or that, the injustice would be remedied. She was soon turning down recruitment agencies with offers of work because of her legal inability to work. She couldn't even take up an internship she'd successfully applied for after a round of competitive interviews. Jayne felt lonely, still struggling to connect with the city. And I, in turn, felt enormous guilt at what I had done to her. I had taken my glorious new wife to the other side of the world to show her a different experience of life and work. It was partly with a view to filling the hole in our childless lives. But now, even this was turning sour.

I noticed none of the London birds were singing. When I asked why, a shopkeeper told me they didn't bother anymore; their voices were drowned out by the noise of the city. Walking home at night, Jayne and I saw groups of young and drunk men and women – hen's nights and stag parties and birthdays. They piggybacked each other and slammed into glass doors and sang at the tops of their voices. Over time, the tube home on a Friday night became the week's very best entertainment, watching overly-refreshed lads in suits struggling to retain consciousness, and short-skirted girls trying to retain their dignity. Jayne and I held hands tightly, remembering what it was like to be so young and carefree.

Unlike Australia, ovulation tracking was not free in England. So Jayne decided to use a phone app to track her cycles and estimate the onset of her 'fertile window'. In Sydney, she'd been told that her endometriosis surgery disrupted the menstruation cycle and that it would take some time to return to normal. So when, early one morning, she checked her phone and saw it had been thirty-one days since her period, she didn't think much of it. And yet, she knew she would have niggling thoughts all day. To save herself the mental expenditure, she decided to tiptoe into the bathroom.

Jayne burst into our bedroom soon after, breathless and tongue-tied. I was sleeping after another late night at the keyboard. The cat, curled up around my feet, woke as well, startled.

'Pete, wake up, see!' she said.

There was a thin stick of plastic in her trembling hand. I struggled to focus my bleary eyes on the small window. After a moment, I saw it – a tiny blue cross that indicated a positive result.

We hugged. Jayne sobbed with joy, gratitude.

'Our lives are going to change forever,' I yawned.

CHAPTER 36

2014

JAYNE'S LIFE CHANGED about a week after she found out she was pregnant. She was nauseous, dizzy, and continually vomiting. The polluted London air and mouldy old flat were not helping.

'It'll be okay,' I said unconvincingly. 'Hopefully you'll feel better soon when we get to Florina.'

We were flying to Greece for Christmas. With Florina so deep in the northern mountains, I was hoping to see snow, and was thrilled at the prospect of spending my first Christmas with brothers. It felt romantic, nostalgic, and had only taken forty years to happen. It's not like I pictured us sitting around a tree opening presents. More like gathered around a cigarette packet trying to stay warm.

Georgios had said we should arrive on the twenty-third of December because 'the fires' would take place that night. These were the Christmas bonfires, an ancient custom, ostensibly to warm the earth for the arrival of Baby Jesus on the twenty-fifth.

I called my parents and told them our news. Mum and Dad were ecstatic. For two people who had worked so hard to simply become parents, they couldn't quite fathom that they would soon be grandparents. Now into their mid-eighties, it wasn't like they hadn't waited. It was also the best tonic for Mum in her recovery; she'd fallen and broken her hip a month earlier. She was now five years cancer-free, but the hip surgery was the second time she'd needed general anaesthetic. I didn't tell my brothers the news. They would hear it in person.

We arrived in Florina to the sight of the town ablaze. I was stunned. The bonfires weren't just small piles of wood haphazardly dumped in piles. They were constructed several storeys high, towers of thick wooden beams that the young men had been building since autumn, stacked with purpose and design like the skeletal frames of new skyscrapers. There must've been about a dozen competing for the title of the tallest. We wandered around town all night comparing heights and seeing how close we could stand to the thousand-degree temperatures. The fires shot into the sky, taller than most of the town's buildings. There was music and dancing on the streets till dawn. Despite all this, Billy remained unimpressed, and preferred to drink coffee and smoke cigarettes at a *kafenion*. Unlike his wide-eyed baby brother, he'd seen it all before.

Georgios took us to eat at nice restaurants and *tavernas*, most of which were owned by his friends. Billy didn't come. 'He can't appreciate good food,' Georgios explained. 'There's no point wasting it on him.'

I didn't like hearing my brother's justification, and was especially upset when he added that Billy had recently developed signs of diabetes.

'I'm making sure he orders the smaller bottle of cola,' Georgios said, 'and substituting pastries with nuts.'

Georgios paid off local café and *taverna* owners so that Billy could 'eat for free'. He advised them to make the same modifications when Billy asked for food or drink. 'Making major changes to his diet won't work,' Georgios explained. 'This way, Billy can't complain.'

We broke our news to Georgios one night after a delicious meal of seafood, steamed wild grasses, roasted red peppers, and *baklava*. He almost wept with joy and hugged Jayne warmly. Her eyes were moist too. She could see how much it meant to him.

Georgios leaned back in his chair and lit a celebratory cigarette. When Jayne excused herself to go outside for some fresh air, he realised his mistake, and apologised. She knew being pregnant in Greece would be a struggle with the country's widespread nicotine addiction. Georgios said he would be more conscious of it in future.

My brother stared out the window into the illuminated *plateia*, the light watery and orange. It still wasn't yet snowing but the forecast was likely. I could tell he was thinking, letting the reality sink in. In seven months time, he would be an uncle.

He turned back to me. 'See, I knew there was a bigger reason for why you came into the family,' Georgios said. 'It was to *continue* the family. Without you, the bloodline would stop. I genuinely believe that Baba foresaw this, far, far into the future.'

I wasn't so sure. 'You don't think our father just wanted to help his sister to become a parent?' I asked.

'Maybe,' Georgios sniffed. 'But I think he also took stock of his own family. He saw Billy sick, and knew that I would probably have to one day give up my own life to care for him. So Baba knew that his only chance was to have another baby and send it far, far away.'

His words were both uplifting and burdensome. On the one hand, I felt more significant, could walk a bit taller, as if my role in the family was affirmed. But on the other, the next seven months would need to progress flawlessly. I looked at Jayne outside the glass trying to stay warm in the subzero temperatures. She was soon retching again, the nausea at its worst after eating. I watched her helplessly. A bulge was yet to appear beneath her puffer jacket.

'Should I tell Billy?' I asked my brother.

'Let me tell him,' Georgios said. 'I'm sure he'll come see you after.'

It snowed the next day. Walking through Florina, Jayne found herself suddenly being escorted by a trio of proud bodyguards. My brothers and I were extra careful that she not slip and fall on the treacherous ground. Billy was the most proud and cautious of all, walking in front like some traffic policeman, even stopping motorists and pointing out that his sister-in-law was 'with child'. Jayne was mildly embarrassed but I told her to enjoy the attention while it lasted. She knew I meant the aggressive drivers who failed to stop at zebra crossings in north London. She'd nearly been knocked down on several occasions.

I'd never seen my home town look so beautiful. Everything

appeared more delicate under snow, reborn. Mum had always told me that winter in Florina was her favourite time of year, and perpetually lamented the lack of snow in sundrenched Australia. I could finally see why.

Dressed in gold chains and black leather, Georgios's childhood friend helped me secure my Greek national ID card – the *taftotita*, which could only be issued by the Hellenic police. I didn't think that applying for a *taftotita* would be a swift process, but my brother assured me that his friend could organise one quickly despite not having a scrap of his own official paperwork. Georgios's friend lived rent-free in a one-room flat that Georgios owned. He had no lease, no bills, and nothing with his name on it. He bummed cigarettes, food, drinks. He didn't own a car, didn't hold a driver's licence, and had no bank account or credit card. He had an unregistered mobile phone that he topped up with pre-paid credit. He had no superannuation, no pension, and spoke more lies than truth. Along with Greek, he was fluent in Russian, Croatian, and assorted other Balkan languages. He used four different surnames depending on whom he talked with, and claimed to have fathered four children to four different women from four different countries. I wanted to touch him to make sure he was real. At the police station, he charmed the female police officer and offered her superior cigars and bottles of French cognac bought across the border. Before I knew it, I had an official Greek *taftotita* in my hands.

'Our country is built on lies and deception,' Georgios told me. 'It's the reason why people like my friend exist. For all intents and purposes, he does not exist. Yet he is larger than life, and my most loyal friend.'

On our last night in Florina, just before New Year's Day, the snow fell with purpose. Returning from dinner at the *taverna*, Jayne went to bed early, sleeping in the bedroom that once belonged to my biological parents. Jayne was growing increasingly tired, her body exhausted from both nourishing a developing foetus and fighting through the nausea associated with forming a robust placenta. I kissed her goodnight and reached for my beanie, an essential for a bald head in snow. I was going out again. In the cramped kitchen, Georgios gave me a look of surprise, Billy one of query.

'Going out walking,' I told them. I had only one place in mind. 'See you in the morning.'

They turned on the TV and settled in for a night of coffee and cigarettes and jokes at the expense of their little foreign brother, trudging around in the snow like a madman. Billy would be shovelling the path clean in the morning, finally putting his brawn to good use.

I walked slowly, careful not to slip on the slick roads and icy pavements. My boots let out a satisfying crunch with every step. The town looked brand new, the parked cars and outdoor café tables and wrought iron fences as if dusted with freshly sifted flour.

I soon arrived at my destination. The Sakoulevas River was in full flow, surging and rumbling beneath my feet as I crossed a footbridge. Other than the ducks and geese, there wasn't a soul in sight.

The air was crisp and clean. I opened my arms wide and filled my lungs. Lemony streetlight illuminated the facades of the neoclassical houses on the river's western side. Behind them was the mountain, leaden with the weight of ten thousand chestnut trees. Georgios said chestnuts produced a better crop when subjected to chill temperatures during the dormant period, so snowfalls were beneficial rather than harmful to the trees.

I returned my gaze to the river where I finally saw what I came for. In the middle of the river floated a 'Greek Christmas tree', traditionally decorated. It was a *karavaki* – a small boat, illuminated with electric blue lights. Greece had started to embrace an old custom of decorating boats instead of trees, which were now considered an imported tradition. By contrast, the *karavaki* was seen as a quintessential Greek symbol. Seafarers had explored the region for thousands of years and turned Greece into a maritime power. During Christmas, when seamen would return home to their islands after a long time away, families would celebrate by decorating small wooden boats. The tradition gradually spread to the mainland and then crept inland, through the Peloponnese, Thessaly and Epirus, and all the way north until it finally reached Florina and its own little mountain river.

The snow kept falling. My legs felt cold for the first time. But my heart was warm, thrumming in time with the river and the idea of becoming a father. It was a concept that was blossoming by the day, growing stronger and more desired. I imagined one day standing alongside a little person, their eyes big and round as they marvelled at the beauty of the iridescent blue *karavaki*. I noticed its bow was pointing north, away from the sea, according to custom. I walked on, following its course up the river.

CHAPTER 37

2015

JAYNE WAS FORTY-ONE weeks pregnant. So we were going for a short walk through the Australian bush in the hope it would bring on the first twinges of labour. We'd already tried acupuncture, raspberry leaf tea, sex, and a ridiculously hot vindaloo. We'd been told that usually the first baby was notoriously late. Thought they were special. Which they were. Being upright and moving was supposed to encourage the baby's head to move down onto the cervix. Our birth plan was written, our bags were packed.

The day was clear but cold; midwinter in southeastern Australia. It was equally cold, but nowhere near as sunny, the day Jayne showed me a little blue cross in our flat in north London. Since then, primitive cells had divided and migrated, forming new body parts in the ambient body temperature deep inside her belly. A child conceived in winter, to be born in winter, so it was no surprise it was reluctant to leave the warmth of the womb. I'd be in no hurry either. We considered a wintery name, but decided against it. At first, I had teased Jayne saying it was twins. My biological dad had been a twin, and Jayne was classified as an 'older mother', which further increased the chance. But it was only one, and for that we were glad.

Three months after we returned from Greece, we broke our West Hampstead lease and returned home to Australia to feather the nest. We were promptly inundated with outgrown baby gear from many friends. We had family support in Australia, and the healthcare system was familiar. Up till then, our ultrasounds had been at the Royal Free, and it was there that we heard our child's fast-thrumming heartbeat for the first time. It was the unmistakable sound of life and made me teary.

I was surprised, and rather shocked, by how much my parents had aged during my relatively short time away. They always seemed to have an increasing number of grey hairs and wrinkles after every one of my overseas trips, but this occasion seemed even more profound. Mum hobbled gingerly on her new hip, while Dad had lost an inordinate amount of weight for some unknown reason. He'd had every diagnostic test and medical scan available but they all came back normal. At times, I had wanted the specialists to find a problem so that at least they could tailor treatment. It was hard to look at Dad, let alone pat him reassuringly on the shoulder. All I felt was bone.

Having been busy knitting in our absence, Mum presented us with perfectly crocheted outfits in neutral colours, yellow and white and green. In contrast to the vast majority of pregnant couples, we'd decided to not find out the gender.

Throughout our pregnancy, my parents remained deliriously

excited. Collectively, they'd waited a hundred and seventy years to become grandparents, and survived two cancers. They rarely left their house anymore, but it was enough to have them nearby.

On this particular day, the winter temperature remained in single digits. We dressed in layers, beanies, scarves and woollen socks. Our street backed onto the bush and a mountain which often hosted joggers, walkers, and mountain bikers in body armour, but also mobs of grey kangaroos. Every morning, our front lawn was littered with new souvenirs from the previous night's soiree. It was often a challenge driving home at night. Drawn by glowing headlights, honour guards of kangaroos lined the roads of suburbia, bouncing along beside the car as I eased my foot off the accelerator. Some of them had the floppy heads of tiny joeys hanging from their pouches, their eyes glowing in the reflection of headlights. The roos bred throughout the year, with peak births in summer. The local government culled the population to sustainable numbers during winter.

I took Jayne's gloved hand in mine as we walked slowly, careful not to slip on any dirt loosened with recent rains. It reminded me of when my brothers and I escorted her across the ice and snow of wintry Florina. Now she walked like she was about to tip over, her centre of gravity shifted forward, her feet invisible. We checked the spot where we once saw a spiny echidna, a ritual we repeated each time we walked up the mountain. We were heading for the place we called the duck pond, which was halfway up a winding single track lined with dead and twisted branches. The crisp air made our cheeks blush pink. We encountered a big grey roo on the track, more than two metres in height. It stood on its rear legs and appeared to be sizing us up for a fight, its ears rotating like satellite dishes. We were, after all, encroaching on its turf. Fortunately, we didn't have to pass the roo to get to the duck pond, and eased ourselves unthreateningly onto its banks. The water was calm, glassy, a mirror. Jayne was out of breath. The roo stared at us a while longer before bouncing off up the mountain, safe in the knowledge that the intruders had been kept at bay.

Mum used to walk me up this same mountain in a stroller when I was a baby. She had chestnut hair then and two natural hips. There was even a photo of us beside the duck pond. To think they tried for eighteen years to become parents; we only tried for two. We had stressed and argued and fought, and our efforts were only a fraction of theirs.

That day, there were ducks but no ducklings. It was still too early in the season, spring another month away. The first new buds had only just begun to appear on the bare bush branches. The golden wattles were in full bloom though, flowering from the start of winter. We sat quietly listening to the warble of magpies who gathered sticks and twigs to build their nests. It would soon be swooping season and the mountain would resonate with the trill of cheeping offspring, demanding another regurgitated feed. And three months later, snakes and shingleback skinks would emerge to warm their cold-blooded bodies on baking hot rocks. At least once a summer we found a snake in our garden. They were a protected species and supposed to only be removed by a licensed wildlife handler. When I was young, we found an adolescent brown snake in the backyard. Browns are one of the world's most venomous breeds of snake. Dad told me to go inside. From my bedroom window, I watched him disappear into his shed and soon heard the distinctive sound of his bench grinder. Minutes later, he reappeared with a freshly sharpened axe. With one firm swing, he decapitated the snake then left its headless body to dry in the sun.

The light faded, and more roos came out to play in preparation for their nightly shindig. Jayne put her head on my shoulder and her hands on her round belly, rubbing gently and humming lightly.

The world was amazing, and this small corner was pretty special. I couldn't wait to show it to my son or daughter soon.

CHAPTER 38

2015

THE LANDLINE TELEPHONE woke me at four o'clock in the morning. I sprung from bed and bolted down the corridor. Something was wrong for it to ring at that hour. Phones never rang at that hour with good news. Following a late-night bout of literary inspiration, I'd had only ninety minutes sleep.

It was Mum; frantic. Dad was having chest pains and difficulty breathing. They'd called an ambulance.

I threw on whatever clothes I could find. Jayne was now also awake; she could barely sleep anyway, and couldn't roll over without the baby kicking like a kung fu master. She offered me reassurance. Dad's health had declined in the previous days with complaints of stomach pains and flu-like symptoms so we'd been somewhat prepared.

It was only a short drive to my parents' house at the other end of the suburb through dark, empty streets. I was relieved when their house came into view with an illuminated ambulance in the driveway. I didn't want to face that scene without paramedics there.

The paramedics were with Dad in the living room. He was sitting in a chair in his flannelette pyjamas and telling them he was having difficulty breathing, a heavy weight on his chest. Mum was also in her pyjamas, sitting and listening. Despite his ailments, Dad continued to order her around. He told her to bring him things, to take things away, and to be quiet whenever he disagreed with what she'd said. His distrust of the medical profession had never abated, had only intensified, and he'd said for years that 'doctors have been trying to kill me'. And yet he'd somehow made it to the ripe old age of eighty-five. Dad always blamed his diabetes for his wild changes in mood. After all those years, I still didn't know whether to believe him.

The paramedics told Dad to calm down and sit quietly while they recorded an electrocardiogram. They gave him some medication. There were no obvious signs of a cardiac event but he was still finding it hard to breathe. The decision was made to go to hospital. Mum and I followed in the car and settled in beside Dad's bed in Emergency, listening to him complain about both immediate and past hardships. I tried to turn his mind to more positive thoughts like the impending birth of his first grandchild. He absolutely adored young children, his face used to light up around them, and he used to interact with them in ways that brought immediate smiles and laughter. But I hadn't seen Dad's smile in a long time.

By mid-morning, Dad was still having trouble breathing and lashed out at me when I asked him questions about his condition. He ordered us to leave the hospital. I was tired and emotional, and only trying to help. Light rain was falling, the sky had no colour. The day was going to be cold, the forecast five degrees, barely the inside of a fridge. I dropped Mum off at her empty house and returned to mine as Jayne left for acupuncture. I crawled into bed with ice cubes for feet, the blood having retreated from my extremities with the stress.

I slept for two hours and was still cold when I woke up. Jayne returned home – still pregnant – and took over the shift, driving Mum back to hospital while I ate breakfast. I arrived mid-afternoon, which had the same colour and temperature as the morning. Dad's condition had improved marginally. He asked Mum to whack him hard on the back so he could expel the phlegm choking his lungs into a blue emesis bag. There was talk of a transfer to another hospital, abnormal blood test results, the implant of a pacemaker, a possible infection. Despite my efforts to focus Dad's attention on the future, he continued to dwell on the past. He repeated himself, forgot things, ordered us around. Mum and I left on only slightly better terms with him.

We ordered takeaway laksa for dinner. I ate reluctantly, philosophising on the fragility of life. Jayne listened half-heartedly; her thoughts were clearly elsewhere. We settled in for the evening, to unwind and soon sleep. We both needed it. My mind was scattered all over the place but I had no energy to get off the couch.

The landline rang at nine o'clock. It was Mum. Dad wanted food delivered. Mum explained that he refused to eat the tasteless gruel they brought him in hospital and was weak with hunger. All he wanted was a cheese sandwich, but a special one that Mum made, toasted, with Vegemite and Greek feta cheese. With one foot in each culture, the snack was true immigrant's fare. The round trip to hospital was an hour and my eyes were closing. I didn't argue, and ended the call. I explained to Jayne what I needed to do. She rolled her eyes and went to bed.

Having gathered my thoughts on the short drive to my parents' house, I let Mum know my displeasure with the situation. Had they forgotten that Jayne was due to go into labour at any minute? Was Dad that self-absorbed? Mum said she was pleading with him but couldn't say no. I suggested the idea of her catching a taxi for once, but she said she'd never caught a taxi in her sixty years in Australia and was too scared to start now.

Dad was in the cardiac care unit on the third floor. He was lying flat out in bed, his eyes closed, mouth half open. His outline was barely visible beneath a thin white hospital blanket, his body reduced to a skeleton. A young woman sat beside him reading a book. Her smile was warm, her eyes bright, skin flawless. She introduced herself as a nurse and explained that she was going to sit with Dad the entire night and keep him company. She was from Nigeria and had a thirteen-week-old son waiting for her at home when she finished her shift at seven in the morning.

Dad stirred and woke. Seeing the delicate aluminium foil package in my hands, he thanked me for the sandwich. He chewed without his false teeth, taking an eternity to dissolve and swallow two careful bites. He rewrapped the sandwich and put it to one side. 'I'll eat the rest tomorrow,' he breathed.

I was disappointed; partly for Dad's lack of appetite, but also for my efforts. I vowed to tell Jayne that he hungrily ate the whole sandwich.

'Eat some more, Dad,' I said.

'No thanks,' he replied. 'But I'll have some banana. Did you bring one?'

I shook my head. Dad looked disappointed. 'I would've eaten a banana,' he added.

He mentioned a possible discharge date which, of course, was according to his own calendar and not any professional medical assessment. I thanked the nurse for looking after Dad and told her that he was 'due to become a grandfather at any minute'. She smiled brilliant white teeth. 'How exciting,' she said.

I drove home. Jayne encountered me in the kitchen as I placed my keys in the bowl. She was holding her lower back and moving warily.

'What's going on here, why are you awake?' I asked.

Jayne smiled gently in a way I'd never quite seen before.

'You better go to bed,' she said. 'I've started feeling contractions.'

CHAPTER 39

2015

'OH. OH RIGHT. Wow.'

My words came out as single syllables. The clock on the wall said it was just after eleven.

'I'm going to try and come to bed soon but the pain may be too much,' Jayne said.

I sat and recorded the time between her contractions – three minutes, with each lasting about forty seconds.

'Stage one of labour,' she said. 'It could be a few hours or few days. Go to bed.'

Jayne added that Mum called while I was out. She was sobbing and saying how much my dad loved me even though he never showed it. He just wasn't one of those men.

I brushed my teeth and slipped into bed. Jayne joined me between the covers but lasted only a few minutes. She said she was going to sit in the living room on the large inflatable exercise ball and keep track of her contractions. I was surprised how quickly

I fell asleep given recent developments but my exhaustion was too great.

I woke at half past three and felt ice-cold sheets beside me. In the living room, Jayne was sitting on her ball, head in her hands. There were chairs everywhere, buckets, towels. She'd showered twice and vomited three times.

'I can't hold out any longer,' she said. 'Call the midwife.'

I was grateful for the four hours sleep. We grabbed our hospital bags and commenced the drive south along a familiar road in darkness. For once, this was a welcomed journey. The contractions slowed during the car trip. Jayne told me she would 'have gas and morphine but no epidural'. There was a parking spot right out front.

The midwife met us at the doors to the birth centre at five o'clock. She showed us to a spacious room with a double bed, large circular bathtub, and ensuite bathroom. We settled in. Jayne sat on the bed, me in a chair. She was wearing one of my long sleeve T-shirts. It was one of the few items of clothing that still fitted her beautifully round body.

'Try to lie down,' I said. 'You need to rest, you're exhausted.'

Jayne tried but the pain was too great. Instead, she rested between contractions and leaned against a vertical surface to see through each wave of pain. Suitable vertical surfaces included the bed, the edge of the bathtub, and me. She showered to ease the sting and was regularly checked by the midwife who found her four centimetres dilated. Three days earlier, she was two centimetres. The baby's heart rate was normal.

We were brought a tray of food, a roast chicken lunch with

bread and dessert. Jayne only wanted the sweet orange jelly so I ate the roast and went to buy her some hard lollies to suck on between sips of water and sports drinks. I texted my mother-in-law, told her we were at the hospital, and asked her to pick up my mum on the way. Then I called my mum and explained the same to her at half the pace. Excitement all round. The baby was coming.

By mid-morning, the pain was even more intense. Jayne had vomited her jelly and sports drinks and requested a cylinder of nitrous oxide. She huffed through every contraction as the gas took away the height of the pain. I massaged the base of her back where the strain was the worst. The midwife checked again; the cervix was slowly dilating, opening an extra centimetre each hour, but it was still the first stage of labour. Jayne panicked, fearing she would be unable to cope with the second stage. I tried to relax her with massage and rotated through a selection of music on a portable stereo. The midwife mentioned women she'd seen who had literally danced their way through their labours.

'No way,' Jayne said swiftly, 'ain't gonna happen.'

She was concerned her waters hadn't yet broken and felt a sudden pain in her lower back. The midwife wondered whether the baby may have been pressing on a nerve and turning to posterior. She guided Jayne to put one foot on the steps leading to the bathtub and to sway in time with the music to keep the baby from turning.

Sensing a moment of respite, I slipped out to the cardiac care unit to check on Dad and the two future grandmothers. I wanted my news to bring some joy but Dad remained focused on his plight even though his symptoms were vastly improved. He said he hadn't eaten much and appeared weak. Mum had brought in delicious home-cooked food but he didn't want any so it sat uneaten by his bedside.

By mid-afternoon, Jayne's pain had intensified even further. Unable to take any more, she requested morphine, but was told it was too late – the only option was an epidural, which could delay the birth several hours. Reluctantly, she agreed. The anaesthetist arrived, explained the risks, which were more than we had realised: headaches, high blood sugar, stomach ulcers, arthritis of the hips, and an increased risk of instrumental delivery by forceps or vacuum. Jayne agreed. The anaesthetist painted her back purple and administered the anaesthetic through a series of careful injections in her lumbar spine. My phone rang; I looked down, saw the name, answered. Dad was calling to ask if there was any news. It was heartening to hear him show interest, and I reasoned that Mum probably had a quiet word to him. I spoke in short sentences and hung up the phone quickly. I missed Jayne breaking her waters, which at that moment was somewhat of an anticlimax.

The big push was soon underway. With a second midwife having joined us, we were now a cheer squad of three. There were concerns when the baby's heart rate plummeted. Naked from the waist down, Jayne was rolled onto her side with her left leg held in the air by the second midwife. The position returned the baby's heart rate to normal. I was in front holding Jayne's hand as she crushed mine. Meanwhile, the two midwives were down at 'the business end' of proceedings, of which I also had full sight. A friend, a father of three, had told me that things were so much more rewarding when you saw the miracle of birth with an unadulterated view. I was brave.

By late afternoon, a head was sighted. I was afraid to look at it directly, imagining that I was looking into the sun. The midwives were cheering on every push. I chimed in when I could but without the same gusto. Jayne ignored me and stayed focused. She had done well to not insult me the entire time. I had expected it too, having heard stories from numerous friends about the moment they became fathers.

'Here,' the first midwife told me, 'reach down and touch the baby's head.' It was with a view to encouraging Jayne to push harder during the second stage of labour.

I extended my arm tentatively, and felt something wet and slimy. They offered Jayne a mirror but she declined. I watched more of the head emerge; an alien being born, from another place, into a strange, unfamiliar world with harsh lights and loud noises. Eventually, the head crowned and I saw slicked-back hair, two ears, two tightly closed eyes, a nose and a squashed-in face covered in shiny goo. From there, it was only two more pushes before a slippery, eel-like body emerged and was placed directly onto the new mum's bare chest for immediate skin-to-skin bonding. Jayne looked at the miracle squealing on her chest and I kissed her forehead on a job supremely done.

'Is it a boy or girl?' the second midwife asked me. 'Take a look, Pete . . .'

CHAPTER 40

2015

MY EYES GRAVITATED to the baby's hairless groin where I saw a set of enlarged gonads. Normally, that would've clearly indicated a boy, but I was suddenly unsure. I was told during antenatal classes that newborn girls' genitalia often became engorged during pregnancy. I was confused, uncertain, and so decided to take a wild stab in the dark.

'Is it a . . . boy?' I asked tentatively.

The second midwife scoffed. 'What do you think?'

I looked again. 'Is it a boy?' I repeated.

I ended up asking four times just to make sure. Yes, it's a boy. You're the father of a son.

We all took a breath. The midwives were overjoyed, I was thankful, and Jayne was exhausted. I took photos. Preliminary checks were made. Ten fingers, ten toes. The first midwife shone a torch to reveal a pair of sleepy blue eyes, which we were told would likely change colour. But everything appeared normal. He was weighed: four kilos in new speak, nine pounds in old. A big bubba, and especially when you considered Jayne's slight frame. He screamed on the scale. Being cold and naked was not appreciated.

The alien stared at us, we stared at the alien. I searched for a resemblance but it wasn't so easy when freshly minted. The eyes appeared familiar, as if my own, and the earlobes were equally floppy. His skin was the softest I'd ever felt. He was bobbing his head on Jayne's chest, an innate process known as blueprinting as he searched for the nipple, for food. The midwives helped guide him until he latched on. But he soon lost the connection, and it would still be a few days before Jayne's milk properly came in. This was just a practice run. We stroked and spoke with him gently, searching for his eyes which he continued to hide from us and the harsh artificial light.

The third stage of labour was quick – the delivery of the placenta followed only minutes later. The second midwife collected the crimson pouch and thick yellow umbilical cord in a stainless steel bowl. She lifted it up to show how thin it was. Whatever bloody leftovers remained in the sack showcased its immense strength. She asked if we wanted the placenta and I immediately said yes. I wasn't precisely sure what I'd do with it but at that moment, I knew I wanted to take the organ home. As a geneticist, I'd seen many mouse placentas, but this was my first human specimen. The midwife dumped the organ into a plastic ice cream tub with a lid and set it to one side. Should I plant it under a tree? Grind it into a powder? Or have it made into some delicate jewellery or artwork?

The second midwife got out her needle and thread – Jayne's perineum had second-degree tearing. I excused myself to go deliver news. This was perhaps the sweetest walk I'd ever made, with three new grandparents waiting nervously for the news in the very next building. It wasn't quite the mental image I had, emerging from the delivery suite to share the news in the waiting room. But it was just as good, and the further walk only prolonged the anticipation.

My feet skipped across the parquetry floor. I was full of adrenaline, with more energy than I'd had in days, but also lighter in spirit. An enormous weight had lifted from my shoulders, one that I'd carried for years. It stemmed from the fear of my parents dying without seeing grandchildren. For years, I'd watched them dote on the grandchildren of near relatives, and sometimes even of strangers, always wanting one of their own. Finally, they had a grandson. Whatever extra time they got with my children – a day, a month, a year, ten years – would be a bonus. And I had always pictured myself hugging my kids at my parents' funerals. I hoped Dad was alright. I walked faster.

I descended a floor, taking two steps at a time, and then started walking east, past the café and postnatal clinic and pathology collection centre and fracture clinic. Up one more flight of stairs, two steps at once, to the third floor. In the cardiac unit, I found my parents and mother-in-law sitting quietly, patiently. They all looked tired, it had been a long day for them too. I stood for a moment, waiting for them to notice me. All three faces were expectant.

'What is it, Panagiotis?' Mum asked. 'Have we got a baby?'

I waited a second for added tension and then said: 'Yes. It's a boy!'

Jubilation. Dad's first smile in eons. Mum's eyes filled with tears. My mother-in-law punched the air and started working her phone. We caused heads to turn in the otherwise calm cardiac unit and got looks of disapproval from the nurses. I showed the baby's first photos on the camera. Mum couldn't stop kissing the digital screen.

I returned to the birth centre. The new family was calm and still acquainting themselves with one another. I started texting the news to friends. Replies came quickly, and many at once. A good friend from London called to send his congratulations. He was one of the first people we told the news of the pregnancy when we were living there, so it was a sense of completeness to have him there as one of the first voices in the room alongside our new baby. I tried to call my brothers but Georgios wasn't answering.

A period of feeding and bonding followed, along with a nappy change, all of which were clumsy and awkward for mother and son alike. But it was still early days. Another tray of food was delivered, more roast, some kind of red meat this time, I couldn't tell whether lamb or beef, but which Jayne and I shared. I fed her mouthfuls while she continued to bond through skin-to-skin contact.

A series of nurses visited the new mother and baby, each with their own test that needed undertaking, another tick in a box or comment on a line. Then it was the turn for the two grandmothers who were both suitably emotional. My mum took her grandson in her arms for the first time, her eyes moist. She spoke in a tone and using phrases that I hadn't heard in years but which were instantly recognisable. It was the same loving lullaby voice I'd heard as a child that soothed me to sleep and magically healed every scraped knee and elbow.

More nurses came and went. The grandmothers left. My eyelids were heavy, sleep was calling. But before that, I stripped down to my waist, lay on the bunk bed in the corner of the room, and had the newborn placed on my hairy chest. He was shivering, the room warm but not ambient body temperature. I was reluctant to touch him at first for fear he'd break, but his healthy birth weight gave me confidence that he was more stable than fine china. His bobble head was noticeably heavy. Suddenly, he cried. It was admittedly a rather adorable sound because it was new, but it made me think I was doing something wrong. Jayne explained that he didn't like being naked and threw a light blanket over us before going to shower. He soon calmed down and began to breathe steadily, soothed by the sound of my heartbeat.

He cried again and I handed him back to Jayne. She got into bed to commence the long and arduous task of feeding. I brushed my teeth, removed my contact lenses, grabbed a couple of hospital blankets, lay down and closed my eyes. I awoke feeling refreshed and slightly guilty at the thought of all those sleep-deprived parents. Still, I knew my time would come.

The next morning, I visited Dad who'd now been moved to one of the wards on the sixth floor. He was hungry for news, but I wished he was hungry for food; he still hadn't eaten much, and had thrown up much of what he'd swallowed. He told me again that he desperately wanted to go home. I told him to wait and just let the doctors do their tests and promised that I would visit again in the afternoon.

I returned to his ward several hours later, flanked on either side by my mum and my wife like a police escort. Both were slow – my mum with her replacement hip, my wife with her post-delivery fatigue. In my arms was a bundle of precious cargo. My son nestled into my neck with his pudgy face, eyes closed tight.

Finally, it was time for the moment I thought might never happen. My dad sees my son, and a grandfather meets his grandson. At that moment, the absence of common blood meant absolutely nothing.

Mum entered the room first and checked behind the blue curtain. Jayne followed, and finally me and my boy, still sleeping in my arms. For a moment, Dad was unsure of what was going on, we'd taken him by surprise. He wasn't used to surprises. But his confusion was only brief before he saw the bundle I was holding. His gummy face smiled. I leaned in to give him a closer look. He asked for his glasses.

'Well,' Mum said, 'what do you think?'

Dad's thin eyes were trying to focus on the new life hovering before them. He stroked my son's smooth cheek with the back of his thick fingers and patted his small, misshapen head.

'Oooh,' Dad said, 'you done good.'

The family gathered around Dad's hospital bed. Photos were taken, with three generations together in the one frame for the very first time. Dad tried to smile but struggled. It didn't help that he wasn't wearing his false teeth, and that he was also from a time when photos weren't often taken so never learned how to smile for the camera. This was something I'd noticed over the years. Mum was the same but on this day there was no restraining her joy or removing her permanent smile. She beamed warmly as the nurse took snaps. I looked at the camera, at the photos, which signified both my past and my future. They were beautiful, but I found it prophetic that the location was a hospital bed. Escorting my elderly parents between medical appointments throughout the day and to hospitals in the middle of the night were memories inseparable from my childhood and adolescence. I remembered my own age of forty-one and reminded myself that I was only three years younger than they were when they became parents. I wondered whether my son would one day care for me in the same way. I hoped so.

Mum and I left the hospital. I kissed my wife and son goodbye. They were getting to know each other with every passing hour. I only hoped I would get a chance to do the same once things calmed down elsewhere in my life.

That night, I finally reached Georgios on the phone. He was overjoyed with the news. He had a nephew. So did Billy.

'He sounds like a little fatty,' Georgios said.

'He's certainly not small,' I said.

'And I also have some news of my own . . .'

Georgios said he had a girlfriend. It was early days but he was optimistic. She had two children of her own and had only recently returned to Florina after living on an island in the Dodecanese for many years.

'We went to high school together,' he said. 'I remember noticing her even then.'

I was thrilled with my brother's news. 'I can't wait to meet her,' I said.

'And I can't wait to meet my new *anipsios*.'

The next day, I took Mum to visit Dad, while I planned to finally take the new family home. Dad was grumpy. He wanted to go home, too. He'd tried to eat but vomited again, and had to fight off the nurses when they tried to give him a shower. He was afraid of falling over in the shower with his matchstick frame. I left Mum to restore calm and sought out a nurse for an update on his condition. She was a friendly nurse who assured me she was familiar with 'difficult patients' like my dad. She explained they still weren't sure of what was going on but that a chest infection was the most likely culprit. He was on antibiotics and antiemetics. If he needed a pacemaker, which was likely, it couldn't be implanted until his infection cleared. So the plan was for observation. His bloods were clear but they were still deeply concerned about his dramatic weight loss. So was I. Given the rate at which Dad was inexplicably disappearing, it did not bode well for the future.

The new family left the hospital. My son's lungs inhaled their first breath of the outdoors and his skin saw the first rays of the harsh Australian sun. I brought the car around and wrestled with the baby capsule, quickly realising I probably should've practised beforehand. My more competent wife took over and we strapped him in. The drive home was slow. We entered through the front door of our house, as prescribed by tradition, even though we normally only ever used the back door.

Over the next three days, I ran a double marathon, caring for young and old alike. Each had a head disproportionately large for their body. Each had unique needs but both were equally helpless. Dad needed a dietary supplement; the baby needed formula milk.

I emptied my wallet on the counter of the local pharmacy each time I walked in.

I prepared a framed photo of the baby with his eyes open to take to Dad in hospital. He sent it away, saying 'the baby doesn't belong in here with the sick people'. Dad was eventually released from hospital, a discharge process that took several hours due to the number of new medications. He was impatient to leave as I tried to understand careful instructions from doctors.. Dad wanted to steal a walking frame from the hospital, claiming it was his, but they were onto him. I pushed him to the car in a wheelchair. I had carried my newborn son out through the same automatic doors three days earlier.

A new generation beckons: my wife, Jayne, with her baby bump in the Florina snow in northern Greece, December 2014.

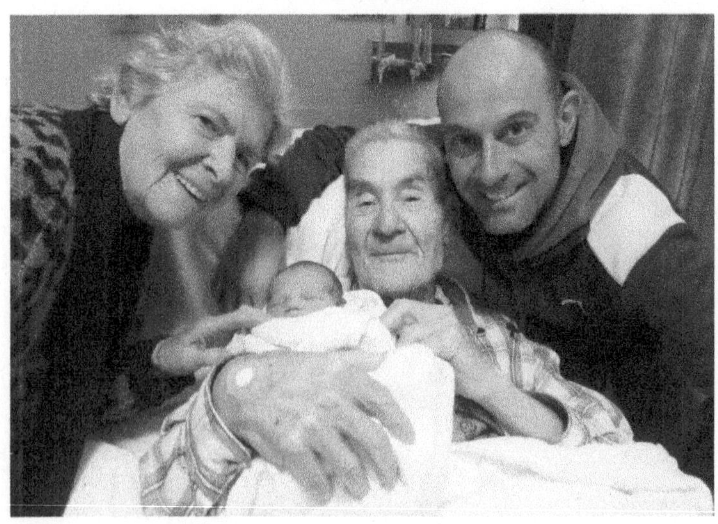

A new generation arrives: my parents with their one-day-old grandson in August 2015 at Canberra Hospital, Australia.

A proud Yiayia and Papou with their eldest grandson in Canberra, Australia, 2015–2017.

Baptising my youngest son at Saint Nicholas Greek Orthodox Church in Kingston, Canberra, Australia, April 2018.

My sons in Canberra, Australia, 2018.

Playing with my sons in Canberra, Australia, 2018.

Me and my sons celebrating their yiayia's 88th birthday in December 2018 in Canberra, Australia. A week after this photo was taken, I told Mum that she would become a grandmother for a third time in mid-2019.

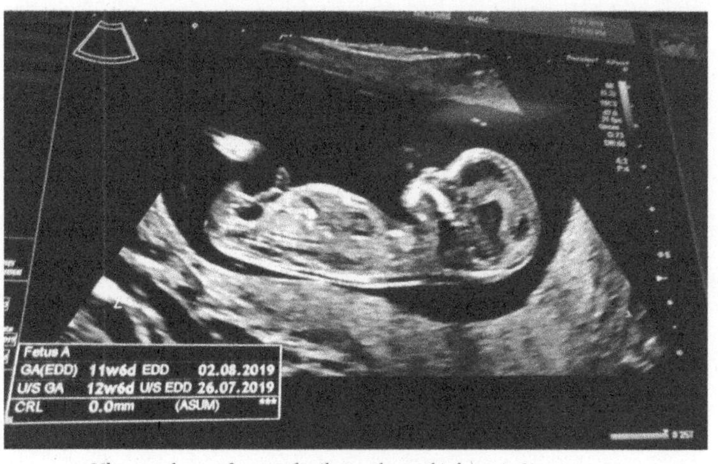

Ultrasound scan of newest family member, a third son, in January 2019.

CHAPTER 41

2016

DAD WAS UNWELL. He wasn't in hospital, he was home, but every day was proving a struggle. I had always imagined taking great pleasure from visiting my parents' house with my kids, seeing them play and grow, witnessing their joy. And that was there to some extent, but it had come to be overwhelmed with a kilo of dread every time I visited.

My father, thin and emaciated, had effectively become bound to his weathered armchair. He struggled to walk the short distance from the living room to the kitchen to make a much-loved Greek coffee, and in the mornings was unable to rise from bed without assistance. Meanwhile, Mum laboured to maintain the family home to her impeccable standards of cleanliness and hygiene, and somehow satisfy her husband's countless rules and demands. The vast majority were irrational and unreasonable and included a ban on outside help. This was despite regular offers from community services, and also from me. I was only allowed to mow their lawn and trim their garden, which was seen as man's work. It was, apparently, a Greek thing. Steeped in cultural expectations, the women engaged in competitive suffering as a means of gaining honour and prestige in their close-knit, gossip-hungry communities. I knew that when Dad did finally die, as with all Greek widows, Mum would make her husband a saint.

In the year since my son's birth, Dad had been hospitalised a dozen times. This included a pacemaker implant, a catheter and urine drainage bag, and countless hypoglycaemic attacks and infections. The arrival of my son had undoubtedly changed things. For the better – the joy he brought into all our lives, especially Dad's, finally a grandfather, a venerable *papou* – but also for the worse. Suddenly, I was no longer just my father's son. I was a father myself and had new responsibilities. Dad sensed this too.

'I will look after myself now,' he told me adamantly.

I debated his decision. I knew it would be both time-consuming and exhausting to be pulled in two different directions, but Dad's health was declining and he was becoming increasingly confused. His extensive list of medications began to baffle him, particularly when he stopped taking pills for his diabetes and needed to self-administer insulin injections. Finding the right dose was an elusive art that required accurate record-keeping and continual decision-making. There was no way he could have possibly navigated such a foreign landscape. And yet, he insisted. He drove himself to doctor's appointments and self-medicated. Mum reminded him to take his pills, his insulin, or reminded him that he'd already taken his pills and insulin and didn't need a second dose. He yelled at her to leave him alone and make him another coffee. He checked his blood sugar repeatedly, forgetting that he'd already checked it. He would later apologise for his outbursts, and blame his blood sugar. On and on it went.

I met with a friendly hospital nutritionist who asked a barrage of questions about Dad's diet. I told her that he ate more nutritious food than both of us combined. She fulfilled her professional duties by recommending a powdered food supplement drunk daily with milk. I bought two large cans, chocolate and vanilla flavoured dust. Dad swallowed them under sufferance, once, twice, then refused to drink more. The full cans sat on the kitchen counter. Finally, Mum started drinking them. Under continual stress and demands from my father, she too had lost an uncomfortable amount of weight.

Over the course of several months, I watched Dad gradually retreat from the world, one routine at a time. He drove, shopped and socialised less, and sat, stared and slept more. He spoke less English and more Greek, most of it directed at his wife, most of it an order or demand. More weight fell away. Dad's bare legs were especially hard to look at, with protruding bones that seemed ready to snap. He started wearing three layers in mid-summer and sometimes even running the indoor heater. The house was a furnace, and caked in the sharp tang of urine from his drainage bag. He transitioned from walking unaided to needing a cane and finally a walking frame. Having mastered supported standing, my son had his own walking frame that he tiptoed around the house with. Dad's frame was aluminium, expensive, monochrome, and had a bench seat on which he could rest. My son's frame was plastic, cheap, multi-coloured, and had a clicking butterfly and caterpillar. The sight of the two of them carefully making their way down the hallway, one uncertain step at a time, would long live with me: gorgeously plump little baby stumps doddering alongside raw spaghetti-thin pensioner legs. Both marched on in diapers.

Dad was soon back in hospital. The diagnosis was a bad chest infection. He was to stay in for treatment and observation. I was somewhat relieved. The hospital was probably the best place for him, and also gave Mum a break at home. But then, two days later, my phone rang.

'We're sorry to report that your father fell and broke his hip,' the nurse said. 'We'll transfer him to the other hospital shortly, the orthopaedic surgeons are all there.'

Dad's pride and stubborn independence meant he had refused nursing assistance to walk to the bathroom. A week earlier, he'd fallen and cut open his head.

I wasn't at all optimistic. How could Dad, in such a weakened state, possibly survive something as serious as a hip operation? He'd go under the gas and never wake up. As they wheeled him into surgery, he was yelling at Mum about needing a new mobile phone, and saying that she should just leave him to die. He was also confused about how long he'd been in hospital, and even said I hadn't been to visit in weeks, despite being there almost every day.

And still, he survived surgery. He'd 'escaped' again. But now, he had another setback to overcome.

We often found Dad sitting up in bed, staring into space, or lying flat, sleeping. Usually, it was the latter. Mum sometimes sat there for hours waiting for him to wake up, was then barked at for doing something incorrectly or not to his liking, and limped home in disgust and disappointment. I knew that much of Dad's anger was frustration at himself, at his own ageing body failing him. As hard as it was to witness, I knew it was healthy. It was a spark. It was life.

Dad started to recount stories of regrets in his life. Things he could've done, should've done, or was prevented from doing. I tried to get him to forget about the past, the things he couldn't change, and instead focus on all the good things he had achieved, and the future, which finally included a grandson. But he couldn't. He went on and on.

He was soon seeing visions of those dearly departed in his dreams. His father and mother, other siblings, aunts, uncles, cousins. Visitations, is what they were called. Somewhere in there, he gave me some life advice:

'Sell your house, son,' he said. 'Live in ours.'

I took this as meaning:

'Don't waste your precious life working to pay off an arrangement of bricks and mortar like this old fool did. Take what I leave you, and go live your life.'

I thought about this intensely. Like so many gravely unwell people before him, Dad was staring into an abyss. I imagined that this often came with a glance over their shoulder and a reflection on what they'd achieved. They wanted to feel their short time on this planet had produced something, that their existence hadn't been futile.

It took four nurses and physiotherapists nearly half an hour to lift Dad using a special harness and move him to a chair. He needed to start sitting up, to return his lungs to a normal functioning position. Prior to this hospital admission, Dad's face had filled out, he looked almost normal again. I thought this was a good sign until I had it explained to me that it was pulmonary oedema, fluid retention. Dad's lungs were filling with fluid, the body struggling to pump blood and get oxygen, a sign of congestive heart failure. His chest infection had also worsened and he was now experiencing blood sepsis, which was blood poisoning from the infection. I was told he was being treated with the strongest antibiotics the hospital had, which was probably meant to reassure me but did nothing more than scare the living daylights out of me. Dad's blood pressure also plummeted when he sat up, which was a further sign of heart problems and a risk factor for another fall if he fainted on standing.

After a month, Dad was clearly tiring of life in hospital. The food was stodgy, bland, what little he ate. Mum visited the fifth-floor orthopaedic ward every day, taking home-cooked meals, but he was quite obviously lonely. He suggested she find a spare bed and sleep there in hospital. Then she wouldn't have to tire commuting each day, and he could see her all the time.

I wanted to decorate Dad's bare room with photos of his grandson. The environment was depressing.

'The baby doesn't belong in hospitals,' he told me. 'He shouldn't have to look at this all day.'

In the end, I crept in one evening while he slept and stuck up a few photos on the wall opposite his bed. When he woke to see them, the nurses said he smiled.

I took Dad's grandson to visit him whenever I could. We stood at the doorway of his room and spoke from there. We otherwise needed to wear protection to step inside, a disposable yellow hospital gown made of tissue paper and dark purple gloves, which always took my unfamiliar mother an inordinate amount of time to put on. The cold, antiseptic paper and plastic added an extra layer of distance between us and Dad. Undoubtedly, the highlight of Dad's hospital stay was the moment his grandson called him 'Papou'. It was as clear as a bell, the first time he'd ever said it, and made the small room shake with joy, which then frightened my son and made him cry. We cuddled away his tears; even Dad had a few. His doting grandmother was instantly and openly jealous. He'd yet to call her 'Yiayia', which were sounds that were harder to wrap his young, inexperienced tongue around. Dad flashed his gummy smile as if he'd won a contest.

❧

Mum and I were summoned for a meeting on a Wednesday morning. This had not previously happened. We were met by a cadre of medical professionals and shown into a small, private room with swipe card access. I quickly discerned that this was where such conversations were had. There was a bespectacled doctor, an intern with a sharp haircut, a senior nurse with a matronly quality, and a soft-eyed social worker, all looking very solemn. We sat and talked for half an hour. The doctor updated us on Dad's condition frankly and without self-censorship. Translating for my frail mother, I felt utterly powerless as I held her trembling hand.

The doctor said that Dad was facing an uphill battle. His heart was weak, his infections weren't clearing, they were turning septic, his blood pressure plummeting, repaired hip not healing, weight vanishing, confusion mounting. It was the lack of improvement that concerned the doctors most of all. At that age, in that condition, Dad couldn't just putter along, staying steady on the scale of health. He needed to either go up and improve, or down. There was no in between.

The thrust of the conversation was about ongoing care for Dad. The staff wanted to make clear that his chances of coming home were basically zero. He was still in the acute care phase, and needed to improve before they could even consider him leaving hospital. And then it would likely be to a nursing home or hospice. And then, even if he overcame those hurdles, his chances of making a full recovery were low. But the staff were willing to respect our wishes, which was partly why they scheduled the meeting – to find out what they were. Did Dad really want to come home? If he did, they'd find a way to make it happen, but they strongly recommended against it.

The doctor leaned in closer to me.

'We're not just looking after your dad here,' he said, 'we're looking after your mum too. She's not young and I think her health will suffer if your father goes home. You see how many people it takes here to look after him, working around the clock. Your mum won't be able to give such care.'

I explained all this to Mum and added that Dad could come home but he was likely coming home to die. 'If that's what you think he wants,' I said, 'then it can happen.'

Mum's face went red, her eyes filling with tears.

'No,' she said, 'I don't want him to come home to die. I'll see his bed all the time and it's all I'll think of.'

I gently asked what she thought Dad's wishes would be, and that it might perhaps be better to help grant him a final wish. What a gift, I said, to allow Dad to see out his days in the same home he'd had for fifty years. But Mum wasn't keen. It was her home, too, and she had to keep living in it. I turned back to the staff, continued the conversation, about medical prognoses and so on. After a few minutes, Mum intervened.

'Okay,' she said, composing herself, 'if he wants to come home, he can come. I'll be okay.'

The doctor then cut in and suggested we actually ask Dad what he wanted. We left the room and gathered around his bed. The doctor explained; I translated. Wide-eyed and open-mouthed, Dad paid careful attention, but I could tell he didn't understand even half of what was being said. In the end, there was no firm decision. The treatment course would continue in the hope that Dad would stabilise. We could then more properly revisit the issue, when something could actually be done. For the time being, Dad was going nowhere. It was all too risky. The staff left and Dad went back to watching TV. The twenty-four-hour racing channel was on.

I noticed Dad's eyes were glassy, unfocused, staring at the screen. He appeared to be watching, but I wasn't sure. Several times I asked him, 'Which horse won, Dad?' and he promptly, and correctly, responded with each winning horse number.

He said he wanted to go downstairs and put a bet on. He

claimed there was a betting shop at the hospital, downstairs in the foyer. I said the doctors weren't allowing him to go but that I would put the bet on for him. He said he didn't have any money in his wallet; I said I had money, just tell me your selection. He said he didn't know which horse he wanted, and needed a newspaper. So I went and bought one, brought it back upstairs, and watched him start to leaf through it. After a few minutes, he tired and went back to watching the TV.

The doctor returned. 'We've got some new test results that are very concerning,' he told me.

It turned out Dad had dangerously high levels of potassium in his blood which could cause paralysis, an irregular heartbeat or heart failure. The likely reason for the high reading was renal failure. Dad's kidneys were now in the firing line, and the doctor said he was too weak for renal dialysis. He proposed treatment with calcium gluconate and calcium resonium to lower the potassium levels, but said they were now only treating symptoms, not the cause. They would re-check Dad's blood later that night to see if his potassium levels had lowered. His latest ECG also showed stress on his heart. I spoke with Dad gently, tried to explain what was happening. He either didn't quite understand or didn't want to understand, and was happy to let the doctors do their work, despite loathing their practice.

Night fell. My uncle and aunt arrived, and we all sat around Dad's bed, listening to him breathe. It was then that I heard it. The sound no one ever wants to hear in a hospital – the dreaded death rattle. Fluids were accumulating in Dad's throat and upper chest, which came from an inability to swallow. He was too weak to cough up the fluid filling his lungs. He asked for vomit bags, tried to cough and spit, but produced little. He was too weak. It was perhaps the saddest moment of the whole ordeal: watching Dad trying to make his body respond to the simplest request, and seeing it fail.

'This is what happens when people are close to death,' my aunt said curtly. 'Now, it's just a matter of time.'

The brusque nature of her words cut me, but my aunt had seen it many times. Worst of all, Dad now had no more anger at the world. It was heartbreaking to see it gone.

CHAPTER 42

2016

WITH AN IRREVERSIBLE process now underway, it was time to surrender what little I knew about the situation and hand it over to an infinitely more powerful force: my Greek heritage and culture.

We gathered around Dad to wait for the inevitable. It was a surreal feeling, me with my family, chatting pleasantly, even gossiping, while one of the circle lay in a sterile bed, dying. And yet, this was what was done. The community came together and waited out of respect, a hushed but respectful vigil. They sometimes even included the dying in their conversation, trying to make the occasion seem as normal as possible. The last sense a dying person loses is their hearing, which was why visitors were so content with sitting around Dad's bed, speaking gently. It was a way of including the dying in life for as long as possible.

We asked if Dad was in pain; he said he wasn't, and had only been soon after his hip operation. He was not on morphine, and only took paracetamol as required, as if he had a headache. He was not hooked up to any machines, intravenous drips or oxygen masks. This was another small mercy for which we were incredibly grateful.

My non-Greek wife arrived, sat awkwardly with the Greeks, listening to us speaking Greek, not understanding, and watching us casually waiting for a man to die, a morbid ritual if ever she saw one. To her, I may have looked at home, but I was sitting just as uncomfortably, trying to make sense of the moment. After a while, my mum suggested Jayne should go, saying she probably needed to get back to our baby, whom she'd left with her own mother for the evening. Jayne got up to leave, wished Dad adieu, and stepped to the door. Then, as if sensing that it wasn't just another hospital visit, she spun back around, faced the bed, and said:

'We love you, Bill.'

We stayed at the hospital a little while longer, watching Dad irregularly lurch forward in bed to manipulate something that he was seeing before his eyes. At one point, I saw him throw off the covers and pour himself an imaginary 'whiskey', before spooning a forkful of 'spaghetti', and peeling and eating a 'mandarin'.

'That's what people do when they're about to die,' said my aunt again. 'They see things.'

It was a form of delirium, changes with the brain chemistry. Mum asked Dad what he could see, and he responded 'the sun' and 'water'. Dad loved the beach, the ocean, was once a fisherman, so all I could think was that he pictured himself in happier times, as a young man who felt the salty wind in his hair as his boat skipped across the waves, and who cooked and ate his catch by an open fire in the sand. Growing tired, we kissed Dad on the forehead, tucked him in for warmth, and said we'd see him tomorrow, leaving the nurses to check his blood pressure and offer a pre-warmed blanket.

I slept restlessly, my son now teething and waking us every few hours in agony. Like his *papou*, he had paracetamol for relief. I returned to the hospital in the morning. Mum was out with my aunt; they had an appointment at the hairdresser, and the nurses insisted they keep it. The TV was on, the racing channel again, with the sound down, the speaker controller next to Dad's ear, muted. Dad wasn't watching, his eyes closed, seemingly sleeping. I coughed accidentally, which made Dad open his eyes. He tried to speak but I had great difficulty understanding him. His words were drawn out, his mouth fixed in a permanent 'O', his jaw sagging. Overnight, his condition had deteriorated even further.

The local Greek Orthodox priest visited. He came to bless Dad and was pleased to find him conscious, responsive. The priests only blessed those communicants who responded. Many didn't. I was pleased to see a spark of life go on behind Dad's eyes the moment he tasted the tiny spoonful of consecrated wine, as if to say: 'Ah, flavour!'

'I was here visiting someone else and heard you were on the floor, so came by to see how you were feeling, hope you don't mind . . .'

This was our sagacious priest's explanation to Dad for his visit. Because dying people were sometimes traumatised by seeing the priest, he now came pre-prepared with an excusatory line. Some Greeks believed the sight of the priest meant they now 'had their ticket' and were cleared for departure, as if the soul was waiting for the priest's blessing before it could finally let the body go.

My mum and aunt arrived, their haircuts grey and neat, although Mum thought hers was too short, too boyish. Dad was now refusing all food and water, which was another sign of the body preparing. Because it no longer required nutrients or fluid, so too had it lost all desire for food and hydration. I again offered Dad a drink; he seemed to reluctantly agree to a mouthful, as if he knew it would make his son happy. Gently tipping forth the blue plastic cup, I fed Dad what turned out to be his very last sip of water. At that moment, as I watched half the water disappear down Dad's angular throat and the other half down his chin, I couldn't help but picture my own son. I'd also fed him water that same morning with his plastic sippy cup, and it produced roughly the same result, soaking most of his robot-themed bib. It was at that moment that I finally shed tears.

We stayed until my mum and aunt tired. Mum wanted to stay all night in case Dad called out for her. But he was growing increasingly quiet and Mum suspected he would just sleep all night, so her presence was less likely to be missed. The nurses assured us they would check on Dad every hour and call if there was any urgency. We kissed Dad on the forehead, saying 'I love you' and 'See you tomorrow'. With eyes closed, he murmured his appreciation, and slept.

The next morning, I prepared to return to hospital. I played with my son, tickling him into a state of delirious laughter on our living room rug. He was changing more and more, a personality emerging, incredibly interactive and also cheeky. He was standing almost independently and would soon be walking, then running, then being chased by a frantic father who feared all manner of mischief and skinned knees. I called my mum; she said she was going to hospital with Dad's brother, and that I should come later. I stepped into the shower, heard my son rush the shower screen, which he liked to bash on while I was in there.

And then, just as I was rinsing away the final suds, my phone rang.

I called to Jayne to answer it. She said it was the hospital. I told her to keep them on the line while I dried off. Wearing only a towel, I took the phone. It was a nurse's gentle voice.

'I'm sorry Peter, but your father passed away. It was only just now, ten minutes ago.'

I rubbed my eyes. This was it, the moment that had been building for years, for decades. I was the first to know and would need to tell Mum. I was momentarily numbed but knew things would now need to be organised. I thanked the nurse and said we'd be there soon. With our son in her arms, Jayne gave me a hug. Still in my towel, I retreated to our bedroom to call Mum. I wanted to catch her before she left with my uncle. I wanted us to all drive there together.

I was too late. When Mum answered her phone, I could hear the noise of the car, of surrounding traffic.

'Mum,' I said, 'Dad's gone.'

She broke down. I couldn't even imagine the pain Mum was experiencing and wanted to be there in person to hold her close and properly share her grief. But then I pictured her in the car with my uncle, her husband's last remaining and closest sibling. He would be hurting, too, perhaps even more than me. Like me, he'd known my dad his entire life, which was twice as long as mine. They'd migrated to Australia together, bought houses around the corner from each other, holidayed together, and raised sons together. They even shared a love of gambling on the nags.

Mum said she wouldn't enter the ward and would wait outside for me to arrive. I called my aunt and organised to pick her up. Despite her raw, unfiltered view of death, it was soothing to have her there so I wouldn't have to make the long painful journey alone.

We met my mum and uncle in the hospital foyer. They hadn't dared to go up to the fifth floor. Mum's face was red with sadness, with instant and intense grief. I held her close and let her sob into my hoodie sweatshirt. We filed solemnly into the lift, went upstairs, filed out again. Mum sobbed as we approached the ward. The nurse who called me expressed his condolences in person and gave us a moment to gather ourselves and dress in the requisite protective clothing.

'I've bandaged his head and jaw,' the nurse said gently. 'His mouth was otherwise open.'

I thanked him and hand-in-hand with Mum, we pushed open the door and went inside.

Mum was shaking uncontrollably as she approached Dad's body, tears in her eyes and on her cheeks, her purple-gloved hands all over his face. I stood behind her, holding her. I found my face softening when I saw Dad lying there, looking quite calm and peaceful, finally free of the body that had run its course.

'His soul is still here, right above us, circling the room,' my aunt said.

The nurse's bandage wrapped around Dad's head, under his jaw, and knotted on the top of his head. It made Dad look like he had a mere toothache. I brushed back his grey hair, felt the coldness of his creased forehead. One eye was open, his left one. Mum reached in and gently pulled it closed, only to watch it flip up again like a stubborn roller blind, much to her frustration.

And so, a quiet sadness filled the room. We settled in again, in plastic chairs around the bed, for hushed conversation with Dad, as if nothing had happened. It was comforting, if not a little eerie. My mum and aunt discussed the body, how Dad looked, his grand head as prominent as ever, his thin body near invisible under the pale blue covers. They talked about upcoming arrangements, the church, relatives, friends. My uncle was emotional. My aunt chastised him lightly, told him to settle down. I imagined this was more out of care and love than anything else. He fired back, unhappy with her criticism, pretended to show the back of his hand, and said he was going home.

Quite unexpectedly, I found myself putting Dad's passing into immediate perspective. I couldn't explain why this happened, but didn't fight the thoughts as they came. For years, I had feared the death of a parent. I thought it would be the worst day imaginable, and that I would crumble into a thousand inconsolable pieces. It wasn't just them dying – it was *me* too, *my* life was also stopping. And yet, there I was, breathing, thinking, seeing. Life went on all around me. People worked their jobs, drove their cars, ordered their coffees, the world kept turning. I had seen friends die in their twenties and thirties, of illnesses and motor vehicle accidents, at the hands of pancreatic cancer and drunk drivers. They never got to marry, procreate, succeed and age. These were true tragedies, lives only half lived, stories half finished. By contrast, Dad had lived a full life with many blessings. He saw youth, moved to another country, became a husband and then a parent, paid off his house, watched his child grow and marry, became a grandparent, and lived long enough to see his face become creased with age. My young dead friends saw only a fraction.

Jayne visited and paid her respects. Mum insisted her adored grandson stay out of the room. She was soon crying again, expressing guilt at not being there at the end, to hold her husband's hand while he slipped away. I held Mum tightly and whispered in her ear, reminding her of the tangible difference we'd made to Dad's life. By rights, he should've died much earlier. For years, I escorted Dad to medical appointments, translating, educating, querying and communicating, all to ensure that my ex-smoking, cancer-surviving, pacemaker-wearing, whiskey-drinking, overmedicated, diabetic, non-English-speaking father could squeeze every last remaining droplet of juice out of life's lemon. And of course Mum had given everything she had; her home-cooked meals and loving care and resilience in absorbing Dad's verbal abuse and demands. Together, we'd done all we could, and could have done no more.

With final kisses, we said our goodbyes.

It was raining by the time we pulled into the driveway at home. All around us were signs of Dad. The sensor light he'd installed. The garage freezer he'd stockpiled full of discounted supermarket meat. His delicate *flitzani* coffee cups and pharmacy slippers. Mum had had six weeks to get used to the house without Dad but it suddenly felt emptier than ever. She looked at the big space for the first time as a widow, as a woman who knew her husband was never coming home again.

I rang Jayne and asked her to visit with our son. Whether Mum wanted to or not, her face would smile the second she saw him. Mum heard me speaking and asked her daughter-in-law to stop at the local shop and buy a jar of coffee and bottle of brandy. Visitors would be coming and those were essential Greek offerings during a time of mourning.

Mum's landline telephone soon started ringing. It had probably been ringing all day, but she was finally there to answer it. Visitors were soon arriving. Brandies were taken by all, a drink to honour the departed.

The vast majority of visitors were old ladies wearing black. They too were either widowed or had husbands in nursing homes with dementia or cancer. Some of them had even lost children. I greeted them warmly, tried to remember their names, failed consistently. Somehow, it was as if my whole life was defined by such women. They were seemingly at every Greek gathering I'd ever been to – not those same women, of course, but rather their collective presence – talking to each other quietly, respectfully. When I was young, I was scared by them. But as I grew older, I found myself developing an immense sense of admiration for them, their stoicism and strength. At times, I even found myself querying whether they possessed some form of mystical power.

Mum's first night alone in the house would not be easy. My aunt offered to stay; so did I. Mum refused, saying she had no choice but to get used to it soon. Looking tired, she went to bed early, but claimed she wouldn't sleep. She already knew she had another long day ahead.

Mum insisted that I take my son and wife to a children's concert we'd pre-bought tickets for. It was only half an hour. Junior needed a breastfeed halfway through the show and was a bit intimidated by the crowd of writhing, squealing, crying little people. But his dad teared up at every song he recognised from his own childhood in a mess of nostalgia and memory.

'It has to be a darker colour for an older person,' she said.

The funeral director said they could even weave through some blue flowers, as if to honour the Greek flag. The overall price was about what we expected, in the thousands. Fortunately, on the advice of his brother, my dad had had the foresight to purchase a twin burial plot the previous year, for himself and his wife. The plots were increasing in price by the day.

As part of the burial arrangements, the funeral director also came to pick up the clothes in which Dad was to be buried. It was something I'd not given much thought. Fortunately, Mum had. She had already selected his best suit, navy, with a matching waistcoast, a pinstripe white shirt and dark red tie. It was exactly what he'd worn to my wedding three years earlier, and my son's baptism three months earlier. A pair of black shoes he'd never worn, black socks, crisp white underpants, and even a hat he'd only recently purchased from a pharmacy and also never worn. In line with tradition, Mum slipped a little money into his wallet. It was to ensure his safe journey to the other side; apparently, there were tolls that needed to be paid. Then she added a notepad and pencil, and a comb for his hair. She carefully laid in his *komboloi*, the worry beads which had brought Dad so much relaxation and meditation. And lastly, his walking stick, which became like a trusted friend in his later years. Watching Mum fussing and carefully arranging the clothes neatly on a chair, my heart ached. She had been caring for her husband for nearly sixty years and knew this was the last thing she would ever do for him. She wanted to send him off looking immaculate, as a final expression of her love.

As I sat there, speaking with the funeral director, answering his questions, my eye was distracted. I couldn't help but be struck by the arrangement of Dad's last clothes, all laid out on the chair opposite. It was as if someone was preparing to go out for the day and they were considering how they might look. I could almost picture my dad standing opposite, carefully scrutinising the outfit. Hmm, this tie, or that one? Which shirt? Dad was never a very formal man, he preferred to wear casual shirts, shorts, singlets, sneakers, sandals. But for major events, he absolutely dressed up. And this was a major event.

The funeral was two days later. Mum and I drove to Saint Nicholas in Dad's car. We lit candles in the narthex and took up our positions in the front row of the church. Dad was already there, waiting for us at the altar. The casket and flowers were fitting and elegant. As was customary, the casket was placed facing east with the feet towards the altar.

Eligibility for an Orthodox funeral was strict. Baptism in a Greek Orthodox Church was required, but this was nullified if the deceased violated one or more of the canon laws, which included suicide or marriage outside the Orthodox Church. If the deceased was to be cremated after death, they were also deemed ineligible. Despite not being overly religious, Dad qualified. Organ donation and donating the body to medical research were also prohibited by the Orthodox Church. The body was sacred.

'The servant of God Vasilios, who has fallen asleep . . .'

It was a stock-standard funeral service. This was something I realised from attending many Greek funerals. No matter whether the deceased was rich or poor, loved or hated, they entered the world in the same way – with a standard Orthodox baptism – and left it the same way. There was no personalisation of the ceremony short of the priest mentioning the deceased's immediate family. I thought this was a shortcoming of the service, and considered asking the priest whether I could say a short eulogy. But, I reminded myself, this was something much bigger than me, and who was I to try to alter something so steeped in tradition. Dad probably would've wanted it that way. *No fuss, just like you do for everyone else, I'm no better or lesser than them, everyone is the same before God.* As with every time I was at church with Mum, I followed her lead, stood when she stood, sat when she sat, crossed myself when she crossed herself. The service included readings, prayers and hymns. The priest swung the censer and led in the singing of the hymn, *Trisagion*. The chanter was in his nineties and had the voice of a songbird.

Mum was strong and stayed composed during the ceremony. I whispered words of support and encouragement in her ear from time to time. But she still cried when she approached the casket, touched it, walked around. We then stood in the front row and received the condolences of the mourners who had all passed around the casket. Some of my non-Greek friends later told me they felt awkward doing that, but were encouraged to do so by the Greeks who did not discriminate and followed the necessary customs for a funeral service.

I was one of six pallbearers at the cemetery. Dad's site was adjacent to a car park, next to a large ornamental rock and freshly planted native garden. I thought it was a splendid location. Because it was further into the cemetery grounds, it made it harder to access, but also isolated it from the nearby industrial suburb.

The priest arrived, delivered a short service, and again recited the *Trisagion*. Mum broke down as the engine clicked into gear and slowly lowered the casket into the grave. Symbolically, she folded a black scarf over her head, which signified the start of the mourning period. It would last for forty days.

I watched from behind dark sunglasses, deeply saddened to see Dad's casket being lowered into the earth. It was a final solemn act, but also came with a sense of relief at its completion.

As with the church service, Dad was buried with his feet facing east, ostensibly so he could sit up and watch the rising sun. A bowl of *koliva*, a dish of boiled wheat with honey, symbolising the cyclical nature of life and the sweetness of Heaven, was emptied into the grave. The funeral director offered a small bucket with soil; each mourner took a spadeful and tossed it into the grave, followed by rose petals. With the help of his attentive mother, even our eleven-month-old son tossed in a few petals, and said a final goodbye to his *papou*.

Jayne handed our son to me. He was calm in my arms, watching the wind push a few errant petals into the grave. It had been a long, emotional day. *I carried my father*, I thought, *but I held my son*.

It felt surreal to imagine I wouldn't see Dad again. In the lead-up to the funeral, I'd seen his face in more photos than I had in ages. Except he was younger, in his seventies, and healthy, his eyes bright, with fat on his bones and colour in his cheeks. It hurt to picture how much he'd aged and become a shadow of himself. Conversationally, Dad had never so much as talked 'with' me as he did 'at' me, telling me his viewpoint on whatever topic. Perhaps that was due to being a man, or perhaps it was due to me not being his blood; I could never be sure. But he'd always been there, a constant force in my life. I knew that Mum would especially need all my support. Despite his many shortcomings, Dad had been good company for her for more than half a century. She told me she'd already started talking to his photo in the evenings, the one I had enlarged and taken to the funeral, and which we'd since hung on the living room wall. The photo now kept her company.

It was only when I thought about the good times with Dad that my eyes got moist. When I pictured him feeding his aviary of canaries, the summers he proudly tended his garden, and the few times he managed to play with his grandson. It was sad to imagine he wouldn't be doing those things anymore.

My father was a good man. He had a rough edge; that was indisputable, even his adoring wife would not debate that. He carried a lot of negative energy just beneath the surface. And yet Dad's qualities were undeniable. He took great pride in his summer garden, which produced tomatoes that tasted like real tomato. He had a deep love for animals; he was fascinated by wildlife documentaries and fed the local magpies, particularly when they had young, calling to them with a knife tapped loudly on a glass jar until they swooped down and took the soft wet morsels of mincemeat from his fingers. He serviced my various jalopy cars for nearly twenty years, often fixing them himself, or towing me home when I'd broken down. He was ingenious enough to fix whatever had broken around the house with whatever scraps he had in his shed. At times, this made our property appear like a junkyard, but the job always got done. He constantly brought groceries for me and Jayne, particularly fruits and vegetables, whether we wanted them or not. He loved the beach and the ocean. He loved to drink a thick shot of Greek coffee, and to while away a long afternoon betting on the horses. He was eternally devoted to Mum and to me. We were only three, but a family nonetheless. I remembered being young and how excited I used to become when Dad came home at the end of the day. When he wasn't there, I was anxious, but that eased the second I heard his key in the door. The family unit was together again, everyone was safe under one roof, and I was happy.

As hard as it had been to bear witness, it was a privilege to see Dad's final days. I marvelled at how the body naturally shut down. Stopped needing food, stopped needing water. I'd only just seen my son come into the world, kicking and screaming and totally unsure of how to function. Dying, on the other hand, had an order to it, a sequence, slow and gradual. I knew that birth had a sequence, too, although much of it was unseen. Birth was chaos, an explosion, suddenly there was this newborn creature, screaming, without the slightest idea what it wanted. By contrast, a body shutting down and preparing for death was like an implosion: ordered, the body closing itself, one organ system at a time.

A memory slowly pushed its way to the front of my mind. I was young, perhaps about seven or eight, and going to swimming lessons at the local public pool. For many years, Dad had lived in Thessaloniki, which was a thriving port. He loved the water, and fishing, and was an adroit swimmer. He wanted me to be the same, to be comfortable and confident in the water, to experience the same joy as he did, floating, swimming, diving. But I never took to the water well. I thrashed like a caught fish and feared drowning more than I appreciated the sensation of swimming, which felt scarily foreign.

The memory was of me floating backwards with a kickboard at the local pool and staring up at the blue Australian sky. As usual, I was struggling, taking in water, squirming, flailing, drowning. Suddenly, Dad appeared in my peripheral vision, walking poolside, his arms outstretched, simulating the act of swimming as he watched me struggle and twitch.

'Relax,' he kept saying, 'breathe, nothing to fear. The water is a safe place. Be free.'

I never mastered the aquatic art and remained a poor swimmer. But Dad's lesson did not go unheeded. In so many other areas of my life, fear became my enemy. With Dad's words in mind, I went on to accomplish more than I would otherwise have ever imagined. I sought out new opportunities and experiences, new countries and knowledge. And now, thanks to Dad again, I feared one less aspect of life – its end.

What an incredible lesson for a parent to teach their child.

CHAPTER 44

2017

MY SON AND I were going for a walk through the Australian bush. I'd done the same thing with his mum nineteen months earlier in the hope the exercise and movement would bring on labour. It didn't, but I didn't consider our son's desire to remain in the womb as a reflection of any aversion to nature. Since his birth, he'd been up the mountain in an all-terrain stroller pushed by his mum, and in a Swedish-designed ergonomic carrier strapped to his dad. But we were a big boy now and could walk independently. Friends had warned me the time would pass quickly. They were right.

Of course, a doddering toddler now meant that any excursion took twice as long. My son walked at half pace and was continually distracted. He stopped to collect sticks, investigate burrows, and point at things in the trees and sky, crimson rosellas and glossy black cockatoos. I marvelled at his inquisitiveness with the world, at his attention to detail, spotting birds looping overhead and rabbits darting through the scrub. On this overcast afternoon, I was hoping to show him some native animals. Kangaroos were most likely; their spherical black droppings were everywhere, here in the bush, on our lawn and throughout the suburb. Spiny echidnas and swamp wallabies and wombats were rarer. But all appeared to be hiding. The mountain landscape was undulating, dotted with scribbly gums, drooping she-oak and red stringybark. Its vegetation was dry, influenced by aspect, slope, fire history, soil depth and human activity. There was even evidence of Aboriginal campsites, deposits of chert sedimentary rock once used to make stone tools.

Slowly, with peeks of the late summer sun on our backs, we made our way up the mountain's western side. On the eastern side stood a vineyard, solar farm, scout camp and shooting range. But between them was a pine forest and labyrinth of mountain-biking tracks.

'That's for when you're older,' I told my son hopefully, imagining the two of us one day riding our bikes together.

But he wasn't listening, and instead fascinated by a squashed bottle cap covered in red fire ants. My own ears pricked at the familiar sound of rubber crunching on dirt as two mountain-bikers came hurtling down the trail. I crouched down low and held my son close to make sure he didn't unexpectedly dart across their path. Dressed in garish fluoro colours and on equally bright aluminium frames, the bikers consciously slowed as they saw us, and we acknowledged each other with polite nods. From the other direction, riding up the mountain, came an old bloke, shirtless, his back the colour of golden bronze. He was puffing hard but still managed a smile.

'Come on,' I urged my son, and lifted my sneakered feet, pretending to jog up the track. He smiled broadly and giggled, commencing to stamp his own feet and trying to run behind me. But his sandals stuck beneath his feet and he struggled. I was careful to turn and position myself to catch him, knowing that he could fall face-first into the dirt at any moment. Still, that was how kids grew and learned, and it was usually not anything that couldn't be fixed with a cuddle after a little cry. Sadly, those moments would also soon be gone.

Having walked up the mountain's fire trail, we finally reached the turnoff for our destination. It took some convincing to coax my son to follow me along the single track veering off to our left. He was now fascinated by a termite mound. The larger trees on the mountain were almost all hollow thanks to termites. He couldn't yet see where I was taking him, but it was somewhere new and special. It was a place that I remembered fondly from my youth and which had stood the test of time despite many years of severe erosion and variable rainfall.

'This way,' I told him, 'nearly there.'

He giggled, showing his precious new teeth, and tried to run. He was eventually undone by an unseen tree root. I rushed to his aid, picked him up, held him close and applied medicinal kisses. His grizzling soon subsided as I carried him the rest of the way and finally showed him my surprise.

At first, he was unsure of the watery expanse before him. The dam was calm, its water dirty brown above a clay base. Fallen branches rested in the water like a giant's slender fingers. My son stood in the protective space between the triangle of my legs, staring out with intense brown eyes. On this day, the dam appeared like the mountain itself: lifeless, without even a thirsty grey kangaroo lapping at its surface. Hoping to have shown him some wildlife at the watering hole, I couldn't help but feel disappointed. A platypus or long-necked turtle would've been a highlight. Instead, the dam was replete with aquatic insects and an introduced species of mosquitofish, now considered a noxious pest due to its impact on native fish populations and frog species.

Hand-in-hand, we walked carefully along the dam's exposed soil banks in a clockwise direction. My son was soon imploring me, wanting to drag me into the water, to drown us both in the murky depths, his curiosity getting the better of his fear. He was pulling on my arm, his face tensing and contorting in agony.

'No, mate,' I told him, 'can't go in there.'

My resistance was wise, but I sensed it was also about to bring on a tantrum. In this situation, Jayne had told me, the best form of parenting was distraction. I looked around, but there wasn't much on offer in the dry, desolate bush. Finally, I peered down and saw the solution, on the ground around my feet.

'Watch this,' I said, and attempted to skip a rock across the dam. It skipped once across the glossy surface before disappearing from sight. I was never a good rock skipper. My son watched attentively but was even more enthralled when I picked up a larger rock and proceeded to simply toss it into the drink with a deep and resonant 'gloop!' He laughed loudly and brushed his hands behind his ears in excitement. He was soon collecting his own pebbles and cheerfully throwing them into the water, sometimes double-handed. It was the best game ever. I revelled in his pleasure, at his sheer unbridled joy from the simple act of throwing rocks into water. It warmed my heart like sunshine through my veins.

It took some time to complete a full circuit of the dam. My son climbed on every log and rock he saw, wanting to be taller like his dad. With bulging nappy hanging out of his shorts, he stopped every few metres to pick up every loose pebble he saw. We then tossed them into the water, listening to them splash, watching the ripples radiate, laughing. My son's arm was still weak, his technique poor, so he had to throw from the dam's very edge. I was careful to make sure he didn't take one step too many, although I was certain his mother would notice the mud on his sandals. She had stayed home to rest, hopefully to nap. Jayne was about to enter her third trimester. Like the first time, the realisation that she was pregnant had been almost as unexpected, but just as joyous. We had tried to explain it to our son and we hoped he understood, but were still expecting his world to turn upside-down in three months time when our cosy house became even cosier.

I sighed lightly. It was moments like these that I wished I could share with my brothers. And my dad.

I wanted my son to appreciate such moments of silence and value small moments of joy. To teach him that life was contained in the skipping of stones across water, the petrichor of the dry bush after rain, and the sighting of a joey's floppy head inside their mother's pouch. But if I was being completely honest, that was actually what he was teaching me.

Tired from throwing, laughing and walking, my son stepped forward to proffer his outstretched arms; the universal sign of 'pick me up'. Having feared another tantrum at the prospect of ending his fun, I was relieved. I hoisted him up; he nestled comfortably into my collarbone, breathing deeply. I carried him home, struggling with his growing weight. At least it was downhill. As I walked, I imagined what it would be like to take our second born up the mountain in a few years time, and perhaps how our son would teach them how to throw rocks into the dam.

CHAPTER 45

2017

JAYNE WAS BOOKED in for an induction. She was again past forty weeks pregnant and there was still no sign of the baby. They'd let her go even longer last time, but not this time. She had gestational diabetes, which makes the placenta deteriorate early. The diabetes forced her to go on insulin, and otherwise curtail her sweet tooth. The baby grew from the size of a poppy seed to a sweet pea, then a strawberry, mango, coconut, pineapple and now watermelon. So we packed our bags and headed for the hospital. Jayne had her birth plan, pregnancy books, electrical nerve stimulation machine, relaxation music and wheat-based heatpacks. I had a pair of old boardshorts, which I tossed into the car at the last minute.

It was so much more civilised this time; like going for an appointment. Fortunately, it was a Monday, which meant our son went to daycare. It was a regular day for him, but he could tell that something was up. Mummy and Daddy didn't usually leave together in the mornings, with a bag packed, and Dad with board-shorts slung over his shoulder. But then again, he'd known for some time that something was awry, that his world was about to change. The baby's room was ready. There had been lots of long, explanatory conversations and new picture books. And, of course, Mummy's growing tummy. We knew it was going to be a testing time for him as he adjusted to not being exclusively in the parental limelight. We expected a change in behaviour. We expected tantrums. We expected him to try to yank the baby's arms off.

I felt anxious as we arrived at hospital and not for the same reasons as Jayne. The last time I was there, eleven months earlier, it was after the phone call to say that Dad had died. Jayne had given me the option of having our second baby in another hospital. A fresh start, she said. I thanked her for thinking of me but said no. It was the hospital she wanted. It was where our first was born, the set-up was familiar, the midwives we knew. I would fight my emotions and somehow overcome my negative association.

We settled into our room on the third floor. Jayne's blood pressure was checked; it was normal. The baby's heart rate was also good. She confided in me that she was worried about being induced, having heard the pain could be more intense than a natural birth. I reassured her that she was in good hands, in a modern hospital with excellent medical staff and the latest technology and medications.

Come mid-morning, the midwife artificially broke the waters. We were told to go for a walk, to climb stairs, to have a strong coffee, perhaps a double shot. Anything to get things moving.

Carefully holding the hand of my spherical wife, we did it all.

We walked between buildings, up and down stairs, to the café, the car park, the other café. I saw the place where I ordered Dad his last cappuccino, and the gift shop where I bought him a box of chocolates, which went unopened. I ended up giving them to the nursing staff in thanks. I avoided the fifth floor altogether. I wasn't yet ready.

Meanwhile, there was nothing happening with the baby. Returning to our room, Jayne was put on a drip of oxytocin and told to do circles on an exercise ball. She was in good spirits, laughing and joking. But we both sensed that was all about to change.

The contractions were soon coming. Jayne was leaning hard on the bed, sucking in lungfuls of oxygen. She was next humming, rhythmically swaying back and forth. I followed my instructions, reminded her of her labour plan, helped with her Ujjayi breathing and use of the electrical nerve machine. I brought cups of water and slivers of ice and rotated through the music selection. The baby's heart rate was continually monitored and the rate of the drip adjusted.

One of the midwives suggested Jayne take a hot shower. She was initially reluctant; she'd tried both showers and baths the first time, which in the end only made her more nauseous. But she eventually agreed. After twenty minutes, I was told to go change into my boardshorts.

I headed down the corridor to the staff bathroom. I was still removing my T-shirt when I heard a sharp knock on the door. A frantic voice said: 'Quick, the baby is coming!'

I finished changing with some urgency and raced back up the

corridor in only my boardshorts. Barefoot and bare-chested, I felt like I was heading to the beach or pool, not a birth. Back in the room, I skipped towards the shower but in my haste missed seeing the water on the floor, overflowing from the bathroom. I slipped on the tiles, only to catch myself against the door frame. The midwives fired me a look of disapproval. At that moment, the last thing they needed was a husband with torn ankle ligaments.

The pushing began, the encouragement and anticipation building. I didn't expect it so soon but was told the baby was coming.

The head appeared, hairy and wet. Jayne was weakening fast, the contractions having doubled, but was told to keep going. As part of the birth plan, I kept reminding her that what she was experiencing was healthy pain, and that every contraction was one less to have, and that soon there would be zero.

After sixteen minutes of pushing, the baby was born. At three hours total, the labour was short but still intense. I was in awe of my amazing wife. Despite being petite, she had now delivered two babies, both in excess of four kilos, both naturally, and only once with an epidural. I vowed to think twice the next time I went to complain of man flu.

It took us a while to compose ourselves and check the gender. We were wet and tired and emotional. It was another boy. We laughed and cried.

We immediately felt more confident with him: holding, soothing, feeding. If only you could have your second child before your first. He seemed to sense our confidence and was instantly calm. Kids, I decided, were like animals: they could sense your fear.

The placenta was birthed, big and blue, bloody and glorious. Last time, I buried the placenta in my parents' front lawn and planted an ornamental plum tree on top. The midwives were overjoyed for their role in a near perfect birth. I could tell that they would soon be bragging about it to their colleagues.

The two grandmothers visited, along with the now bigger brother, excited, uncertain. Jayne told me to hold the baby; she had prepared for this moment, and knew our first-born would rush headlong into her arms the moment he saw her. He did exactly that but soon turned to greet his new baby brother, whom I held out for him to see. It was touching to see him embrace his newborn sibling. No doubt it wouldn't be long before they were fighting over toys, then bikes, then car keys. More than anything, I was glad to have given my children the gift of a sibling. I didn't want them to grow up an only child like their dad.

Gifts were exchanged. Bigger brother offered a plush monkey comforter, which matched his own beloved teddy one. Meanwhile, baby brother gifted two toy Bananas in Pyjamas, as if to signify the newly formed team of B1 and B2. Their parents, fortunately, came prepared.

I handed the new baby to my mum, who was soon sobbing lightly. I knew she was thinking of Dad, who would never get to see his second grandchild. At eighty-six, Mum complained about her many aches and pains and yet somehow always found the energy for the new generation. She picked up by hand every single biscuit crumb that my son dropped and still smothered him with kisses. Deep down, she knew she was incredibly lucky.

Jayne glowed with post-birth hormones, but was at the same

time reflective. She felt a sense of loss about the pregnancy being over, because it was such a unique experience, full of anticipation.

'I want to bottle this short time with the new one,' she told me.

'Time flies,' I replied.

Having a big healthy baby was a blessing, but it also meant they would be little for an even shorter time. Our first-born about to move from the Nursery room to Tiny Tots at daycare was another reminder of that.

I told my brother the news that night.

'He sounds even bigger than the first!' Georgios said.

He was bigger; nearly four-and-a-half kilos in new speak, almost ten pounds in old.

'He'll be beating up his older brother before you know it,' Georgios said.

The next morning, as I prepared to leave the hospital with my sleeping newborn and sleepy wife, I knew I had something to do. I excused myself and took a detour via the fifth floor. My heart was racing, palms sweaty, mouth dry. Slowly, I walked the corridors, one careful step after another. I sat in the visitor area, pretending to watch the TV and read a magazine. I even saw a few familiar faces on the nursing staff. They recognised me instantly and asked how I was doing. When they asked why I was back at the hospital, their faces lit up. What wonderful news, they said.

It sure was.

CHAPTER 46

2017

IT WAS MY eldest son's third Christmas. And, as his dad, I'd come up with unquestionably the best gift ever.

My son hadn't really understood his first two Christmases, but was much more cluey the third time around. He knew the significance of lights and trees, of reindeer and tinsel, and recognised Santa like a celebrity; which, in a way, he is at that time of year. Early on the morning of the twenty-fifth, my son was overwhelmed with presents from loving relatives. He seemed to derive almost as much pleasure opening each carefully wrapped box as he did the eventual item, all plastic and colourful and maddeningly noisy. But there was something missing – a present from Dad.

I was no fan of Christmas. Over the years, I'd seen it become an increasingly commercial holiday that seemed to cause more stress than joy. I saw people rushing to the shops in the lead-up, and then saw charity bins overflowing by New Years. I saw gift pets abandoned at shelters in January. Families got together, they ate and drank and argued and fought. Loneliness was felt more acutely. But I also understood that Christmas was a time for children. I enjoyed it when I was one myself and fully intended to pass on the tradition.

'I've got a present for you as well, son,' I told him, 'but I'll give it to you later today.'

He looked up at me, his young face a combination of excitement and confusion. What was silly old Dad talking about?

By late morning, I showed him. I was taking my son on his first bus ride.

The allure of the long vehicular monster that snakes its way through suburbia looms large when you're a kid. My son eagerly pointed out every bus he saw like it was the first he'd ever seen. Little kids sing songs about buses at daycare. My son already had several toy buses which he regularly destroyed with unbridled enthusiasm. And yet, Jayne and I worked out that he'd never actually been on a bus, and had only ever ridden in cars, and once on a plane. When the realisation dawned on us, I knew there couldn't have been a more fitting Christmas present. And when I heard that bus services were free on Christmas Day, the gesture felt that little bit more romantic. After all, the best things in life had the same price tag.

Hand-in-hand, we walked excitedly to the bus stop. Despite the day being hot and dry, my son insisted he wear his favourite shoes – bright red gumboots – to honour the significance of the occasion. As with most Christmases, the streets were quiet, with only a few isolated cars on the road. A middle-aged jogger puffed past. Two young kids on bikes rode by: 'Merry Christmas!' they proclaimed like two Dickensian urchins. 'Merry Kissmas!' my son called back in his beautifully underdeveloped pronunciation. This saying of festive greetings was a wonderful new game to him. The louder you said it, the wider you smiled, the more you were winning at the game of Christmas.

We got excited with the sound of every rapidly-approaching engine, but our hopes were constantly dashed. Where was the bus? Is that the bus? No. Wait, what about that one? No, just another car. Sigh. Was the bus ever coming? Dad, you promised.

And then . . . the bus arrived. My son was so overjoyed that it took us a while to get on board.

The driver wished us a gentle 'Happy Christmas'; she was wearing a Santa hat. My son fired off his most impassioned festive greeting yet and flashed a joyous smile of precious new teeth. Feeling the full force of my son's charm, the driver returned the favour. This cute little guy just made working Christmas Day slightly more bearable.

We took a seat somewhere near the front where my son could see the traffic lights change. 'Red top . . . green go!' was another favourite new game. The bus was almost empty but soon began to fill with passengers as we approached the city. A group of young international students boarded with laughter, staring into each other's phones. A painfully thin junkie rattling with nervous energy took a seat at the back. An elderly man reeking of alcohol boarded wearing his own Santa hat and ruddy Rudolph nose. A man in a wheelchair and his carer occupied the disabled space. But I didn't see any other kids. Hmm, maybe this gift was a little odd after all.

And yet, my son's eyes were everywhere, soaking it all in. He admired the large bus windows and colourful seat patterns, and felt the rumble of the diesel engine behind his dangling red gumboots. He watched people press the bell to disembark and I explained to him how the system worked. It made him want to press the bell too; more than anything. I let him as we approached our final destination.

It was a short stop. We got off, stretched our legs, and immediately got back on for the return journey. The Christmas Day service was a special loop that ran hourly and the city was near deserted, with only convenience stores and petrol stations open for business.

Riding home, I savoured familiar sights of tree-lined streets that I once walked to high school. We passed by the homes of old schoolmates I no longer spoke with, or even knew their whereabouts. I saw the house of my teenage crush, and remembered all the times I rode past on my Malvern Star racing bike hoping to catch a glimpse of her reading a book on the verandah. But I never did.

Leaning over, I pulled my son towards me and held him close. He curled up, comfortable and safe, watching the world go by. The day would come when a bus ride would be just a bus ride. Anxious journeys to school, mind-numbing commutes to work, and tiresome shuttles to the airport. Until then, I drank in such moments. The window was narrow.

We returned home. As expected, my son took some convincing to get off at our stop. I promised him we'd ride the bus again. And yes, before next Christmas. For even though this was ostensibly a present for him, it was secretly also a gift for me: of a priceless new memory that I would carry with me always.

CHAPTER 47

2018

IT WAS TIME to demolish Dad's shed. He'd died eighteen months ago and wasn't coming back.

I regretted having to do it. Dad had spent many enjoyable hours in that shed, drilling holes, hammering nails, sharpening tools and axes on his bench grinder, all while listening to the racing channel on the radio. But that was long ago. Dad didn't enter the shed in his final years; it was too hazardous even for him, along with anyone else who was brave enough to step inside. The air was hard to breathe, infused with years of sawdust and industrial chemicals and fine metal particles. The wood was rotting and the metal was rusted. As lamentable as it was, the decision was clear. It was up to me to somehow undo that beautifully grotesque marvel of backyard engineering.

With crowbar in one hand, sledgehammer in the other, I approached the shed with trepidation, as if it somehow knew the irreversible process that was about to begin. Mum watched from the kitchen window warily. She, too, was sad to see the shed go, as if her husband of sixty years was dying a second time. But she was realistic, and sympathetic to her only child, who she knew was grossly underprepared to perform such a hazardous operation. Undaunted, I put on my gloves, lowered my safety goggles, applied my dust mask, and went in.

I began by removing the shed's innards: its tools and paint tins and gas cylinders and ladders. Examining the tools, I decided which to retain as keepsakes, perhaps even mount on a wall at home. Some of the hacksaws and hammers and hand planes remained in good nick, along with the concrete trowels and spirit levels. Many also appeared instantly familiar, as if I could picture them in Dad's hands, his palms creased with dark lines. But I blocked out those visions and stuck to the task. I threw out broken metal files, jam jars filled with tiny screws, old doorknobs and ashtrays, rusted filing cabinets. I kept an arc welder, electric drills, spanner and wrench set, industrial rubber boots, radio still programmed to the racing channel. I tossed frayed extension cords, kept a metal vice, discarded a broken fridge, retained a working one. The skip bin I had hired for the weekend was large enough to fit the sun and yet somehow began to fill. As I tried to position items, I soon realised that maximising the skip's limited space was an art, and not unlike a perfectly packed suitcase.

Rifling through old drawers, I couldn't afford to be too discerning, scrutinising the potential value of literally thousands of separate items, screws and nuts and light bulbs and nails and spare betting slips. These were all things that Dad had collected with a view to using later, but later never came. I stopped when I found items of real value. These included a black and white photo of Dad's parents, his mother's Australian passport from 1968, and a construction contract he signed in June 1975 when I was a year old. I certainly remembered my *yiayia* and Dad explaining that he even went to the trouble of naturalising her. I think this was with a view to her staying in Australia permanently since all her six children had migrated. My *yiayia's* passport said she was five foot five inches tall, with blue eyes and brown hair, and born in 1898 in the village of Maroneia in the Greek municipality of Thrace. Dad's work contract quoted a salary of '$180.00 per week', with work hours 'from 8.00 am to 4.42 pm Mondays to Fridays and 8.00 am to 12.30 pm Saturdays, inclusive with lunch from 12 noon to 12.45 pm'. I pictured Dad sitting at the kitchen table late one night and reading his contract with a smile on his face and hope in his heart while his toddler son slept soundly in his cot.

I continued sorting and dodging hazards, both beneath my feet and above my head. The ground was littered with rusty nails, bent and upturned, while a multitude of items hung precariously from the ceiling, all from homemade hooks which Dad rigged with tiny individual pieces of wire. I was soon unearthing rounds of live ammunition, shotgun shells, and finally a long artillery belt, all leftover from Dad's former hunting weapon. He surrendered it to police during the national gun amnesty of 1996, which followed the deadliest mass shooting in Australian history at Port Arthur in Tasmania. I remember him taking me hunting once on a cousin's property not far outside town. He shot a rabbit and made me carry it home. Two hours later, my forearm was numb.

And then, in the furthest, dirtiest corner of the shed, I stumbled upon my own personal history. There lived my plastic baby walker and wooden rocking horse, a He-Man action figure, a small transistor radio I once had in my room, and a key ring that came with my first Superstar Bumblebee BMX bike. And in an old ice-cream container, under a patina of dust, I found my collection of original Smurf figurines. These were given away at service stations with purchases of petrol and held enormous sentimental value. I remembered pestering Dad to buy petrol from those specific outlets so that I could choose another precious figurine to take home. The first movie I ever saw at the cinema also featured the Smurfs, and was one that Dad took me to see. He failed to understand my fascination with the tiny blue creatures, which were my first real obsession, but he let me stockpile the figurines because he loved me.

With the shed's contents emptied, the fixtures were next. The wooden storage cabinets were former household furniture; rotted, they came away from the walls with minimal effort. Most of the wooden shelves offered similarly little resistance, disintegrating with a single whack of the sledgehammer. The brackets were another story, fastened to the shed's frame with insanely tight defiance. Trying to loosen them nearly burst a blood vessel in my head. It was the same for the dozens of individual metal sheets that formed the shed's internal walls. Dad used angry six-inch nails to fasten them, which only came free after extensive crowbarring. Progressing deeper into the shed, I saw where Dad ran out of concrete for the floor and the earth reappeared as dirt. It was a similar situation for the frame overhead, with irregularly sized bits of wood hammered onto other irregularly sized bits of wood, extending the frame back until the shed reached the boundary.

I stopped for a breather, for Mum's syrupy Greek coffee and feta cheese toasted sandwiches, and pondered Dad's workmanship. Dismantling his shed had been like undoing an industrial patchwork quilt welded together using a combination of steel, aluminium sheeting and rotted wood. The bird aviary in the opposite corner of the backyard was much the same. Dad had used bricks, concrete, steel and aluminium, and made it able to withstand a Category 5 cyclone. He'd secured the aviary to the back fence with about a hundred pop rivets that I had to individually undrill; this was an exercise in blinding frustration, and resulted in half the fence coming down with the aviary. The skip was filling up rapidly now, and still the shed remained standing.

My electrician godbrother arrived to disconnect the shed's power. I had called him to come and marvel at his *nouno*'s inventiveness, which extended to jerry-rigging a single wire from the house to the shed and then spreading it throughout the interior like an enormous spider's web. My godbrother was both astonished and horrified. He kept chuckling to himself as he unhooked wires. He said he wanted to show the shed to his young apprentices as an example of what not to do.

'Frankly,' he said, 'I can't believe how this wiring didn't start a fire and burn the whole bloody thing to the ground. And kill someone.'

Wearing my bike helmet for protection, I climbed a ladder and used a hammer to painstakingly loosen the roof's various components, which were a collection of incongruous corrugated steel panels. Dad fastened them to each other with homemade metal staples. The scorching Australian sun reflected off the roof, burning my knees and boiling my brain. I realised it was a mistake to undertake this task during summer.

Finally, it was time. I picked up my sledgehammer, loosened my shoulders, reapplied my goggles and mask, and moved in.

The shed came down all around me, beams falling, splintering like matchsticks. I was surprised by how little effort it took, perhaps because of the multitude of individual pieces comprising the shed's structure, which ultimately weakened it. Like the aviary, the shed's biggest issue was its attachment to another structure; in this case, the garage. But that was double brick and, unlike the corrugated steel fence, going nowhere. Hearing the sledgehammer's approach, a frightened possum scurried out of the roof cavity. I knew it had been living in the shed for some time, knocking down paint tins and peeing on my mountain bike during all-night possum parties. The frightened evictee raced up a telephone pole and was immediately surrounded by a family of squawking magpies. I discovered two panels of asbestos in the roof, which I needed to wet before carefully removing. I would need professional help to remove a few metal struts which Dad had somehow welded to the Earth's core.

With the sun now sitting low and orange in the western sky, it was a slow and tiring process to drag away the shed's skeletal remains. The wooden beams were especially hazardous, with long, crooked nails and Dad's homemade staples jutting out at all angles. I filled the skip to the top, watched it overflow, sighed, and eventually stacked a neat pile alongside in anticipation of the next skip delivery. A neighbour leaned over the fence, argued with me about all the noise I was making and threatened to call the police. Another neighbour complimented my efforts and offered to pay their half of the new fence.

I returned to the vacuum where Dad's shed once stood, now just a few broken bits of wood and concrete that needed sweeping. It was then that it hit me – I had just removed one of Dad's few remaining earthly footprints. The shed had been a place he'd spent so much time in, and which was unique to him. It brought him immense joy, and had been a living extension of him. And I'd erased it, one misshapen scrap of metal at a time.

I paused to reflect. It may have been a good shed once. But not anymore. Like its former owner, it had aged to an unfortunate state of disrepair. In a way, seeing the shed like that had been rather heartbreaking. It was better to remember it in its prime, when a much younger man had busied himself within its walls, tinkering and problem-solving all afternoon, and ultimately emerging with something that gave him great pride.

'Sorry, Baba,' I said to the empty space, 'it had to be done.'

Jayne arrived pushing a pram, her back aching. She looked at me oddly. It was the look she gave whenever she caught me talking to myself. Despite being married for years, I still felt embarrassed. She admitted she thought it was a bit strange, but that she also understood why I did it.

'Look,' Jayne said, 'it's Daddy.'

Our two-year-old had been asking to see me, having missed his errant father all day, while his six-month-old brother slept soundly in his carrier, strapped to his mum's chest, completely oblivious to the destruction going on around him. It was incredibly sad that my dad only got the chance to meet his first grandchild. But it was that same grandson who now raced to embrace me, and I lifted him high into the air, my biceps screaming. They would hurt even more the next day.

I carried him to see what had been keeping his dad away. But my son wasn't interested, and I couldn't really blame him. It didn't look like much now – just a dirty piece of uneven concrete, with the waft of industrial chemicals still on the breeze. But then, closing my eyes, I pictured my kids playing in the space where Dad's shed once stood, perhaps on a new patch of green lawn or some climbing equipment. And I thought he'd like that.

CHAPTER 48

2018

MUM WORE AN emerald green dress to my youngest son's baptism. It was the same dress she'd worn to my eldest's baptism two years earlier, and also to my baptism forty years before that. She'd been saving it for these very occasions. All three baptisms were in the same Greek Orthodox church.

This baptism was a small but heartwarming occasion. I especially loved sharing the tradition with my non-Greek friends. The ceremony was deeply symbolic, and the church interior stunning, every inch intricately decorated with gold, multicoloured icons, warm woods, an enormous chandelier, a deep red rug. After the ceremony, at the lunch in the adjacent hall, an old friend approached me. She said it was her first Orthodox baptism ceremony.

'It was lovely,' she said. 'I think it's especially nice to have a celebration like that for babies. Although I'm not religious and never have been, I think faith and having ceremonies are lacking in the modern world. There's something quite meaningful about it and I love that it brings people together.'

I looked out across the hall, at all the people we'd brought together. There was a mix of cultural groups, along with gourmet sandwiches, craft beer, chocolate cake, and polite conversation. It was nice enough, but it did make me lament the past and the wild family celebrations in tiny halls that I remembered as a child. I pictured the room packed with people, at times fighting to get to the food before the best platters were emptied. I saw bottomless carafes of wine, a frenetic *bouzouki* band, big moustaches, plates being smashed, and dancers swirling in an endless, dizzying corkscrew. I saw my mum dancing, leading the circle, twirling a handkerchief high in the air above her head, and my dad watching, talking to a friend and smoking a slow, meditative cigarette. I even pictured Billy pretending to dance a solo *zeibekiko* while Georgios got down on one knee and clapped along encouragingly. I was glad I had insisted on buying some Greek beer for the baptism party and serving traditional *mezethes*, dense meatballs and oily *dolmades* and delicate *spanakopita* triangles. I even plonked a stereo in the corner and played Greek music. It was, I thought, the least I could do to honour the ghosts of celebrations past.

Three years after that cold, grey morning in West Hampstead, our lives had come to be ruled by a pair of dictatorial but otherwise healthy boys. The littlest one refused to sleep, while his other brother refused to share the spotlight with his younger, cuter version, and whacked into him whenever our backs were turned. They drove us mad but filled our hearts to bursting, and I had no doubt that my own mum and dad once felt the same. Simply becoming parents challenged each generation, but we both found solutions, whether it was through the scalpel of a surgeon or the generosity of a family member. Each answer came after much trial and error, and reflected a moment in time and the available technology, or lack thereof.

My brothers saw their nephews in photos, which was enough for now. Billy had some stuck up on the fridge with magnets, which Georgios said he talked to each day. I sent them money whenever Georgios asked; the local Western Union office knew me well. At times, Georgios said he hadn't been paid in over a month, and that Billy's disability pension was in jeopardy. I helped upgrade their car from the Romanian jalopy to a German saloon. Georgios said he'd finally given up smoking, and had since gained some weight. I was pleased even though he probably still drove without a seatbelt.

'It's a strange feeling,' he told me. 'I've smoked since I was fifteen. Billy and I used to have to hide our cigarettes from Dad. He never told us not to smoke because it was bad for us. He only said we couldn't smoke until we were older.'

In the meantime, I taught my sons how to speak Greek, readying them, in the same way my parents once prepared me. They even watched children's cartoons dubbed into Greek, traditional nursery rhymes and modern-day characters. My eldest was already enamoured with the Smurfs and had even begun stealing and hiding my vintage figurines. I had always considered myself as Greek-Australian, a true product of nature and nurture. But would my kids feel the same? Would they feel any sense of 'Greekness' in their watered-down lineage? Their connection to a country other than Australia was even more distant from its roots. And yet, their Hellenic DNA was still there, in their olive skin, in their deep brown eyes and unpronounceably long surname. At the end of the day, it was up to them. All I could do as a parent was guide and educate them.

I was no longer the centre of Mum's universe. This was understandable, but still came as a shock; I'd gotten so used to it my whole life, it was all I'd ever known. At times, I felt decidedly peripheral to domestic proceedings. There wasn't much a father could do to soothe a screaming newborn who only wanted the breast, or a crying infant whose pain could only be fixed by Mummy's kisses and cuddles. I was probably once like that too. All I could now do was sigh and go put on another load of washing.

I had now been a dad for three years. I'd fathered through joy, frustration, anger, exhaustion, sadness, mourning and cloudy childhood memories, which slowly began to stir with every new experience with my kids. Together, Jayne and I developed an appreciation of the emotional and physical labours of parenthood. We learned the value of parenting with resilience and compassion, and did so each day with the hope that we would one day pass this knowledge on to our children. I knew they could not replace the fatherly love that I'd lost; I would always live with that piece of my heart missing. But they did help me grow a new, separate love, a vast compartment of my heart that belonged solely to them. And Dad's legacy lived on. He had taught me how to be a father.

Dad had come to me in a dream the night before the baptism. Perhaps it was because I'd been thinking about him, and how much he enjoyed the one he'd been able to attend. I hadn't dreamt a lot about Dad since he died, but this one was vivid. Jayne and I were at the beach with our youngest. Dad was sitting alone on a nearby bench looking down at the ground. He often did that when he sat, weighed down with his thoughts. He was dressed in a jacket and pants, which was unusually formal and overdressed for him on a hot summer day. But then I remembered that Dad felt very cold towards the end of his life due to his weight loss. I insisted he come down to the water with the three of us. He was reluctant at first, content where he was sitting, and also aware of his limitations. But I could tell that he had a longing. He still loved the beach and ocean. And now, he also had a new grandchild to introduce them to. Slowly, I helped Dad off the bench until he stood. He struggled to walk unaided. But he managed, one measured step after another. Standing close by, at the water's edge, Jayne and I watched as Dad took our son into his arms and gently eased himself into the ocean. It was our son's very first time in the sea. He felt safe in his *papou*'s arms, laughing and feeling the sensation of the cool water as it splashed against his soft white skin. For a moment, Dad looked lighter, too, if not weightless, moving effortlessly in the water, tasting the salt. After a few minutes, we helped him out of the surf and he handed our son back to us. Dad was now dripping wet, his clothes sodden. But he was smiling broadly. I woke up smiling, too. Dad never got to meet his second grandson in the flesh, but he did in my dream. They were together for a moment in a place where he felt perfectly comfortable and eternally joyous.

After the baptism, we cleaned up the church hall and prepared to go home. I feared the worst. Our youngest was overtired while the eldest was hyped on sugar. We were also all exhausted from organising and hosting the event. Jayne took our youngest home to settle him for sleep, while I took his brother to Yiayia's house to burn off his excess energy.

Mum sat on her bed, removed her jacket and shoes, and curled her arthritic toes on the thick blue rug. I heard them crack with relief. She now went to at least one funeral a week, events which often took all day, and which took their toll. Baptisms weren't as emotive, but they still exhausted a grand old lady who was closing in on ninety. For over forty years, she'd wanted nothing more than to love as a mother and be loved by a child. And now, as she approached her tenth decade of life, Mum was still loving and being loved. She loved her two grandsons with the energy of a thousand suns, and who then returned her adoration with their curiosity and joy at visiting Yiayia's house. And her son was also finding new ways to love and admire his mother as he saw her cooking traditional recipes for his children, reading to them, or teaching them Greek. One day, I hoped to tell them: 'Without that lady and the lengths she went to to become a mother, I wouldn't be here and neither would you.'

But the day would also come when my kids would hear about the other woman in their ancestral tree whose sacrifice was all in the name of family. My mum would always be my mother, but her sister-in-law's kindness to have and donate a baby was never far from my thoughts. I never met Anna, but I knew what she did, and that would never be forgotten. We were a family born from one great act of kindness. My biological mother's framed photo was still on the wall, next to my biological and adoptive fathers' photos. Mum said she spoke to it every day, and continued to give her unending gratitude. I did too. It was an almost unspeakable generosity that changed the course of so many lives.

It was also simple mathematics. While it usually only took two people to bring most lives into the world, for me it just happened to be four. Take away any one of those vital components and the result would've been different. I had four parents. The older generations weren't so obsessed with the idea that biology and genetics trump all else.

I came into Mum's bedroom and flopped onto the armchair near the window. The April day was clear but cool, the late autumn light fading. Hearing our descendant tearing along the hallway, pushing a toy truck and yelling at the top of his lungs, Mum and I smiled at each other. Her house was again tumbling with life.

'He's going to be a handful,' she said.

'He already is,' I replied.

'Just like you were,' she added warmly.

'Thanks! Then his future is clearly bright.'

'Shh,' she said, 'he'll hear us.'

But it was too late. My son appeared, peering tentatively around the door frame. It wasn't often that Dad and Yiayia were in this room, talking quietly, almost privately. He wanted to know what was going on, what we were hiding from him.

'Welcome!' Mum said. 'You found us.'

He sugar-rushed in and headed straight for his *yiayia*, who was fortunately sitting down. At times, he had charged her as she walked, and had come close to pushing her over with the force of his love. Mum kissed the top of my son's shaggy head, his hair thick and lustrous. He still had remnants of the blue lollipop bomboniere stuck to the corners of his mouth. Mum moistened two of her fingers and wiped them away, much to his chagrin.

Extracting the cushion from behind my back, I threw it playfully at my son's head and made him laugh. He fell forward onto the blue rug, writhing and squealing with glee. When he finally composed himself, he looked up at the framed photo on the wall opposite Mum's bed. It was of three brothers, all standing amid the ruins at the Prespa Lakes. The younger two were looking directly at the camera while the eldest was distracted, his eyes to the sky, following a flying bird or passing plane or slow-moving cloud.

After a while of intense study, my son pointed at the photo. He looked at me with curious eyes and said: 'Who are those two people you're with, Daddy?'

EPILOGUE

2019

JAYNE AND I were going out for a rare brunch together. It was our 'date night' brought forward in the day, which stemmed from having tried to go out for dinner a few times and the kids refusing to sleep. Switching from dinner to brunch meant that kitchens were at least open by the time we made it out. On this occasion, our date came with an added bonus. We were going to discover the sex of our unborn baby.

The third pregnancy had come as a minor surprise. Having grown up as an only child, I'd always wanted to have a bigger family, as if to make up for lost time. So Jayne and I tried for a third without too much thought about the timing. We didn't expect success so soon, but no expectant parent ever does.

We didn't find out the gender with our first two babies. We wanted to retain this last little pocket of mystery – there are so few left in the world. But the third time was different. Jayne wanted to mentally prepare for the baby's arrival, and we wanted to explain

– at least to our eldest – whether to expect a baby brother or sister. He was now three years old and would understand. We'd also struggled with boys' names in the past and didn't want to put ourselves through the stress if the baby was a girl.

Most people learn the gender at the twenty-week ultrasound scan when the baby's genitalia become visible. But we had decided to find out after ten weeks using a genetic test known as non-invasive prenatal testing. The test detects cell-free placental DNA present in maternal blood, which reflects the presence of trisomies and three common genetic conditions: Down syndrome, Edwards syndrome and Patau syndrome. For Jayne, Edwards syndrome had always been on her mind because her younger brother died soon after birth. There was no screening for such genetic conditions in the 1980s, but medical science had come a long way thanks to basic discoveries with lab mice.

Fortunately, Jayne's doctor reported that the three trisomy tests all showed low risk. We were incredibly relieved. Jayne had been considered in a higher risk class for genetic disorders given her age. But her doctor withheld one vital test result. She didn't reveal the constitution of the 23rd chromosome pair, the sex chromosome, which non-invasive prenatal testing also examined. Instead, she handed us a sealed white envelope with the outcome. And it was this little envelope that we took along to Saturday brunch.

Increasingly extravagant gender reveal parties were now becoming popular. There were countless internet videos of expectant couples slicing cakes, setting off smoke bombs, and smashing open piñatas to expose either pink or blue colours, or sometimes both in the case of twins. But we knew that wasn't for us. We instead opted for something more understated and private.

We ended up down by the water at one of the city's hip new cafés. As we ate, Jayne and I absently discussed such topics as schools, superannuation, career goals and the boys. All the while, the crisp white envelope stared at us from the café table. It could tell we were distracted. We paid our bill hurriedly and got moving.

I suggested we drive to a tourist lookout over the city and open the envelope there. But Jayne had an even better idea.

'Okay, let's bet,' she said as we drove. 'What do you think it is?'

It felt like a loaded question. The night before, I'd had a vivid dream that it was a girl.

'Um . . .' I paused. 'I'll say a boy, based on my track record.'

It was also an assessment based on my bloodline. There hadn't been a female baby born in my family in nearly ninety years. Mum was the last, way back in 1930.

'I'll say a girl,' Jayne replied. 'At least this way, one of us will be right.'

Georgios had also said it would be a girl when I told him the news.

We arrived at the suburban oval and parked under an old white gum tree. It was where I had parked some ten years earlier to play in a summer mixed soccer team. That day, I'd walked to the oval with sports bag in my hand and was introduced to my attractive new teammate. This time, I walked to the same spot with her hand in mine and the sealed white envelope in the other.

Having endured a week of forty-degree temperatures, we didn't want to spend any longer on an exposed oval than we needed to.

Jayne could barely work her fingers and open the envelope for all her nervous energy. This wasn't quite the frantic birth suite after a prolonged, exhausting delivery. But it would be just as memorable for other reasons.

Thrusting open the page, our eyes expectantly scanned the data. There, beneath the trisomy test reports was printed a single letter:

'M'

It was another boy. We exclaimed with elation, surprise, and a little sigh. The cricketers on the adjacent oval looked over at us with curiosity.

We couldn't deny that having a girl would've been a different parenting experience that we would have embraced. But all children are different, including our two young boys already. There would be no reason to believe it wouldn't be the same with a third. Hopefully, they would all grow up as good mates and look out for each other. And the third would always be a little special as the youngest.

We could plan now. We could give away all the hand-me-down dresses and skirts we'd been gifted and try to find a suitable boy's name. At the end of the day, we wanted three healthy kids, and we got what we wanted. We were quietly grateful that it wasn't twins.

On a personal level, I had to admit that the outcome had a nice symmetry to it. I would soon be the father of three sons, and was one of three brothers. But because I was adopted, I missed out on seeing how three brothers grow up together. I missed the games, the laughter, the pranks, the teamwork, the arguments, the tears, the jealousy, the competition. I had thought about that ever since the day I learned of my adoption. Finally, I would get to experience the dynamic of three through my own boys. I imagined that I might even have a soft spot for the youngest and littlest one, *o micros*, since he would be the same as me, the third of three brothers.

Jayne and I drove home to see our two sons whom we'd left in the care of their two grandmothers. They looked at us anxiously. I had a plan. Taking our eldest into the bedroom, I asked him to find his blue bunny and pink bear. I told him that we'd take them into the living room and when I asked him, to step forward to pick the blue bunny. He nodded his understanding and said: 'Okay, Daddy.'

The family watched us emerge. I lined up the two soft toys and asked my son to pick one. With a cheeky smile, he looked around the room, stepped forward and grabbed the pink bear. The grandmothers squealed with delight until they saw Jayne and I shaking our heads. Meanwhile, our eldest ran off down the hall with the pink bear, laughing.

I clarified the situation. Both grandmothers were equally overjoyed, agreeing that a healthy baby was the most important thing, although Mum was a little emotional. She would remain the family's last female descendent. At least, for now.

'Maybe when the boys grow up, they'll have daughters,' she said hopefully. 'And then you'll have granddaughters.'

I smiled. 'And you'll have great-granddaughters,' I said.

Mum stared wistfully into the distance, her eyes glistening.

'I don't think so,' she said. 'But I played my part. The family was once failing but is now thriving. I am proud.'

Acknowledgements

DEEP THANKS TO Dexter Petley of Jericho Writers for astute editing and patience; to Irina Dunn for assistance and guidance; to Jennifer Belle at The New School in New York City for being the spark that lit the torch; to Carol Major at Varuna in Sydney for early instruction and feedback; to Lee Gordon, Anthony Ferguson and Maurits Zwankhuizen for helpful comments on the manuscript; to Irfan Master for moral encouragement; to Jayne for enduring support and belief; to the boys for their joy and madness; and to Chris and Jen at Salt for being such phenomenal publishers.

This book has been typeset by
SALT PUBLISHING LIMITED
using Neacademia, a font designed by Sergei Egorov
for the Rosetta Type Foundry in the Czech Republic. It
is manufactured using Holmen Book Cream 70gsm, a
Forest Stewardship Council™ certified paper from the
Hallsta Paper Mill in Sweden. It was printed and bound
by Clays Limited in Bungay, Suffolk, Great Britain.

CROMER
GREAT BRITAIN
MMXIX